Spatial Planning in
the Small Economy

Helen B. O'Neill

The Praeger Special Studies program—utilizing the most modern and efficient book production techniques and a selective worldwide distribution network—makes available to the academic, government, and business communities significant, timely research in U.S. and international economic, social, and political development.

Spatial Planning in the Small Economy

A Case Study of Ireland

PRAEGER SPECIAL STUDIES IN INTERNATIONAL ECONOMICS AND DEVELOPMENT

Praeger Publishers   New York   Washington   London

PRAEGER PUBLISHERS
111 Fourth Avenue, New York, N.Y. 10003, U.S.A.
5, Cromwell Place, London S.W.7, England

Published in the United States of America in 1971
by Praeger Publishers, Inc.

Library of Congress Catalog Card Number: 70-161911

Printed in the United States of America

TO MY MOTHER

I wish to record my thanks to the professors, staff, and students of the Department of Economics of McGill University.

I owe a particular debt to Professor John Iton for his penetrating criticism of the first draft of the book, and for the generous manner in which he put forward many helpful suggestions.

For encouragement and useful discussions at various stages during the writing of the book, I am grateful to Professor Kari Levitt and to Professor E. F. Beach of the Department of Economics of McGill University; to Dr. William O'Riordan of the Department of Political Economy of University College, Dublin; to Anthony O'Neill, architect and town planning consultant, Dublin; and to the many government officials in both parts of Ireland who gave so generously of their time and experience.

I am also indebted to my students in University College, Dublin, especially those in the graduate seminar on the economics of land use planning in the Department of Town Planning. I can only hope that they learned as much from me as I learned from them.

Finally, I wish to thank Ita O'Byrne for the cheerful and efficient way in which she typed the manuscript.

LIST OF TABLES

LIST OF CHARTS

LIST OF MAPS

IRISH TOWNS
WITH
POPULATIONS
OF MORE THAN 5,000

Spatial Planning in the Small Economy

IRISH PROVINCES
AND COUNTIES

INTRODUCTION

The causes and the problems of growth and development have preoccupied economists since the days of Adam Smith. Admittedly, that interest waned during the late nineteenth century and the early part of the twentieth century, but it has been revived, and indeed intensified, during the last two decades.

Most areas of the subject have been thoroughly investigated. Theories, models, plans, and strategies have been devised and tested and, in many cases, used successfully as the basis for implementing national development goals. One aspect has, however, been relatively neglected until recent years. Though geographers and physical planners have emphasized its importance, economists, in general, have all but ignored the spatial element in the growth process. The purpose of this book is to highlight this aspect of development and to consider it, especially, in its relation to the problems of small, open economies. The spatial aspects of Irish economic development are examined as a case study, but it is with the hope that the conclusions will prove to be of more general interest and application.

A model--considered appropriate to explain the sectoral and spatial process of development in a small, open economy--is presented and later compared with the Irish experience over the last forty years. The regional and urban problems of development are then investigated, and since most of these are assumed to be locational in character, the question of the optimum industrial and demographic locations are discussed in some detail and the results of the research carried out in this connection for the present study examined. Finally, a tentative regional development policy is suggested.

3

The model is a stages theory of development and leans heavily on two distinct schools of thought: the Structuralist group in Latin America as represented by Dudley Seers[1] and the more cosmopolitan "regional science" group as represented by John Friedmann.[2]

Three themes are central to the Structuralist approach. The first theme is the Marxian historical view of economic development that emphasizes the importance of past experiences as an explanation of the current economic and social structure of the country and as a guide to the strategy of future development both possible and probable. Development is seen as a process occurring in distinct stages without, however, being constrained by Rostovian rigidity;[3] the sequence and duration of the stages may vary from country to country. A second concern of the Structuralists is the increasing importance of the large international corporation as an instrument of investment in developing areas. Though the economic advantages that derive from inflows of foreign capital are acknowledged, the attendant disadvantages associated with foreign influence--notably the decrease in economic, and even political, independence and undue influence upon consumption patterns and wage rates through the demonstration effect-- are considered to be a very high price to pay for economic growth.

A third theme that runs through Structuralist writings is the center-periphery notion of the international economy as one divided into two distinct subeconomies. These are respectively the center (or metropolis), consisting of the developed, industrialized, largely urban areas (chiefly in North America and Western Europe) and the periphery (or hinterland) of the underdeveloped, primary-producing economies in the rest of the world. In the latter, production is concentrated in the mining or agricultural sector and is geared in the main to the needs and policies of the center, involving, on the one hand, adequate supplies of raw materials for industry and, on the other, ready outlets for its finished products. These policies are implemented by the trade flows between center and periphery whose composition and direction cement the status quo and incidentally inhibit the development of intraregional trade inside the periphery because of the similarity of individual productive structures. This approach may be usefully extended to explain both the cause and the effect of economic transformation at all levels; world, continent, nation, and city. Friedmann, following a line traced by Gerald Meier and Robert Baldwin,[4] Raul Prebisch,[5] Harvey S. Perloff and Lowdon Wingo, Jr.,[6] and T.W. Schultz,[7] argues that the spatial structure of developing economies is characterized by relationships whereby a powerful central region reduces the rest of the space economy to the role of a tributary area, draining it of resources, manpower, and capital. The problems arising from the resulting regional imbalances and the behavior, through time, of interregional disparities provide an enduring area for discussion. Many writers have made contributions, in-cluding Gunnar Myrdal,[8] who argues that development leads to a widening of income differentials between regions, both nationally and internationally. Simon Kuznets[9] claims that this applies only in the early stages of development and that the gaps narrow as economies reach maturity. Both conclusions are altogether too dogmatic according to B. Okun and R.W. Richardson,[10] who claim that the outcome depends upon a wide variety of factors, including initial levels of development in the various regions, their respective rates of growth or decline, and the effects of interregional flows of labor and capital over time. There is scope for further research into these important questions.

THE MODEL

For a model explaining the process of industrialization and urbanization in a small, open economy like Ireland, four stages are proposed: (1) the agrarian economy, (2) the transitional economy, (3) the urbanized industrial economy, and (4) the urbanized service economy.

Stage 1: The Agrarian Economy

The country is a colonial or neocolonial-type economy with strong center-periphery relationships operating both externally and internally. It is open in the sense that very low tariffs and other import restrictions prevail and exports and imports both constitute a high percentage of gross national product. The banking system lacks independence, the currency being backed by reserves held in the center country and the monetary policy being purely reactive in nature. An outmoded land tenure system operates involving uncertainty of titles.

The repercussions on an economy that forms part of a colonial free-trade system extend to all facets of its economic life. Under a free-trade regime both industry and agriculture have access to world-wide export markets and benefit accordingly. Nevertheless, especially with respect to agriculture, production is generally geared to the needs of the main importer at the center rather than to those of the peripheral exporter. The only industries that prosper are those that can compete internationally and, among these, many are almost wholly dependent upon imported raw materials. When the economy is small, other industries catering exclusively to the home market are almost impossible to foster owing to free-trade conditions in the domestic market. Membership of the colonial club also affects the mobility and price of the factors of production. Unless racial discrimination prevails, labor will move freely to the center or other parts of the system, resulting in upward pressure on money wage rates in the periphery. Capital is subject to Myrdal's "backwash" effect. Because of the lack of investment opportunities at home*, capital tends to move to the center with its prospects of higher and safer returns. Local projects have, therefore, to compete with those at the center and elsewhere for funds. Further, the flow of local savings is meager because incomes are low and unevenly distributed and the capital and shares markets are undeveloped.

An economy may be described as agrarian if at least 50 percent of the labor force is employed in the primary sector and the contribution to total output (gross national product or gross domestic product) made by industry is less than 10 percent. The vast majority of the population lives in settlements of 1,500 or less, and less than 10 percent of the population lives in centers of 100,000 or more. There is very little regional integration and the problem of regional dualism is accentuated if the economy is largely dependent upon a single primary product that is exported unprocessed to the center. In this event, the main center within the country is in most cases a port located advantageously with respect to the center to facilitate exports of primary products to it and imports of manufactured goods and also, perhaps, raw materials from it. This is also the administrative center. Because of the lack of regional integration within the country and the low level of communication, other urban centers can also thrive, even if they lack industry, when they serve as local service centers. If transportation and communications in general improve, the distance between centers will decrease and the smaller of these centers will decline relatively and sometimes even absolutely.** The operation of these forces will also cause the influence of the main urban center to increase.

In so far as industry exists, its chief products consist of consumer goods, principally food, drink, and (perhaps) textiles. The leading export industry, as mentioned above, is an unprocessed product from the primary sector; the principal imports are consumer goods. Depending upon climate and resources, imports may also include fuel and locally unavailable foods, such as cereals. In a small,

---

*There is a reluctance to invest in land because of the uncertainty of titles and a reluctance to invest in industry because of low returns except in large undertakings.

**Contrary to popular belief, however, a center rarely disappears from the map.

open economy with some industry, raw materials are also an important item on the import list.

Stage 2: The Transitional Economy

Once a shock has been introduced into the system, (for example,
political independence, war, or a world economic slump), the status
quo is disrupted and the process of deliberate industrialization and
guided economic development begins. Increased urbanization accompanies this process. The percentage of the population living in centers
of 100,000 or more increases steadily and by the end of the period
will rise to more than 30 percent of the population. This phenomenon
is facilitated by the drift from the rural areas to the towns and cities
on the one hand and, on the other, by the internal growth of urban
settlements due to industrialization and the resulting increase in employment opportunities and incomes. Employment in agriculture
drops sharply and this process continues until a floor, set by demand
and the minimum amount of labor required to produce the desired
output, is reached.

These twin processes of industrialization and urbanization proceed in phases which may be distinguished from each other.

The first phase involves the accelerated production of consumer
goods, the new industries manufacturing import replacements, such
as food products, clothing and shoes. Protection is mild and relatively haphazard at first, probably as a result of bilateral agreements
between the peripheral country and the center. Because of the lack
of local raw materials and the consequent necessity of importing
these and machinery, there tends to be a heavy concentration of production at the main city and port. Nevertheless, these consumer-
goods industries are mainly market-oriented; thus, many firms are
scattered among smaller locations throughout the country. This
"scatteration" is further facilitated by the incomplete communications network, which involves not only a relatively poor transportation system but also permits the existence, even in a small country,
of imperfect competition between regions. In turn, this gives rise
to large differences in profit margins between firms in the same industry.* What might be called a fixed-income syndrome operates
among enterpreneurs. Inertia prevents them from penetrating the

---

*This factor was brought to my attention by Dr. R. C. Geary of
the Economic and Social Research Institute in Dublin.

market beyond their own locality. This phenomenon is manifested
in the form of inelasticities of supply among many industrial products despite the existence of fairly high tariffs and other instruments
of protection. Location decisions tend to be as much noneconomic
(on an emotional, personal-preference basis) as economic in character. This, too, permits the growth of industries at subcenters even
far removed from the main concentration. Some infrastructure,
particularly that concerned with public utilities, such as electricity
and gas, is necessarily also located at scattered points throughout
the country.

The second phase in the industrialization process involves the
production of a wider range of consumer goods and also the production of intermediate and even capital goods. Resources set a limit
to the scope of production but imports of materials can extend this
limit. Protection on finished goods is of necessity increased sharply
and aimed specifically at preventing competition with locally produced
goods. The tendency towards concentration of production at the main
center and port is strengthened by the necessity to import raw materials and by the increasing interdependency of the new industries
which are, therefore, not as footloose as those in the earlier period.
In a sense, these new industries might be described as import-ori-
ented--analogous with resource-oriented in the traditional litera-
ture--and just as tied, therefore, with respect to location. Unless
other, relatively large settlements had grown up prior to this stage,
the relative dominance of the main center would now increase. This
tendency is strengthened by the lack of alternative centers to absorb
the rural outflow and by the improvements in transportation and
communications generally throughout the economy. Indeed, unless
the main center is comparable in size and structure to the industrial
centers of nearby countries, the flow will bypass it and emigrate.
The smaller the economy and the greater the dependence on international trade, the stronger is the tendency towards locational concentration at the main city.

Once the production possibilities for the home market have
been largely exhausted, a third phase in the industrialization process
is reached. Determined efforts will be made to widen the market and
to take advantage of economies of scale through exports of industrial
goods. The policy of large-scale and somewhat indiscriminate protection will have to be changed, in return for similar concessions from
trading partners, in order to gain access to foreign markets. The
economy will become more open with respect to these countries--
though not necessarily to the world as a whole, as the arrangements
may simply involve small regional free-trade areas. The erosion of
nationalistic attitudes and the abandonment of autarkic economic
policies will facilitate the inflow of foreign capital and technology if

it is required to promote the fairly massive industrialization efforts.
Foreign companies will then move in to set up branches within the
economy. Misgivings voiced by certain elements within the community
about the dangers of a foreign takeover will be dismissed by the prag-
matists who will point to the unlikelihood of independence in a small,
open economy in any event. This will tend to mask the real disadvantages inherent in a branch-plant type economy. These center on the
somewhat violent reactions which can be touched off in the local economy when recessions occur in the investing countries or in the economies to which these countries sell. Unless subsidiaries are large
in relation to the parent plant they tend to be the first to contract
activities when trading conditions deteriorate. However, even if the
size of subsidiaries is small the attendant disadvantages might be
mitigated by linkages within industrial groups. Individual firms do
not in general provide significant employment opportunities. Further,
multiplier effects upon the whole economy become important only
when a firm or an industry becomes part of the local market, either
by being based on local raw materials or by becoming big enough to
induce other linked processes to it.* So linkages bind the diverse
parts of the new industrial structure together and help it to put down
permanent roots in the developing economy. The oft-mooted sugges-
tion that small countries should concentrate on the production of components or services of a subcontracting nature can be dismissed for
the same reasons and also because of the increasing tendency of
large corporations to subcontract within their own industrial group.

Once there has been a shift in the composition of exports from
primary products to manufactured goods, the tendency towards locational concentration at the main city will increase. Industrial production will now tend to be market-oriented in the international sense;
this will increase the advantages to be gained from location at the main
port.

Stage 3: The Urbanized Industrial Economy

Once industry contributes more than 25 percent to total output
the economy may be described as industrialized, and once at least
30 percent of the population live in centers of 100,000 or more it may

---

*An example is a food-processing industry inducing the setting
up of packaging and canning activities and later engineering and perhaps steel production. Of course, the chain of linkages cannot be
pursued very far in a backward direction in a small economy.

be called urbanized. In general, according to Kingsley Davis,[11] the later each country becomes industrialized, the faster is its urbanization. There is a very close correlation between the two phenomena. When the economy is small it will continue to be dependent on imports of raw materials due to the skewed nature of its own resource base. It will most certainly always continue to be dependent on exports as a means of widening the market and the possibilities of specialization. The objective now is to become internationally competitive. This involves achieving economies of scale which, of course, are usually possible in many industries only after the market has been widened through exports. The small, open economy may not proceed very far in this direction. The small size of the domestic market and, to a lesser extent, the lack of native raw materials will prevent the development of large-scale intermediate and capital-goods industries. Certain types of industry, such as those represented by steel mills and automobile plants, may be entirely precluded.

If the economy is of the branch-plant type, as a result of foreign investments, it is already vulnerable to economic forces in the center countries. It cannot survive as an industrial entity on the basis of "cheap labor" alone. As incomes go up and trade unionism spreads, there is a danger of inflationary price and wage increases occurring. Innovation is essential to keep ahead; imitation may not be good enough.

The main center's dominance within the domestic market is now powerful as a result of the new structure of industrial production, the bias towards industrial exports, and the improved level of communications. However, there is hope for smaller centers, a hope based on the still-relative importance of consumer goods and therefore of domestically oriented products in the industrial structure. Profit spreads still exist within industries because of the prevailing remnants of imperfect competition and apathy among producers. Nevertheless, capital movements from abroad and foreign competition in the form of international retail outlets and the freer entry of imports will narrow the gaps. This process will be accelerated by mergers and by rationalization moves within industries. Competition from without will damage monopolies within. Tariff reductions and common-market arrangements will complete the process.

Stage 4: The Urbanized Service Economy

The most notable feature of this stage in the development of the economy is that industry begins to decline as a percentage of total output. As a result of accelerated automation, industry also becomes less significant as an employer of labor. The economy

becomes increasingly oriented towards services, and within the tertiary sector itself important shifts take place. Personal services
and such professional skills as computer programming assume increasing importance in the sophisticated urban society while the
lengthening of the educational process and the widespread diffusion
of health services increase the demand for teachers and doctors.

If we define urbanization as the ratio of the urban population to
total population, the rate of urbanization also begins to slow up at this
stage and the process will eventually come to an end. Rural-urban
migration will cease and city growth, which continues at a rapid rate
and produces the megalopolis, becomes a function of general population growth.

Space becomes an absolutely scare factor of production. The
emphasis of policy-makers is placed on issues concerning urban
renewal, amenities, the use of leisure, and the "quality of life." The
necessity for economizing in the use of scarce resources will not be
eliminated by economic development; the range of choices facing man-
kind will simply be different.

The model explains the spatial pattern likely to result in a small,
open economy at various stages in its economic development. It concludes that in the absence of intervention the production structure
tends to be highly concentrated from a locational viewpoint. Even
though the small size of the market may preclude the setting up of
capital-goods producing industries to any significant extent and, further, although the predominance of light industries permits more
scatteration, the tendency towards concentration exists nevertheless.
Where the country itself is small in relation to its neighbors and
particularly in relation to the center, the only hope of absorbing the
rural outflow within the economy is to allow the main urban settlement
to grow into one of comparable size to the cities of neighboring countries. This will have detrimental effects on smaller cities and will
further aggravate the locational imbalances. The inevitable result is
a dominant central city surrounded, perhaps, by a thriving but small
region with the rest of the country forming a rural hinterland inter-
spersed here and there with smaller urban centers, many of which
are stagnant.* The only way of avoiding this outcome is by deliberate
government intervention, preferably during the transitional stage.

----

*A stagnant area is defined as one wherein the forces leading
to decline are equally as strong in the long run as those leading to
growth.

DYNAMIC IMPLICATIONS OF THE MODEL

The foregoing analysis is essentially static but an examination of the forces which determine rural-urban migration and the ability of urban centers to absorb this flow would help to explain the processes of industrialization and urbanization between the various stages.

The absorptive capacity of urban centers depends upon their ability to provide employment for the unemployed and the under employed of the rural areas. Urban industrialization and the consequent increase in job opportunities increases the demand for labor inside relative to that outside and attracts migrants to the city. The extent to which these find employment defines the effective absorption capacity of the urban area. This, in turn, is determined by its size and the structure of its productive activities. Effective absorption capacity probably involves a certain minimum size of urban center and in the small, open economy would allow the growth of only a few relatively large centers outside the main city. That is, it probably also depends on regional urban concentration. The actual absorption may be calculated for any period as follows:

$$A = (P_2 - P_1 - B + D)$$

where P_2 and P_1 are respectively populations at the end and at the beginning of the period, B is the number of births, and D is the number of deaths. Given that urbanization is the ratio of urban to total population, or an increase in this ratio, then the process of urbanization has a beginning and an end. It reaches a limit when the rural population falls to the minimum required to operate the agricultural sector, given the technology and the nature of output. Rural-urban migration then becomes insignificant and, indeed, may later be reversed as is evidenced by the growth of the so-called dormitory suburbs. Once rural-urban migration ceases--that is, once the process of urbanization comes to an end--city growth becomes a function of general population growth.

Another important determinant of the growth of an area is the amount of exports it sells to other areas. This applies at the national, the regional, and the urban levels. Borrowing a concept from physics, W.J. Reilly[12] states that trade and commercial activity between urban centers is proportional to their masses (populations) and inversely proportional to some power of the distance between them, the relevant index being dependent upon their internal structure.

We have already seen that urban absorption capacity depends upon population size, industrial structure, and the degree of regional

urban concentration. The greater the extent of regional urban concentration, the greater the distance from each regional urban center
to the limits of its hinterland. The tendency may, therefore, be for
the commercial activity of these hinterland areas to be lost to the
urban area in favor of smaller, mainly service centers. However,
the general growth of the economy and rising incomes would lead to
improvements in transportation, and the decrease in the distance
factor would lead once more to an increase in the attraction of the
regional city as a commercial center.

Once again we see that economic development increases the
tendency towards urban concentration. This tendency, we have already
noted, will be stronger in a small, open economy because the smaller
the size, the more open in general is the economy and, consequently,
the more powerful are the forces of concentration in production at
one or two centers conveniently located for trading purposes. In
general, the smaller the area the greater is the dependence on exports
as a motor of growth, given that a varied consumption pattern is desired and, thus, that imports are necessary on a continuing basis.
We may conclude that the extent to which growth is externally induced
increases inversely with the size of the area under consideration.
Another important determinant of the size and growth of imports and
exports is the income elasticity of demand at all spatial levels--re-
gional, national, and international. These differ depending upon the
size and distribution of income and the extent of urbanization and
industrialization at each level.

THE NEED FOR GOVERNMENT INTERVENTION

Unless there is a deliberate policy to promote other centers in
the peripheral areas during the transitional stage of economic development, polarization at the center increases as industrialization proceeds. The problems associated with regional dualism are not be
solved by economic development alone and the disparities in per capita
incomes, infrastructural facilities, social amenities, and political
power widen. Social unrest may result and, in extreme cases, may
be avoided only by a narrowing of the regional disparities.

One method of doing so is to avoid interference at the wealth-
creation stage and to provide, later on, large transfers of funds from
the growing center to the lagging peripheral regions to help iron out
the resulting disparities in incomes and amenities.

The alternative method is a deliberate policy of interference
with the automatic mechanism. It involves the promotion of development and, therefore, of industrialization in the periphery during the

transitional stage. In some cases this may be accompanied by a concurrent policy involving a curtailment of growth at the center.

Because of the powerful attraction of the central city in a small,
open economy and its ever-widening influence, development of the
periphery involves the creation of industrial and commercial nuclei
which are capable of competing with the center, if not on a national
level, then at least within their own regions. The greater the degree
of integration of the economy, the greater is the sphere of influence
of the center; the greater this influence, the harder will it be for other
centers to compete with it even on a regional basis. Further, the
smaller the economy and the higher the level of its development, the
greater tends to be its degree of integration. Therefore, the chances
of success in the promotion of other centers of industrial and commercial growth will lessen as development proceeds beyond the transitional stage. As a result, these induced centers of growth, these
so-called growth poles, have to be sufficiently large to enable them
to compete with the center; the smaller the economy in terms of area,
population, and national income, the smaller is the number of growth
poles that the economy can effectively promote.

Ideally, these induced-growth centers would contain an integrated
group of linked industries and would be located according to economic
and social needs. The relative importance of the two criteria would
depend upon many factors. An economic choice might involve picking
a thriving town (that is, choosing one whose past performance and
future potential indicated strong growth possibilities). A social or
political choice would involve picking a town in a lagging region or
building a new town in order to substitute intraregional movements
of labor and capital for interregional flows of the factors of production. It might also call for the building up of a large center in the
periphery to act as a countermagnet to the center in order to avoid
the disadvantages of locational concentration.

As has already been pointed out, because of the predominance
of light industries in the small, open economy a scattered pattern of
location outside the main center tends to result, in the absence of
government intervention. The lowering of trade barriers during the
later stages of development would cause many of these industries to
disappear due to the forces of external competition. Consequently,
absorption of the unemployed locally would not be probable.

The smaller the country the earlier would tend to be the stage
of industrialization at which the economy would halt. Then, the lack
of interference by the government or the incorrect choice of growth
points would result in locational imbalance and a "regional problem."
Thus, the timing of government intervention is crucial. It must occur

during the transitional stage and not later than that period when intermediate and capital-goods producing industries are being established.
The more advanced the stage of industrialization the greater are the
internal linkages and, thus, the greater are the forces leading to urban
concentration and central dominance. It is much more difficult to
induce alternative growth centers at the later stages in a small, open
economy.

NOTES

1. Dudley Seers, "The Stages of Development of a Primary-
producing Country in the Middle of the Twentieth Century," The Economic Bulletin of Ghana, VII, 4 (1963), 57-69. Other members of the
group include Prebisch, Veliz, and Sunkel.

2. John Friedmann, Regional Development Policy: A Case
Study of Venezuela (Cambridge, Mass.: MIT Press, 1966).

3. W. W. Rostow, The Stages of Economic Growth (New York:
Cambridge University Press, 1960).

4. Gerald Meier and Robert Baldwin, Economic Development:
Theory, History and Policy (New York: John Wiley and Sons, 1957).

5. Raul Prebisch, The Economic Development of Latin America
and its principal problems (New York: United Nations [ECLA], 1950).

6. Harvey S. Perloff and Lowdon Wingo, Jr., "Natural Resource
Endowment and Regional Economic Growth", in Joseph J. Spengler, ed.,
Natural Resources and Economic Growth (Washington, D.C.: Resources
for the Future, Inc., 1961).

7. T. W. Schultz, The Economic Organization of Agriculture
(New York: McGraw-Hill, 1953).

8. Gunnar Myrdal, Economic Theory and Underdeveloped
Regions (London: Duckworth, 1957).

9. Simon Kuznets, "Economic Growth and Income Inequality,"
American Economic Review, XLV (March, 1955), 1-28.

10. B. Okun and R. W. Richardson, "Regional Income Inequality
and Internal Population Migration," Economic Development and Cultural
Change, Vol. IX (January, 1961).

    11.   Kingsley Davis, "The Urbanization of the Human Population," Scientific American, CCXIII, 3, (September, 1965), 43.

    12.   W. J. Reilly, "Methods for the Study of Retail Relationships," University of Texas Bulletin No. 2,944.

THE SMALL, OPEN ECONOMY

There are three criteria by which a country may be defined as small: area, population, and total income. It is difficult to be dogmatic about concepts which are essentially relative in character, both over time and space; nevertheless, William Demas' view[1] that a small country is one with a population of less than 5 million and a usable land area of between 10,000 and 20,000 square miles may be taken as a useful yardstick at this particular point in time. Out of one hundred and twelve countries recently classified by the United Nations as under-developed, ninety-one had populations of less than 15 million and sixty-five had populations of less than five million. It seems appropriate, therefore, to focus attention on the concept of size. Further, it is probable that the spatial aspects of economic development in small countries will have many features in common.

The concept of openness may be measured by the relationship between external trade and internal production. Table 1 shows the relationship between exports and gross national product (GNP) in certain selected countries in 1966 while Table 2 shows the relation-ship between total trade and GNP for a further group of countries in 1959. Both tables highlight the expected correlation between the size of a country and its dependence on foreign trade, irrespective of its stage of economic development.

Ireland is a small island, 32,000 square miles in area, with a total population of less than 4.5 millions. It is divided into four provinces: Leinster, Munster, Connacht, and Ulster. These, in turn, are subdivided into thirty-two counties, Leinster having twelve, Munster six, Connacht five, and Ulster nine.

TABLE 1

Exports as a Percentage of Gross National Product for Certain Selected Countries in 1966

Country	Exports as percent of GNP
United States	5
Argentina	7
Japan	10
France	11
Italy	12
South Africa	13
United Kingdom	14
Germany	16
Sweden	21
Netherlands	34

Source: Data derived from author's research.

TABLE 2

Exports and Imports as a Percentage of Gross National Product for Certain Selected Countries in 1959

Country	Exports as percent of GNP	Imports as percent of GNP
Ceylon	33.0	29.0
Burma	19.0	19.0
Taiwan	17.0	12.0
Japan	10.3	10.0
India	6.9	4.8

Source: Data derived from author's research.

Until 1922, Ireland formed part of the United Kingdom, but since that date the island has been divided politically into two distinct parts. The larger of these, the Republic of Ireland, is 27,000 square miles in area and has a population of 2.8 million.*

The smaller part, Northern Ireland,** has a total area of approximately 5,500 square miles and a population of 1.5 million. It has remained an integral part of the United Kingdom, but Ireland has severed all political ties with it.

In 1965 the GNP of the Republic was approximately £1,000 million and the gross domestic product (GDP) of Northern Ireland was approximately £560 million.***

International trade is of vital importance to both economies. In the Republic, total exports and imports combined amount to over 70 percent of GNP, and in Northern Ireland, merchandise exports alone constitute 82 percent of GDP, while merchandise imports are almost equal to it. In other words, merchandise trade alone for Northern Ireland is nearly twice the size of its total domestic production.

By all criteria, therefore, the two parts of the island may be considered small and open. Indeed, even if one considers them as a unit, the whole island is a small, open economy.

THE CENTER-PERIPHERY RELATIONSHIP

In Ireland, strong center-periphery relationships operate both externally and internally.

----

*It contains the provinces of Leinster, Munster, Connacht, and three of the counties of Ulster. (See Map 1.)

**Northern Ireland is composed of the remaining six counties of Ulster. (See Map 1.)

***The chief difference between GDP and GNP (apart from in direct taxes) is that if earnings rising from production go abroad, they are omitted from GNP but remain in the GDP. Conversely, dividends from foreign production received by local residents enter the GNP but not the GDP.

Externally, the connection between both parts of the island and Great Britain is very strong. There is full mobility of the factors of production between Ireland and Great Britain and no passports are required for travel between the two islands.* The Republic's banking system remains closely tied to that of Great Britain and, despite recent attempts designed to make it more independent, its monetary policy reflects its essential dependency.

Part of the explanation for the large investments of foreign capital in Irish industry lies in the fact that exports enjoy free entry into the British market and, in the case of Northern Ireland, into European Free Trade Association (EFTA) countries as well.

As might be expected in an increasingly independent economy, the degree of geographic concentration of the Republic's external trade has lessened since the 1920's. Nevertheless, as can be seen from Tables 3 and 4, almost 70 percent of its exports in 1966 went to Great Britain and over 50 percent of its imports originated there. In fact, most of Ireland's trade is either to or through Great Britain. Although Table 5 does not show the origins of imports and the final destinations of exports in detail for Northern Ireland, it can be concluded that the corresponding degree of geographic concentration for its trade has not altered significantly since the 1930's. Moreover, and as one would expect in the case of largely competitive economies, the amount of trade carried on between both parts of the island is relatively small. Despite this, however, cross-border movements of people now number 50 million annually and a significant proportion of tourist earnings in both areas comes from this traffic. Further, despite the recent political upheaval in Northern Ireland and its government's declared opposition to the idea of the eventual reunification of the island, cooperative efforts in the field of overseas tourist promotion and electricity generation have recently been launched.

Within both parts of the island, strong center-periphery relationships also operate. Both Dublin and Belfast dominate their respective territories with respect to political influence, population, and economic activity.

---

*However, work permits are necessary for all nonresidents seeking jobs in Northern Ireland--evidence of the very high rate of unemployment which normally prevails there and which reached a height of 8 percent early in 1969.

TABLE 3

Domestic Exports of the Republic of Ireland
by Destination Expressed as Percentage of
Total Domestic Exports for
Selected Years Between 1924 and 1966

Destination	1924	1933	1944	1953	1963	1966
United Kingdom	98.0	93.7	99.0	91.8	72.0	69.4
of which Northern Ireland	14.5	11.5	19.3	15.1	15.1	11.7
United States	0.5	0.8	0.94	2.1	7.8	6.9
Canada	0.06	0.1	-	0.3	1.6	0.9
Countries now constituting EEC	0.7	2.6	-	2.9	7.5	11.0
Countries now constituting EFTA (excluding United Kingdom)	0.1	0.6	0.06	0.5	1.2	1.2
Other countries	0.64	2.2	-	2.4	9.9	10.6
	100.0	100.0	100.0	100.0	100.0	100.0

Source: Trade and Shipping Statistics of Ireland for the years
cited.

TABLE 4

Imports of the Republic of Ireland by Origin
Expressed as Percentage of Total Imports for
Selected Years Between 1924 and 1966

Origin	1924	1933	1944	1953	1963	1966
United Kingdom	81.1	69.8	47.0	50.7	51.0	51.8
of which Northern Ireland	11.4	5.8	2.8	1.3	4.7	3.7
United States	5.4	2.9	10.4	9.0	6.0	9.4
Canada	2.1	3.0	17.5	3.1	2.4	2.6
Countries now constituting EEC	3.9	9.6	-	12.4	15.4	13.5
Countries now constituting EFTA (excluding United Kingdom)	1.0	2.2	2.6	4.3	4.1	3.4
Other countries	6.5	12.5	22.5	20.5	21.1	19.3
	100.0	100.0	100.0	100.0	100.0	100.0

Source: Trade and Shipping Statistics of Ireland for the years
cited.

TABLE 5

Trade of Northern Ireland by Countries

Exports

Class	Declared value of all goods exported direct to all places outside Great Britain expressed as percentage of total exports				Estimated value of goods exported to Great Britain and to other countries via Great Britain expressed as percentage of total exports			
	1938	1946	1956	1965	1938	1946	1956	1965
Total Exports	10	7	6	9	90	93	94	91
Live animals	0.5	0.3	0.5	2.0	9.0	6.0	6.0	2.0
Food and drink	2.0	0.3	1.0	1.0	17.0	13.0	20.0	15.0
Basic materials	1.5	0.4	0.5	1.0	2.0	3.0	2.0	2.0
Manufactured goods	6.0	6.0	4.0	5.0	62.0	71.0	66.0	72.0

Imports

Class	Declared value of all goods imported direct from places outside Great Britain expressed as percentage of total imports				Estimated value of goods imported from and through Great Britain expressed as percentage of total imports			
	1938	1946	1956	1965	1938	1946	1956	1965
Total Imports	27	18	23	25	73	82	77	75
Live animals	4.0	4.0	3.0	2.0	0	0	0	0
Food, drink, and tobacco	13.0	9.0	12.0	12.0	17.0	16.0	15.0	11.0
Basic materials	7.0	3.0	5.0	5.0	6.0	8.0	7.0	7.0
Manufactured goods	3.0	2.0	3.0	6.0	50.0	58.0	55.0	57.0

Source: Northern Ireland, The Trade of Northern Ireland (Belfast: Ministry of Commerce, 1938, 1946, 1956, and 1965).

As a capital city, each occupies the seat of government and acts as the administrative center for its area.

In 1966, 25 percent of the population of the Republic lived in the Dublin urban area, while 37 percent of Northern Ireland's population lived in the urban area centered on Belfast.*

As can be seen from Table 6, the demographic dominance exercised by Dublin and Belfast in their respective areas increased steadily up to the 1950's but the position of Belfast in this respect now appears to have reached an equilibrium, no doubt reflecting the fact that it is the main center in a much more urbanized economy.

Both parts of the island are areas of heavy out-migration. In the case of the Republic, the flows of emigrants have been greater than the natural increase of births over deaths for almost every intercensal period since the great famine of the 1840's. As can be seen from Table 7, this had resulted in persistent falls in total population and in the populations of the individual provinces until 1961. The notable exception was Leinster Province, wherein Dublin is situated. All the individual counties, with the exception of Dublin, have persistently been areas of net outward migration. Dublin and the neighboring counties of Kildare, Meath, and Louth are the only ones to have shown steady increases in population since the 1930's. Dublin itself is the only county of net immigration--that is, the only county where the increase in population was due not merely to internal growth but also to net inward movements of population which it attracted from the periphery.

In the case of Northern Ireland, as Table 8 demonstrates, the total outflow of emigrants, though high, has been consistently less than the natural increase of births over deaths since 1891, thus leading to a steady increase in total population over the period.

Table 9 shows the migratory movements on a county basis. In contrast to the Republic, four out of the six counties of Northern Ireland are areas of net inward migration, with Antrim and Down, not unexpectedly, displaying the greatest gains. Most of the migrants from the peripheral western counties moved to these eastern counties

---

*Throughout this book Dublin is taken to include: the contiguous county boroughs of Dublin and Dun Laoghaire together with their suburbs and environs. Belfast is taken to include the county borough of Belfast plus the urban areas adjoining the city. These definitions are considered more useful within the context of the present study.

TABLE 6

Population of all Ireland, the Area now Constituting the
Republic of Ireland, the Area now Constituting Northern
Ireland, and the Populations of Dublin and Belfast as Percentages
of Republic and Northern Ireland Populations,
Respectively, for Selected Years Between 1881 and 1966
(population in thousands)

Area	1881	1891	1901	1911	1926	1936a	1951	1961	1966
Ireland	5,175	4,705	4,459	4,390	4,229	4,248	4,332	4,243	4,369
Republic	3,870	3,469	3,222	3,140	2,972	2,968	2,961	2,818	2,884
Northern Ireland	1,305	1,236	1,237	1,250	1,257	1,280	1,371	1,425	1,485
Dublin as percent of (2)	8.5	10	11.6	12.7	15	17	21	23	26
Belfast as percent of (3)	16	21	28	31	33	34	37	37	37
Percent urbanized in Republicb	8.5	10	11.6	12.7	15	17	21	28	30
Percent urbanized in Northern Ireland	16	21	28	31	33	34	37	37	37

a1937 for Northern Ireland.
bUntil 1956, Dublin was the only center in the Republic with a population greater than 100,000. From that date Cork exceeded that figure and thus the percentage of the population which is urbanized consists of the percentage of the population living in Dublin and Cork. Belfast continues to be the only city in Northern Ireland with a population exceeding 100,000.

Source: Data derived from Ireland, Census of Population (Dublin: Stationery Office, 1881, 1891, 1901, 1911, 1936, 1951, 1961, and 1966).

TABLE 7

Rate of Decrease in Population, Natural Increase, and Net Emigration Per Thousand Average Population Per Annum in the Provinces of the Republic of Ireland, 1926-66

Intercensal period	Total			Leinster			Munster			Connacht			Ulster (part of)		
	Decrease in population	Natural increase	Net emigration	Decrease in population	Natural increase	Net emigration	Decrease in population	Natural increase	Net emigration	Decrease in population	Natural increase	Net emigration	Decrease in population	Natural increase	Net emigration
1901-11	2.6	5.6	8.2	+0.8	4.4	3.6	3.9	6.2	10.1	5.7	7.4	13.1	4.3	4.8	9.1
1911-26	3.7	5.2	8.8	0.7	4.7	5.5	4.4	5.6	9.9	6.7	6.1	12.8	6.6	4.0	10.6
1926-36	0.1	5.5	5.6	+6.0	6.4	0.4	2.9	5.3	8.2	5.1	5.0	10.1	6.8	3.4	10.2
1936-46	0.4	5.9	6.3	+4.9	7.8	2.9	2.7	5.0	7.7	6.4	3.9	10.3	6.0	3.7	9.7
1946-51	+0.4	8.6	8.2	+8.6	10.7	2.1	4.1	7.5	11.7	8.8	6.3	15.1	8.4	6.2	14.6
1951-56	4.3	9.2	13.4	+0.4	11.7	11.4	4.9	7.9	12.8	11.2	6.3	17.4	14.2	5.4	19.6
1956-61	5.6	9.2	14.8	1.0	12.1	13.1	6.5	7.7	14.2	12.4	5.9	18.3	16.2	4.5	20.7
1961-66	+4.6	10.3	5.7	+12.0	13.5	1.5	+2.3	8.7	6.4	8.5	5.0	13.6	8.7	5.6	14.2

Source: Ireland, Census of Population (Dublin, Stationary Office, 1901, 1911, 1926, 1936, 1946, 1951, 1956, 1961, and 1966).

TABLE 8

Intercensal Variations in the Population of Northern Ireland

Intercensal period	Population at beginning of period	Births registered	Deaths registered	Excess of births over deaths	Intercensal variations in population	Net movements outward
1871-81	1,359,190	355,301	250,951	104,350	-54,374	158,724
1881-91	1,304,816	312,249	240,339	71,910	-68,760	140,670
1891-1901	1,236,056	314,795	246,161	68,634	+ 896	67,738
1901-11	1,236,952	309,502	230,506	78,996	+13,579	65,417
1911-26	1,250,531	431,148	317,545	113,603	+ 6,030	107,573*
1926-37	1,256,561	280,641	199,806	80,835	+23,184	57,651
1937-51	1,279,745	402,187	243,744	158,443	+91,176	67,267*
1951-61	1,370,921	298,808	152,459	146,349	+54,121	92,228
1961-66	1,425,042	182,529	85,050	97,479	+59,728	37,751

*Including deaths in H.M. Forces which occurred outside Northern Ireland.

Source: Northern Ireland, Census of Population (Belfast: H. M. Stationery Office, 1966).

26

TABLE 9

Numbers of Immigrants and Emigrants for Each County and County Borough in Northern Ireland, 1961-66

Area	Resident population at census date 1966	Immigrants	Emigrants	Migration balance	
				Number	Percentage of resident population
County Boroughs					
Belfast	393,797	15,680	36,399	-20,719	-5.3
Londonderry	55,399	1,733	3,963	- 2,230	-4.0
Counties					
Antrim	311,457	28,915	12,993	+15,922	+5.1
Armagh	124,748	5,035	4,646	+ 389	+0.3
Down	285,105	23,350	13,296	+10,054	+3.5
Fermanagh	49,866	1,310	2,614	- 1,304	-2.6
Londonderry	118,317	6,077	5,372	+ 705	+0.6
Tyrone	136,263	3,096	5,913	- 2,817	-2.1

Source: Northern Ireland, Census of Population (Belfast: H.M. Stationery Office, 1966).

of Antrim and Down and to Belfast city. As mentioned earlier, the census figures for Belfast are somewhat misleading because by far the greater part of the movement out of Belfast city in recent years has been to areas directly adjoining the city. Once again, therefore, we can see that, just as in the case of the Republic, the main urban center exercises a very strong pull on the peripheral areas.

The dominant position of the main center in each economy is further demonstrated in Table 10, which shows the proportion of economic activity (measured in terms of net output and employment) located in Dublin and Belfast during the period 1936-64. The supporting data is taken from the respective censuses of industrial production. These data include not only the manufacturing sectors but also the service sectors of each economy, but, of course, do not cover very small firms. An examination of the location of all manufacturing firms will be carried out in Chapter 4.

Of the large firms thus covered, 33 percent in the Republic were located in Dublin in 1964.

An examination of the location of net output in the Republic shows that the degree of its concentration in Dublin declined from 54 percent in 1936 to 43 percent in 1964. If, however, we include County Dublin in the calculations (and from the point of view of manufacturing activity this is reasonable, since many factories are located outside the city boundaries but are obviously an integral part of the urban industrial complex), then we find that the degree of concentration has declined by only 7 percent, that is from 56 percent to 49 percent over the period.

As regards employment, while we find that the degree of concentration is not so marked within the city, the decline in concentration has been slight over the period. Again, when we include County Dublin in the calculations, we find that the degree of concentration has actually risen steadily since 1936. More significantly, the firms in County Dublin lead all others with respect to average output and average numbers engaged per establishment.

As might be expected in a smaller area, the dominant position of Belfast, with respect to the degree of concentration of net output and employment, in its territory is much greater than the corresponding position of Dublin within the Republic.*

_____

*Belfast, in this instance, includes the county borough area only as defined in the Census of Industrial Production and thus the

TABLE 10

Distribution of Net Output and Employment in Dublin and in
Belfast as Percentages of Total Net Output and Employment
in the Republic of Ireland and in Northern Ireland
for Selected Years

Area	Net output				Average numbers engaged			
	1936[a]	1946[b]	1956	1964	1936[a]	1946[b]	1956	1964
Dublin city	54	43	48	43	43	42	42	40
Dublin city and county	56	46	53	49	45	45	46	46
Belfast	69	65	60	n.a.	63	60	57	n.a.

[a] 1935 for Northern Ireland.
[b] 1949 for Northern Ireland.

Source: Data derived from Ireland, Census of Industrial Production (Dublin, Stationery Office, 1936, 1946, 1954, and 1964).

It is, therefore, clear that not only is there a strong center-periphery relationship operating externally between both parts of the island and Great Britain but that this type of relationship is also at work inside the two small economies. The main center within each acts as a powerful magnet upon its periphery drawing to itself resources and population and attracting the bulk of industry which, in turn, enables it to absorb these inflows.

This pattern of urban growth, involving a concentration of population in a small number of very large centers, is, of course, not unique to Ireland. In many countries of Africa, Asia, Latin America, and the Middle East, a very high proportion of the total urban population is concentrated in one or two large agglomerations or "primate cities" and the dominating influence which these centers exert on their national economies is a source of concern to economic planners in these countries.

According to a United Nations report, the settlement pattern in Africa, which is "generally assuming the form of an expanding metro-politan region with a primate urban core surrounded by a tributary hinterland. . .being drained of its material and human resources,"[2] appears to be typical of developing countries. Disquiet is also felt by planners in Latin America about the implications of such an urban pattern, and the problems are seen to be chronic unless new techniques are developed to correct them. To quote from the United Nations observers again: "The rapidity of concentration of population in a few large centers has been viewed with apprehension as the source of a complex of problems that seem almost insoluble. At any rate the available techniques of urban planning, administration, and provision of social services seem to be making no headway towards their solution and a continuation in present trends in population growth and redistribution will make their dimensions even more intractable."[3]

The tendency towards urban concentration appears to be par-ticularly acute in small countries like those of the Middle East where the rural-urban migrations tend to bypass the medium-size towns and to settle in the relatively few large urban centers in the region. In Jordan, which had a population of 1.7 million in 1965, only one of the country's seven census districts, Amman, grew more rapidly than the country itself between 1952 and 1961 and, according to the estimates of the U.N. Economic and Social Office in Beirut,[4] over

---

apparently rapid rate of decline in industrial concentration therein recorded in recent years is due to the ommission of the new indus-tries located outside the legal limits.

26 percent of the population will be living in the capital city by 1980.

The effects of the operation of an external center-periphery
relationship between the developing and the developed areas of the
world has been postulated in the model as one of the causes of the
spatially unbalanced growth experienced by many developing countries.
This would appear to be in agreement with the opinion of observers
on the Asian scene who claim that the excessive concentration of
urban population in the larger agglomerations of Asian countries is
explained by the fact that "the commercialization of the peasant economies of Asia has proceeded from a few port towns linking vast raw
material-producing hinterlands with external markets in industrializing
countries."[5]

Thus, the motivation behind most regional planning schemes in
developing countries appears to stem from the belief that the growth
of one or two primate cities in these countries produces an unbalanced
spatial distribution of population and of economic activity--a consequence which is considered undersirable in the long run and which,
therefore, calls for corrective action in the form of regional and
urban planning.

THE APPLICATION OF THE MODEL TO IRELAND

In attempting to relate the Irish experience to the model it
must be kept in mind that up to 1922 the island was a unified economy,
forming an integral part of the United Kingdom. After that date it
was divided into two separate political units, which, in terms of past
experience and subsequent trends, have many contrasts.

The two areas, therefore, do not necessarily fit into the same
stage of development during the same time period. However, this
study claims that, despite the undoubted contrasts, from a spatial
point of view the island is still essentially a unit and, therefore, that
policy-makers should take congnizance of this. Otherwise, if and
when the island is again reunited, it will be too late to reverse the
repercussions of autarkic and interregionally competitive spatial
policies.

Throughout the nineteenth century, Ireland was a member of
the British colonial empire. The operation of the free-trade system,
of which it thus formed a part, was geared in the main to the needs
of the center in Great Britain, with Ireland fitting into the agricultural
periphery of the system. The demand at the center for cattle, for
example, led to a shift in agricultural production in Ireland from
tillage to pasture and the production of livestock. The main export

item became live animals--that is, an unprocessed product from the primary sector.

Certain areas within Ireland prospered, in particular the capital city, Dublin, and the city of Belfast, together with its neighboring towns.

Three large industries, shipbuilding, linen, and brewing and distilling, provided the bulk of output in the secondary sector. In many respects, however, they were not really an integral part of the domestic economy. The first two industries, shipbuilding and linen, located in the northeastern area, centered on Belfast, relied upon imports of steel and flax for their raw materials, and sold most of their output abroad. Brewing and distilling, concentrated in Dublin, also benefited greatly from free access to world markets, although they were not quite so dependent on imports for their raw materials. Thus, the two main centers, together with the linen towns in the hinterland of Belfast, formed a relatively prosperous enclave within a largely agrarian economy as a result of the operation of free trade. With the exception of a couple of other thriving industries producing biscuits and ropes, the free-trade regime did not facilitate industrialization based on domestic resources or catering exclusively to the home market. Competition from imports, which flowed in unimpeded by tariffs, effectively precluded the growth of local and necessarily small-scale industries.

Near-perfect competition also prevailed in the factor markets and both labor and capital sought employment at the center, where the opportunities seemed more apparent and the returns more lucrative.

According to the report of the Commission on Emigration, the amount of investment in Ireland was very low during the nineteenth century.

"Investment in land was ruled out so long as titles were uncertain. Investment in industry was impeded by the lack of obvious openings. Even when such openings did exist they had to compete with those found abroad. In the U.K. there were innumerable opportunities for the investment of capital that offered both a degree of security and a prospect of profit that could not be mached at home. Irish investors, therefore, looked increasingly abroad, and opportunities at home, even when they were sound, were neglected."[6]

Urbanization was proceeding at a steady pace but its pattern was not uniform either throughout the country or between the six counties now constituting Northern Ireland and the remaining

TABLE 11

Town and Rural Population of Ireland, 1841-1926

Census year	Ireland		26 Counties		6 Counties	
	Town	Rural	Town	Rural	Town	Rural
1841	1,215	6,960	1,002	5,527	213	1,433
1851	1,279	5,273	1,033	4,079	246	1,194
1861	1,174	4,625	895	3,507	279	1,184
1871	1,241	4,171	895	3,158	346	1,013
1881	1,292	3,883	898	2,972	394	911
1891	1,293	3,412	853	2,616	440	796
1901	1,436	3,023	887	2,335	549	688
1911	1,523	2,867	920	2,220	603	647
1926	1,596	2,633	944	2,028	652	605

Source: Ireland, Commission on Emigration...1948-54 (Dublin: Stationery Office, 1955), p. 10.

twenty-six counties now making up the Irish Republic.

Up until 1881, less than 10 percent of the total population was living in centers of 100,000 or more, but between that date and 1921 (the year before independence) the proportion increased from 10 percent to 20 percent. However, whereas in the northern six counties the figure more than doubled from 16 percent to 38 percent, in the twenty-six counties, which up to that date had been truly agrarian, is started from a lower base of 9 percent and increased to only 15 percent by 1921.

The vast majority of the population lived in centers of less than 1,500 but the internal growth of towns and the drift from the land led to an increase in the ratio of town to rural population. Again, as can be seen from Table 11 the experience of the northern six counties can be contrasted with that of the rest of the country.

Between the 1840's and the 1920's the proportion of the population
of Ireland living in towns of 1,500 or more increased by almost one-
third but this was caused by the three-fold increase in town population
in the northern six counties since the town population in the twenty-
six counties actually fell until 1901. The trends in rural population
were similar, both parts of the country being affected to the same
extent. The Emigration Commission report[7] points out that, despite
many differences between the two areas, the demographic experiences
of Northern Ireland and of Leinster Province were remarkably alike.
The report attributes this to the favorable reaction of the growth and
size of Dublin and Belfast on the rural population of the areas adjacent
to these cities.

Despite the regional imbalance with respect to industrialization
and urbanization thus apparent in the country until the 1920's, a number
of other centers, relatively far removed from the two main ones,
managed to grow and to prosper. Two of these, Londonderry in the
north and Cork in the south, had some important industries but such
others as Limerick, Sligo, Tralee, and Waterford thrived mainly by
acting as service centers for their surrounding hinterlands.

The status quo was disrupted in 1922 when the twenty-six counties
now comprising the Irish Republic became politically independent.*
The remaining six counties chose to remain within the United Kingdom;
Ireland was thus divided into two separate economies--a relatively
industrialized and urbanized northeast and an independent state which
was, to a large extent, still essentially agrarian in character. An
examination of Table 6, showing the degree of urbanization in each
economy in the 1920's, highlights the contrasts between them while
the data in Tables 12 and 13 reinforce these contrasts by showing the
differences in the relative importance of the three sectors as employers.

Indeed, it is apparent from a comparison of these tables that in
1966 the Republic was not as developed in terms of the breakdown of
its labor force as Northern Ireland was forty years earlier. For this
reason, and also because Northern Ireland, as part of the United
Kingdom, did not pursue an independent development program, the
examination of economic development policy in Ireland, at least until

-----

*Upon independence, the twenty-six counties became the Irish
Free State. They did not leave the Commonwealth and become a
republic until 1949, but for the sake of convenience and terminological
consistency that portion of the island will be referred to as the
Republic throughout this book.

TABLE 12

Sectoral Breakdown of the Labor Force
in the Republic of Ireland, 1926-66
(in percentages)

Year	Agriculture	Industry	Services
1926	53.0	13.5	33.5
1936	49.3	16.6	34.1
1946	47.1	16.7	36.2
1956	39.3	23.2	37.5
1966	32.2	26.7	41.1

Source: Data derived from Ireland, Census of Population (Dublin: Stationery Office, 1926, 1936, 1946, 1956, and 1966).

TABLE 13

Sectoral Breakdown of the Labor Force
in Northern Ireland, 1926-66
(in percentages)

Year	Agriculture	Industry	Services
1926	27.0	36.0	37.0
1937	n.a.	n.a.	n.a.
1948	20.0	43.0	37.0
1956	17.0	46.0	37.0
1966	11.3	42.0	46.7

Source: Data Derived from Northern Ireland, Census of Population (Belfast: H.M. Stationery Office, 1926, 1937, 1948, 1956, and 1966).

the 1950's, will be confined mainly to a study of the Irish Republic.
Since then, Northern Ireland has embarked upon a vigorous program
of development and thus the comparisons and contrasts which will be
made throughout this section will be more specific when they refer to
the final phase of the period under review.

In an effort to achieve economic development in the Republic,
the government set in motion a two-pronged program designed to
encourage industrialization. On the one hand, a policy of mild protection was adopted and tariffs were imposed on a haphazard collection
of imports which included boots and shoes, glass bottles, soap and
candles, clothing, wooden furniture, and confectionery products, with
the object of promoting the domestic production of these consumer
goods. On the other hand, the government set about providing the
infrastructural facilities which it considered essential to induce
industrialization during this first phase of its transition towards economic development. The first important project was the Shannon
hydroelectric scheme begun in 1927 and completed in 1931.*

Between 1926 and 1929 there was a fairly general expansion of
industry. The most important manufacturing industry, with a total

------

*Much argument in the literature on development strategy
centers on the question of balance between social overhead capital
(chiefly transportation and power) and directly productive activities
(chiefly industry), and A.O. Hirschman in The Strategy of Economic
Development (New Haven: Yale University Press, 1959), Chapter 5
discusses at length the advantages of "development via excess capacity"
(of SOC) and "development via shortage" (of SOC). Although, in
general, Hirschman appears to favor "development via shortage" (of
SOC) as a means of inducing action, he acknowledges that this may
not be feasible in an economy which hopes to attract foreign capital
or one within which there are serious regional imbalances. "The
foreign investor can choose among dynamic centers of many countries
and is likely to give some preference to those where shortages are
least harassing. This consideration also applies within a country that
has several developing centers competing with one another. In such
a situation the positive response to excessive SOC may be high for
one center because of the competition of the others. In other words,
the choice of DPA investors is likely to be made primarily on the
basis of the comparative SOC endowments of the different candidate
areas. . .and development via excess capacity is definitely the choice
in this case." (pp. 95-96). In view of the subsequent encouragement
in the Republic of foreign capital inflows, the early emphasis on SOC
investments was probably sound in the long run.

net output of £5 million, was still brewing, followed by bread and flour confectionery, building, printing, tobacco, and a variety of other consumer goods. The production of vehicles, which ranked ninth in terms of net output, led in terms of growth, and other growth industries included sugar confectionery, clothing, electricity, soap and candles, and wood furniture, most of which were benefiting from the new policy of protection.

The second impetus to industrialization in the Republic came in the early 1930's. This was caused first by the spread of the world depression and the consequent reduction in international trade, but second, and more importantly, by an economic "war" between Ireland and Great Britain.* This led to the adoption of a self-sufficiency policy and to the extension of protection to cover a wide variety of consumer goods, including domestic hollow-ware, cutlery, pottery, electric lamps, cement, sugar, flour milling, semimanufactured clothing, textiles, leather, and various manufactures of wood, rubber, aluminum, wire, and iron.

Although not necessarily due to the effects of the tariff alone, the value of net output in the industrial sector rose from £23 million in 1926 to £33 million in 1936, while total employment in this sector rose from 103,000 to 154,000. However, the increases in net output and employment in manufacturing alone were even more significant during this period. The ranking of individual industries had not

---

*According to the provisions of the treaty signed in 1921 between the United Kingdom and the area now constituting the Republic of Ireland, the Irish signatories agreed to make certain annual payments to the British government after independence, principally in respect of war damages to British property in Ireland, and land annuities, that is, repayments of monies which had, up to that date, been paid directly by Irish farmers to the British government which had bought out British landowners. With the coming to power in 1932 of the party which had opposed these conditions in the 1921 treaty, these payments were stopped and the British government, in an attempt to recoup its losses, imposed punitive duties on imports from Ireland. The Irish government retaliated by imposing correspondingly high duties on imports from the United Kingdom and the economic "war" which followed completely disrupted trade between the two countries. From being Britain's best customer in 1932, the Republic of Ireland fell to fifth place by 1938. The dispute was finally settled by the Anglo-Irish Agreements of 1938, the first of which was a financial agreement and the second a trade agreement which was to lay the basis for future trading relations between the two countries.

changed appreciably and the emphasis was still almost exclusively on the production of consumer goods. Meanwhile, the spread of the world depression, coupled with the absence of an independent protectionist policy, had adversely affected industrial production in Northern Ireland, and net output and numbers employed fell in most industries in the early 1930's. The leading growth industry there was electrical engineering, followed by bacon, distilling and brewing, shipbuilding, and chemicals, reflecting a much more developed industrial mix than that obtaining in the Republic.

During this early period, imports of some consumer goods (notably flour, bacon, sugar and confectionery, footwear, and furniture) gradually began to fall in the Republic but there was no corresponding increase in industrial exports. Indeed, in many cases, despite massive protection, home production fell short of demand in the local market. There is strong evidence to support the view that in the case of many manufacturing industries this was due not so much to a lack of effective demand either at home or abroad as to inelasticity of supply caused in many cases by inertia on the part of the home producers. As the report of the Commission on Emigration[8] points out:

> The number of existing industries in which output is suffi-
> cient to meet home demand wholly or substantially was
> very small. In many cases, for a variety of reasons, pro-
> duction falls substantially short of home demand despite
> the protection given by tariff or quota. These revenue
> receipts, substantial though they are, are not a complete
> indication of the quantity of such commodities imported.
> Where the required amounts of protected goods cannot be
> obtained from Irish factories, licences are granted to
> import the goods free of duty and the number of such
> licences issued is considerable. Where protection is
> given in the form of a quota limitation of imports, the
> size of the quota, and hence of permitted imports, indi-
> cates the extent to which home production falls short of
> domestic demand and so gives some idea of the expansion
> which is still possible even in industries already estab-
> lished and protected. . . . Some other protected indus-
> tries, with the market similarly reserved for them, are
> selling their products at fully competitive prices in the
> home market, but because of the trouble and risk of
> export trade have not tried to sell elsewhere [my emphasis].[9]

Because of the lack of heavy industry and the shortage of most of the minerals and fuels used in industrial production, imports of capital goods and of raw materials and fuels rose sharply in the Republic as industrialization proceeded. Increased prices of consumer goods adversely affected agricultural costs of production and reduced the competitiveness of exports from the primary sector. Nevertheless, the industrialization of the economy was considered of prime importance and protection of new industries was continued after World War II and through the early 1950's. By this time, important shifts had already taken place within the manufacturing sector. Although 75 percent of the volume of output still came from the production of consumer goods, over 8 percent represented the output of consumer durables and 15 percent capital-goods production.

The progress recorded in industry was not accompanied by a corresponding development of the economy's main sector. Agriculture was neglected. The volume of gross and net agricultural output fell between the late 1930's and the early 1950's and the increase in the value of net output was the result of substantial increases in agricultural prices during this period. Meanwhile, the drift from the land gathered momentum.[10]

The decline in agricultural population, which had proceeded at an average rate of approximately 4,000 per annum up to 1946 accelerated in the succeeding five years when it reached a rate of over 14,000 per annum. In contrast to the previous twenty-year period, when migration from agriculture was mainly confined to small holdings, in the 1946-51 period it was felt with equal severity on all sizes of holdings and in all areas of the country. However, the counties which were worst affected were those which lacked larger towns and which showed the least increase in manufacturing employment such as Leitrim, Monaghan, Mayo, Longford, and Donegal.

The urban population of the Republic as a whole increased but, as can be seen from Table 14, the larger cities and towns were gradually garnering an increasing percentage of total population. Concentration in Dublin was increasing steadily and many of the smaller towns tended to decrease in size.

An examination of census data showing the percentage of people born and remaining in the area of their birth provides an indication of the extent of internal migration. In the late 1940's only 65 percent of the population of Dublin (city and county) was Dublin-born while over 75 percent of the population in the rest of Leinster was born in that province. The corresponding figures for Munster, Connacht, and the three counties of Ulster were 85 percent, 90 percent, and 88 percent respectively, showing that inward migration into Dublin was high while movement into the provinces outside Leinster was negligible. The same pattern was repeated on a county level, the only counties showing in-migration being Dublin and a few of the counties contiguous

TABLE 14

Distribution of the Population in the Republic of Ireland by Type of District, 1926-66

(in thousands)

Type of District	1926			1936			1946			1956			1966		
	Number	Population	Percent	Number	Population	Percent	Number	Population	Percent	Number	Population	Percent	Number	Population	Percent
County Boroughs															
Dublin*	2	443	14.9	2	513	17.3	2	551	18.6	2	650	22.4	2	735	25.5
Cork	1	78	2.6	1	81	2.7	1	90	3.0	1	114	3.9	1	125	4.3
Limerick	1	39	1.3	1	41	1.4	1	43	1.5	1	52	1.8	1	58	2.0
Waterford	1	27	0.8	1	28	0.9	1	28	0.9	1	29	1.0	1	30	1.0
5 County Boroughs															
Towns with population of:	5	588	19.8	5	663	22.3	5	698	23.6	5	845	29.2	5	948	32.7
over 10,000	7	87	2.9	8	106	3.6	8	111	3.7	10	145	5.0	10	152	5.3
5,000 - 10,000	14	88	2.9	17	104	3.5	17	108	3.6	17	105	3.6	19	123	4.3
1,500 - 5,000	76	201	6.7	72	188	6.3	72	193	6.6	67	191	6.6	70	196	6.8
Rest of country		2,008	67.6		1,908	64.3		1,843	62.4		1,611	55.6		1,465	50.8
Republic of Ireland		2,972	100		2,968	100		2,953	100		2,898	100		2,884	100

*Dublin, as defined in this study, contains two boroughs, Dublin and Dun Laoghaire.

Source: Ireland, Census of Population of Ireland (Dublin: Stationery Office, 1926, 1936, 1946, 1956, and 1966).

to it. In general, and again with the notable exception of Dublin, the urban centers failed to absorb effectively the rural exodus and consequently the flow tended to bypass the local towns and to emigrate to urban centers abroad. By the mid-1950's, emigration was proceeding at the rate of 40,000 per annum. Obviously, the emigrants were seeking industrial employment and the fact that the relatively industrialized areas of Leinster succeeded in absorbing some of the migrants emphasizes the important connection between urbanization and industrialization during the process of economic development.

The expansion of industry up to the mid-1950's was widespread and affected all provinces equally, with the result that the percentage distribution of industry between the provinces did not change significantly and manufacturing remained concentrated in the east and most particularly in Dublin. Most of the larger capital-intensive industries were located in the main city, reflecting, among other things, the increased dependence on imports of raw materials and machinery and the advantages which the main port conferred on exporters. Thus, despite government policy favoring decentralization,* industry remained heavily concentrated in Dublin.

The third impetus to industrialization in the Republic came in the form of an endogenously induced crisis in the late 1950's. It was the culmination of a series of setbacks in the economy which had led to virtual stagnation in the earlier part of the decade. The need to import capital goods and raw materials for industry and the failure of exports to keep pace led to a series of balance of payments deficits which caused the external reserves built up during the war years to be virtually depleted. The failure of incomes to rise appreciably caused government investment expenditure to fall, and in 1958, GNP fell in real terms. Self-confidence had evaporated.

It had already become apparent that the existing tariff policy was no longer effective as a means of promoting new industries, as the production possibilities for the home market had already been largely exhausted. The application to join the European Economic Comminity (EEC) reflected the growing realization that further

---

*In the early 1950's, policies were put into operation authorizing grants towards the cost of buildings and equipment in the underdeveloped areas of the Republic (chiefly the counties on the western seaboard). The Industrial Grants Act of 1956 extended these benefits to the whole country but continued to favor the underdeveloped areas by restricting the size of grants given to the rest of the country. For a fuller discussion on regional policy, see Chapter 3.

development of the economy involved participation in a wider international community and the abandonment of autarkic economic policies.
A program was now needed to carry the economy into the third phase
of industrialization, involving the export of manufactured goods.

Accordingly, in 1958 the government initiated its first Program
of Economic Expansion in an attempt to revitalize and transform the
economy and to halt the emigration of agriculture's displaced workers
who were unable to secure employment in the industrial sector which
was not growing at a rate fast enough to absorb them.

The Control of Manufactures Act, which specified that the con-
trolling interest in all industries should be held by Irish nationals,
had already been repealed to facilitate the inflow of foreign capital;
the drive to encourage such investments was now intensified. Policies
involving capital grants and increased credit facilities for productive
investment, together with tax reliefs on export earnings were put into
effect. This marked an important shift in emphasis in investment
policy from the earlier concentration on infrastructure and social
overhead capital to investment in directly productive activities, particularly in the field of manufacturing industry. By the end of the
plan period, in 1963, the modest target of a 2 percent increase in GNP
had been achieved twice over. Most of this increase came from the
industrial sector, the net output of which increased from £146 million
in 1958 to £221 million in 1962; the main contribution to growth within
this sector came from the production of manufactured goods. Industrial
exports increased sharply and the percentage shares of machinery,
textiles, clothing, and chemicals in total exports all rose.

Progress towards a more open economy was further advanced
during the period of the second Program of Economic Expansion, which
was planned to cover the period 1964 to 1970. It was based upon the
assumption that Ireland would be a member of the EEC by 1970 but
the immediate stimulus came in 1965 in the form of the Anglo-Irish
Free Trade Area (AIFTA) agreement signed between the Republic and
the United Kingdom. It specified that in return for annual tariff
reductions of approximately 10 percent, over the subsequent decade,
on British goods entering the Republic, the United Kingdom agreed to
the immediate abolition of the few remaining tariffs on Irish exports
to it.

The overall projections contained within the second program
were generally in line with the achievements of the first plan period
and once again the main impetus to growth was expected to come from
the industrial sector. Although the increase in employment was set
at a modest rate of 1 percent per annum and migration from agriculture
was expected to approximate 9,000 per annum, it was hoped that

emigration abroad would be reduced to 10,000 per annum by 1970--
that is, to half the rate prevailing in the 1960's and one-quarter of
that in the 1950's. Both exports and imports were expected to rise
faster than GNP but the actual increase which took place in the latter
and the abandonment of the possibility of EEC entry by 1970 were
together largely responsible for the failure of the second program to
reach its targets. In 1969 it was replaced by the third Program for
Economic Expansion, which charts the years 1969 to 1972. The industrial targets contained therein lean heavily on expectations from new,
and predominantly foreign-controlled industry.* Nearly 30 percent
of the additional output, nearly 45 percent of the growth in exports,
and more than 40 percent of extra employment are expected to come
from new firms. The contribution to growth from existing domestic
firms is expected to take the form of increased productivity, and output
per worker is expected to rise by 3.5 percent per annum. Indeed, the
overall increase in employment, despite the emphasis on labor-
intensive investments, is expected to rise by only 16,000 by 1972, a
fall of 36,000 in the agricultural sector being more than offset by a
rise of 31,000 in industry and 21,000 in the rest of the economy. These
modest projections are based upon the realization that underemployment
on the land means that immediate progress towards full employment
will consist of moving people to better-paid jobs rather than of
increasing the total numbers at work.

Despite the replacement of the second program, however, an
examination of the economy's position in the late 1960's shows that it
could be described as both industrialized and urbanized, and thus that
it has arrived at the end of the transitional stage in its economic
development. Over 26 percent of the labor force is employed in industry while 32 percent of the GNP originates in that sector. At the same
time, the economy has entered the urbanized league, since 30 percent
of its population lives in centers of 100,000 or more.

Although it cannot claim to be regionally articulated, the third
program nonetheless emphasizes the necessity of regional policies
fitting into the overall national plan and complementing it by providing
conditions favorable to economic development and population growth
in all parts of the economy but especially in areas which might act as
counterattractions to Dublin. In accordance with government policy
laid down in 1965, which emphasized the advantages of large centers,

------

*This reflects the experience of the 1959-69 decade during
which four-fifths of all investment in new industries came from
foreign companies--of which 40 percent were British, 20 percent
German, 16 percent American, and 5 percent Dutch.

or growth poles, in attracting industry and related economic activities, the industrial incentives scheme was redesigned with the objective of inducing investment at certain selected large centers.

While the underdeveloped (chiefly western) areas are to continue to benefit from higher rates of industrial grants, the recent policy shift emphasizes the development of the economy as a whole and specifically indicates that this would be best achieved by the concentration of investment in a limited number of centers.

Meanwhile, a similar policy change has occurred in Northern Ireland. Although by most criteria the area could be considered both industrialized and urbanized in the 1920's, the high rate of unemployment and the continuance of emigration indicated (as they still do in both economies) an urgent need for further industrialization efforts. For more than two hundred years the leading industry had been linen but when it began to decline the towns which had been built on its prosperity faced the possibility of depression and population loss. Accordingly, in the 1950's, policies designed to encourage the development of new industries were initiated.

As in the Republic, these policies included grants for plant and machinery, the building of advance factories, and tax relief. Most of the new industries which have been set up during the past decade represent branch-plant activity by British manufacturers who have expanded into Northern Ireland in response to the many inducements offered. These include not only the aforementioned grants and tax concessions but also a surplus supply of labor and adequate space should further expansion be justified in the long run. In general, the new industries have tended to locate in Belfast and adjacent towns, thus aggravating the relative decline in the less-developed western area and, in particular, in the city of Londonderry, where chronic unemployment among males periodically sparks serious social and political unrest.

There has been less emphasis on labor intensiveness in Northern Ireland than in the Republic and, as a result, the average cost per head of creating new jobs is noticeably higher.

It is felt that the dangers inherent in a branch-plant type of economy could be overcome if the branches were big in relation to the size of the parent plant and involved relatively heavy capital outlays which would help to ensure a long-term commitment to the area.

In contrast to the Republic, which lacks an industrial tradition and where technology and skills are still being developed, Northern Ireland in its recent development efforts has succeeded in putting traditional skills to use, in both the old and the new industries. The technical skills of the declining linen industry are being used in the new leading industry producing manmade fibers and textiles, and the traditional engineering skills are employed not only in the revived shipbuilding industry but also in the machinery industry which makes equipment for use in the new textile-producing firms.

It is because of the heavy capital commitments involved in the new industries and the fairly limited employment opportunities offered by individual projects that the government in Northern Ireland has chosen the same type of investment policy as that recently adopted in the Republic, that is, the concentration of investment in a limited number of selected centers.

Since the late 1950's, the continued drift from the land in Northern Ireland has led to a decrease of 35,000 in the agricultural sector, but the decline of old industries and the failure of the newer ones to absorb all the displaced workers has caused total employment in the industrial sector to fall in recent years. An examination of Table 13 shows that this has involved a fall in the percentage of the labor force employed in the industrial sector. This phenomenon should not be likened to what has recently been happening in the United States nor interpreted as heralding the arrival of the urbanized service-oriented stage of development. Although it has already proceeded much further than the Republic along the road to industrialization, Northern Ireland still has a long way to go before it reaches that stage of development.

Thus, the advent of the 1970's finds both parts of Ireland now industrialized and urbanized although, of course, in neither is the process yet complete.* The problems of unemployment and emigration have not yet been solved in either area. The dependence on foreign trade will increase owing to the small size of both markets and the

---

*Kingsley Davis, in "The Urbanization of the Human Population," Scientific American, 213, 3 (September, 1965), 43, claims that the later each country becomes industrialized the faster is its rate of urbanization. "The change from a population with 10% in cities of 100,000 or larger to one in which 30% lived in such cities took about 79 years in England and Wales, 66 in the U.S., 48 in Germany, 36 in Japan, and 26 in Australia. The close association between economic development and urbanization has persisted." The process took about 80 years in Ireland, but the experiences of the two parts of the island were very different. In the Republic the process took 75 years, from 1891 to 1966, but in Northern Ireland it appears to have been accomplished in about 40 years (from about 1871 to 1911).

lack of industrial raw materials and fuel. The recent moves towards
free trade and the resulting increase in competition on the home
markets, coupled with the increased importance of foreign capital,
not only in the productive sectors but also in the field of retailing,
have all tended to weaken the position of the small local firm. To the
extent that these are located in smaller centers of population and
relatively far removed from the main cities, these towns tend to stag-
nate and decline.

We have already seen that with respect to population and economic activity, polarization on the east coast is evident. An examination of the distribution of personal income by county for each of the
economies in 1960 displays the same pattern of regional imbalance
and bias towards the center.* Table 15 shows the degree of concentration of total and per capita incomes in the east and in County Dublin in particular. This concentration is more pronounced in the case
of income arising** (36 percent in County Dublin) than in the case of
personal income*** (30 percent in County Dublin) illustrating the
size of the income transfers (£ 33 million in 1960) made from the center
to the hinterland to help redress the regional income disparities.
A similar tendency towards polarization at the center operates in
Northern Ireland. Almost 70 percent of personal income**** was
produced in County Antrim in 1960, while the hinterland areas of
Fermanagh and Tyrone accounted for only 7 percent between them.

Thus we can see that the dominance of the two main centers in
their respective territories has persisted over time and an examination of expected developments in the future suggests that this tendency would continue in the absence of regional policies designed to

---

*In this case, owing to a lack of data at the city level, the center
is equated with the county wherein it is situated.

**"Income arising" is defined as the income created within the
borders of each county and is very like "earned income." As well
as income in cash, it includes income in kind.

***"Personal income" is defined as income receivable by house-
holds from all sources whether earned or not, and thus includes emigrants' remittances, social welfare payments, and dividends received.

****The data on personal incomes for Northern Ireland are not
comparable with those for the Republic. "Personal income" in the
Northern Ireland table refers to income subject to taxation and, therefore, does not include incomes exempted from taxes.

TABLE 15

Distribution of Income Arising and Personal Income
by County in the Republic of Ireland in 1960

| County | Income arising | | Personal income | |
	Total (£000)	Per capita	Total (£000)	Per capita
Province of Leinster	287,850	216	290,014	218
Carlow	5,743	172	7,185	215
Dublin	185,334	259	164,631	231
Kildare	12,454	193	14,703	227
Kilkenny	10,977	177	13,585	219
Laoighis	7,469	164	9,280	204
Longford	3,621	116	5,297	170
Louth	12,559	186	12,156	180
Meath	11,382	174	14,512	222
Offaly	8,440	163	10,320	200
Westmeath	8,151	154	10,842	204
Wexford	12,460	148	15,582	185
Wicklow	9,260	158	11,921	203
Province of Munster	144,198	169	168,361	197
Clare	9,623	129	12,435	167
Cork	60,896	184	65,901	199
Kerry	15,927	135	20,510	174
Limerick	23,094	172	27,395	204
Tipperary	21,202	170	26,424	212
Waterford	13,456	187	15,696	218
Province of Connacht	53,918	127	71,544	168
Galway	20,467	136	26,950	178
Leitrim	4,106	120	5,709	167
Mayo	14,128	113	19,201	153
Roscommon	7,673	128	10,223	170
Sligo	7,544	139	9,461	174
Province of Ulster	27,534	124	35,481	160
Cavan	7,399	128	9,459	164
Donegal	13,702	119	17,626	153
Monaghan	6,433	134	8,396	175
Republic of Ireland	513,500	181	565,400	200

Source: E. A. Attwood and R. C. Geary, Irish County Incomes in 1960. Paper No. 16 (Dublin: Economic and Social Research Institute, September, 1963).

TABLE 16

Distribution of Personal Incomes
by County in Northern Ireland, 1959-60.

County	Number (000)	Amount (£ million)
Antrim	272.3	172.1
Armagh	24.6	12.9
Down	50.6	28.2
Fermanagh	8.4	4.3
Londonderry	37.3	20.1
Tyrone	22.3	11.7
Northern Ireland	415.5	249.4

Source: Northern Ireland, Report of the Commissioners of H.M. Inland Revenue for the Year 1961 (Belfast: H.M. Stationery Office, 1961).

counteract the automatic mechanism.* However, in both parts of the island many such policies have already been proposed or initiated.

Nevertheless, in many respects they would appear to be competitive and thus wasteful. The basic assumption of this paper is that, from a spatial point of view, the island is essentially a unit and, therefore, that regional policies in both areas should be harmonized. In the next chapter this concept of unity will be considered in more depth and the nature of the policies already proposed or initiated will be examined in order to determine the extent to which they are likely

---

*The preliminary results of a survey by Michael Ross (of the Economic and Social Research Institute in Dublin) on the behavior of personal incomes in the Republic between 1960 and 1965 were released at the end of 1969. They show that the per capita income disparities between rich and poor counties widened during the period. County Dublin increased its lead over the rest of the country by growing almost half as fast again as the average of the other twenty-five counties and almost one-fifth faster than its nearest rival, Waterford. In addition, its population rose by three times as much as that of any other county.

to succeed in providing an optimum spatial distribution of population
and economic activity in the whole island.

NOTES

1. William Demas, The Economics of Development in Small
Countries, With Special.Reference to the Caribbean (Montreal: McGill
University Press, 1965), p. 22.

2. United Nations, 1967 Report on the World Social Situation
(New York, 1969), p. 154.

3. Ibid., p. 131.

4. Ibid., p. 171.

5. Ibid., p. 160.

6. Ireland, Commission on Emigration and Other Population
Problems 1948-54 (Dublin, Stationery Office, 1955), p. 26. Reluctance
on the part of wealthy nationals to invest in the local economy during
the early stages of economic development has been noted by many
economists including Myrdal. Indeed, as Adler points out in The
Under-developed Areas and Their Industrialization (New Haven: Yale
University Press, 1949), this reluctance often continues even when
industrialization has got under way. Local entrepreneurs then insist
upon government subsidies and guarantees before they are willing to
take investment risks in the local economy.

7. Ireland, Commission on Emigration and Other Population
Problems, 1948-54 (Dublin: Stationery Office, 1955), p. 10.

8. Ireland, Commission on Emigration and Other Population
Problems, 1948-54 (Dublin: Stationery Office, 1955), p. 158.

9. Ibid., p. 162.

10. The failure of agriculture to match the progress achieved
in the industrial sector and, thus, its tendency to constrain growth in
a developing economy is a fairly general phenomenon. Commenting
upon the uneven growth rates achieved by different regions in Asia in
the early 1960's, the U.N. 1967 Report on the World Social Situation
(op. cit., p. 112) notes: "Several countries have made excellent progress while others demonstrated the capacity for it, but in others
progress in economic growth was slow or actually declined. It was
largely the failure of one sector agriculture that accounted for the

poor economic performance in the region generally and in particular countries. The backwardness of agriculture is the main constraint on Asian economic growth.''

THE CAUSES OF REGIONAL DUALISM

As we have already seen, development does not affect all parts of the economy equally. Powerful forces make for a spatial concentration of development around the original growth nucleus. The operation of the market, which might be expected to lead to an equalization of returns to the factors of production in all regions through the mobility of factors and commodities and, thus, to a diffusion of growth over space as well as over time, leads instead in many cases to a reinforcement of regional imbalance.[1]

It is generally assumed that mobility leads to an increase in the marginal product of labor in areas of out-migration and to a decrease in areas of in-migration and, thus, that the returns to labor tend to be geographically equalized by labor movements.

The fact that this does not always happen may be due to the relatively large investments of capital usually undertaken in areas of in-migration. It would appear that, in practice, capital inflows often tend to have a greater effect on wage rates than do labor outflows. In this connection also, we may note the interesting distinction which E. Von Boventer[2] draws between the different effects on the spatial distribution of economic activities caused respectively by commodity movements, factor movements, and commuting. He states that high labor mobility allied to low goods mobility leads to agglomeration; high goods mobility plus low labor mobility causes dispersion; and commuting allows concentrated production and dispersed consumption.

Another factor operating to prevent the market from producing equilibrium is the failure of diminishing returns to set in at the center. Friedmann claims[3] that this is what causes the center to grow and to attract capital, despite its presumed social diseconomies. It results in the overestimation of investment profitabilities there by entrepreneurs (the majority of whom are located at the center) and their failure to perceive opportunities elsewhere. It has already been noted* that local entrepreneurs on the periphery may benefit, especially in the early and protected stages of economic development, from imperfections in the market but this generally results in the location there of small-scale manufacturing units with limited growth potential and resource-oriented activities which also tend to decline in relative importance as development proceeds. The center tends to attract the large-scale, capital-intensive, and export-oriented industries which lead to cumulative growth.

Finally, the fact that services such as finance, education, government, and research are concentrated at the center attracts and holds entrepreneurs there, turning it into a permanent nucleus of technological progress and giving the industries there an advantage over those on the periphery.

Even where the local market forces succeed in working towards the spatial transmission of growth, they tend to be outweighed by the more powerful international forces emanating from the foreign center and lead to geographical concentration in the small, open economies in the periphery. This strengthens the tendency towards regional dualism, or the division of these economies into backward and progressive regions which, if allowed to persist, will have detrimental effects on their overall economic development. This is why regional development policies must be applied to alter the inefficient spatial relationships which tend to inhibit national growth.

REGIONAL CONCEPTS AND REGIONAL PROBLEMS

Before approaching the consideration of alternative forms of development strategies, it is appropriate first to examine briefly the whole concept of the region and the various kinds of regional problems which are encountered.

It is customary to distinguish between two main kinds of regions: homogeneous regions, which are defined as areas delineated on the basis of certain common characteristics, such as terrain, type of agricultural production, or level of per capita income;[4] and structured or polarized regions, which are delimited on the basis of interdependency

---

*See p. 7.

or range of influence and represented by the extent of the flows of people, information, and goods.[5] While it is useful to be able to identify these two types of regions, one feels that an inordinate amount of the literature on regional science has been devoted to the problem of regional delineation.[6] One is inclined to agree with Friedmann that the exercise is of only secondary importance. In any event, boundaries are not static and as both characteristics and relationships alter over time, regional boundaries shift.

For planning purposes, however, it is useful to have information on the extent of both homogeneity and interdependence within regions. Friedmann distinguishes between five types of development regions delimited on the basis of common prospects and problems of development. The first is the core region, reminiscent of Perroux's growth pole, and describes an urban economy with a high potential for economic growth. Four ranks may be distinguished within the hierarchy: the national metropolis, the regional capital, the subregional center, and the local service center. Their many problems include the maintenance of growth, the absorption of immigrants into the labor force, and the organization of a pleasant and efficient living environment. One method of delimiting core regions is by measuring the extent of daily commuting.

The second class of development region identified by Friedmann is the upward-transitional area. Such areas include all settled regions whose natural endowments and location relative to core regions suggest the possibility of greatly intensified development. They, too, attract immigrants but their development is generally induced because of increased demand at the core. Their problems are those associated with rapid growth and their solution calls for agricultural adjustments, including more intensive farming and improved marketing arrangements, as well as increased urbanization and industrialization.

Downward-transitional areas, the next category, are old-established settlement regions whose essentially rural economies are stagnant or in decline. They may also be declining urban areas with aging industrial structures and overpopulation relative to existing production possibilities. Being areas of out-migration, the problems of downward-transitional regions include those of a relatively large dependent population and of adaptation to new external conditions.

Resource frontier regions are areas of new settlement, rich in minerals and other valuable resources and generally located relatively far away from existing core regions.

Finally, there are special problem regions which, because of the peculiarity of their resources or location, demand a specialized development approach. They include regions along national borders, water

resource development regions, military zones, and areas suited to the
intensive development of tourism or fisheries.

The types of regional problems most often encountered in developed economies, such as overconcentration around capital cities (Paris,
or the Amsterdam-Rotterdam-Hague triangle), lack of investment in
areas close to national borders (the France-Belgium border inside the
EEC), areas of chronic underdevelopment (Italy's Mezzogiorno), and
areas of industrial decline (Britain's northeast), are all capable of
being examined within the context of Friedmann's regional classification.

REGIONAL DEVELOPMENT STRATEGIES

The solution to regional problems and the choice of regional
development strategies must be adapted to the current phase in the
development of the national economy. Tackling individual problems
in isolation or failing to fit regional into national goals may aggravate
spatial imbalances and jeopardize the development of the overall
economy.

The search for the optimum inducement mechanisms to promote
growth leads Hirschman[7] to explore the relative merits of balance
versus imbalance between regions during the process of economic
development. He identifies three principal patterns of regional
allocation of public investment: dispersal, concentration on growing
areas, and attempts to promote the development of backward regions.
The policy of scattering investment among a large number of small
projects and areas has a strong appeal for politicians (who are dependent on widespread support from voters), particularly in the early
stages of economic development, when it is often necessary that the
benefits should appear to be fairly equitably spread throughout the
whole economy. Later, there is often a shift in policy towards the
concentration of investment in areas of rapid growth where shortages
of infrastructure or social overhead capital have become acute.
This, in turn, induces a concern with the problems of backward areas
which have become relatively worse off as a result of concentration
in the progressive regions. Thus, Hirschman believes that the tendency
of public investment policy to cause regional imbalance can also be
relied upon to reverse the process eventually and that this accounts
for the widespread concern of governments with the development of
backward regions within their economies.

Friedmann criticises equally forcefully the strategy of "con-
trolled imbalance" advocated by Hirschman and that of "concentrated
decentralization" recommended by Lloyd Rodwin,[8] on the grounds
that the dichotomy between balance and imbalance is just as false as

that between concentration and dispersal. He maintains that the recognition of Hirschman's state of optimal imbalance (and its differentiation from plain inefficiency) would be difficult in practice and, further, that the concept of balance is not clear. Is it total investment in each region, or investment in each sector, or investment per capita that should be balanced? Should all regions grow at the same rate or should the more backward grow at a faster rate in order to catch up? Each course of action has different policy implications and will produce different results. While Friedmann advocates a policy of selective concentration of development efforts, he feels that Rodwin's policy of concentrating investment in a few growth centers on the periphery may not be sufficient to promote either regional or national development. Concentration of investment in a few points which promise the best potential for growth is necessary in order that these core regions, or growth points, should develop a countervailing pull of their own in competition with the central region. Nevertheless, at the same time, appropriate strategies must be developed for every type of region and these must all be put to work simultaneously. The problems arising from regional growth or decline cannot be tackled in isolation and an effective regional policy must deal as a system with the separate developments of core regions, upward-transitional and downward-transitional areas, resource frontiers, and special problem areas. A partial solution to structural poverty in downward-transitional areas may involve intensified investment programs in adjacent core regions but the fate of these regions, in turn, will rest upon the ability of the nation to maintain minimum acceptable standards of living in areas of decline. The main problems in the metropolis will relate to urbanization and urban renewal, land use, public utilities, housing, and transportation, while the policies appropriate for upward-transitional areas will involve the reorganization of agriculture, interregional transportation, industrial development, and absorption of immigrants. In the downward-transitional areas, emigration and population resettlement, community development, and rural land-use adjustments will demand priority treatment. The interrelatedness of these problems emphasizes the need for regional policies to be introduced on a national scale. The total collection of regional strategies must be reconciled so that, taken together, they are consistent with the goals of the overall national plan. National planners will then be able to test proposed investment projects for their locational efficiency and their consistency with other planned investments. As Friedmann points out, the long-term objective of regional policy should be the gradual elimination of the periphery on a national scale by substituting for it a single interdependent system of urban regions and the progressive integration of the space economy by the extension, on a national scale, of a system of efficient commodity and factor markets.

THE RELATIONSHIP BETWEEN ECONOMIC
AND PHYSICAL PLANNING

One of the difficulties encountered in the implementation of regional development strategies is the incompleteness of the dialogue between the two disciplines of economic and physical planning. Until recently the division of labor was almost complete. Economic planning, which operates from the central government level, took a sectoral approach to the problem of development, emphasizing capital use and seemingly implying that if capital were allocated efficiently the optimum location of industry and population and the optimum pattern of land use would follow automatically. Physical planning, on the other hand, which operates at the city or local government level and emphasizes land use, often failed to take account of broader economic development issues and, thus, to relate urban planning to the needs of national strategies.

There has occurred in recent years a helpful shift in viewpoint. Economic planners have become increasingly aware of the importance of the spatial dimension and of the need for positive manipulation of land uses in place of the former negative approach of leaving such decisions to private investors and local government. The necessity of operating "from the top down," of translating national objectives into local realities, constitutes the essence of national planning implementation. At the same time, the physical planners are realizing the importance of fitting individual urban plans into the national planning strategy and that working "from the bottom up" involves central government control. A physical master plan and national urban policy could be devised and coordinated with the economic development program.

Industrial location, the provision of infrastructure for industry, and the improvement of communal amenities are important elements in both types of planning. Their instigation is the result of economic decisions but their execution is a physical activity which, in turn, has economic consequences. An economic decision, for example, on the allocation of grants to attract industry will result, very often, in a location which has to be specific. This, in turn, implies physical repercussions, not only with regard to the location of the activity itself but also with regard to the provision of the necessary ancillary activities, whether of a directly (servicing industry) or an indirectly (schools and housing) productive nature. These will have physical repercussions on land use and social and economic effects with respect to investment, internal and external migration, employment, and incomes.

Because it is maintained that regional planning is crucial during the transition stage of the development process, it is then that the fusion of economic and physical planning is essential. In the field of regional planning the two disciplines find common ground. Cooperation between them prevents bottlenecks (industries without adequate housing and educational facilities, or ports without tributary roads) from jeopardizing development programs. A national urban policy must be formulated which is consistent with the goals of social and economic development.

Charles Haar, Benjamin Higgins, and Lloyd Rodwin[9] have suggested a method for implementing such a program. The first step, in their opinion, is the formulation of a general policy statement--for example, that urban development will be concentrated in a small number of cities rather than dispersed over many centers, or that the growth of the capital city is to be contained and alternative urban centers are to be developed. The physical development objectives must then be set out and tested for feasibility. The institutional arrangements will vary from country to country and will depend, among other things, upon the relative importance and level of performance of the private sector. In general, the more underdeveloped the country the more important is the role of the central government in providing overhead capital, industry, housing, and amenities. Legislation will probably be required to authorize the preparation not only of a national development policy but also of development plans by local or regional units. The agency responsible for the overall physical development pattern would undertake certain functions. First, it would review the principal physical development resources, problems, and needs of the country and present a set of physical development policies consistent with the national economic development program. The feasible alternatives would then be evaluated, taking into account social objectives, the present trends in the distribution, functions, and prospects of cities and towns, the economic and demographic trends, resource limitations, transportation needs, and the requirements of the industrial and agricultural plans. The various measures necessary to implement the alternative goals, such as economic incentives, compensation and other costs, techniques of control, and the determination of priorities are then analyzed. A choice is made from the alternative proposals and it becomes the basis for official policy and provides the criteria for development in the future. A helpful aid to planners would be the publication of a manual explaining the methods for producing master plans and the preparation of a model study for a specific area which would provide useful guidance, especially to local development teams. The implications of alternative policies and the reasons for the final choice should be presented to the community, since public support is necessary (particularly at the local level). Finally, according to Haar,

Higgins, and Rodwin, the program must include provision for frequent and vigilant reassessment of its progress and continuous coordination between the work of physical, social, and economic planners in providing criteria for investment decisions.

The importance of regional planning during the transition stage of economic development and the consequent necessity of coordinating economic and physical planning during this period has already been emphasized. But the question arises: if economic planning fails, does it follow that physical planning is then neither necessary nor feasible? The constraints on physical planning are largely endogenous to the economy but those on economic planning, especially in a small, open economy, are manifestly more often exogenously created. They are less controllable than the former and, therefore, less capable of being surmounted. But even if economic planning miscarries due to external forces it is still a worthwhile pursuit, if only because of the national self-knowledge and sense of purpose which it generates. Physical planning is still necessary and its repercussions, which will be felt for decades, are economic as well as physical in character. Nevertheless, it must be realized that the execution, and thus the feasibility, of physical plans depend upon economic decisions, that is, on some degree of economic planning, however loosely interpreted.

It thus seems reasonable to conclude, once more, that during the transitional stage of economic development the two planning procedures are closely intertwined.

REGIONAL POLICY IN IRELAND

The first attempt at a conscious regional policy in Ireland was made in the late nineteenth century. The roots of some of the problems are buried deep in history. The Cromwellian Plantations of the seventeenth century resulted in the banishment of a large proportion of the Irish population to the poor and relatively infertile counties of the western seaboard and, consequently, that part of the country became overpopulated in relation to other productive resources.* Despite continuously heavy out-migration from Donegal, West Galway, and Mayo counties since the great famine of the mid-1840's, high rural population densities persisted and individual holdings remained small

---

*Cromwell's infamous dictum "To Hell or to Connacht" summarizes succinctly the narrow choice presented to the dispossessed natives whose lands were "planted" by his followers in the more fertile parts of the island.

relative to those in the rest of the country. In 1891, the Congested
Districts Board was set up to help solve the problems of those very
poor areas and its activities were gradually extended until they covered
the counties of Donegal, Leitrim, Sligo, Roscommon, Mayo, Galway,
Clare, Kerry, and West Cork. In 1923 the board's functions were
transferred to the Land Commission and thus the efforts to improve
conditions in those areas continued uninterrupted after independence.
The main policies which were implemented related to improvements
in land and livestock, the reallocation of small farms into more economic
holdings, the migration of groups of families to larger farms in the
midlands, and the building of roads and light railways. Because of the
uneconomic size of holdings in general and the consequent tendency
for many of the heads of the remaining households to migrate to Great
Britain periodically to supplement their incomes, the need for additional
employment opportunities was obvious. The Underdeveloped Areas
Act of 1952 provided for special grants for buildings and equipment in
order to promote the establishment of small-scale rural industries in
these areas but the success of this scheme was limited and the high
rate of emigration, both seasonal and permanent, persisted; it persists
today, leading to a continuous fall in the populations of most of those
counties.*

As already noted in Chapter 2, during the late 1950's the government in the Republic became concerned with the need for structural
transformation and industrialization throughout the whole economy
and preferential treatment for the underdeveloped western areas,
while still maintained, was made gradually subservient to the needs
of the national economy as a whole. Thus, the Industrial Grants Act
of 1956, which made provision for grants to industries in all parts of
the country but fixed the maximum for firms outside the "underdeveloped" areas at £50,000, was modified in 1959 and again in 1963 in
order to implement this new policy. While the maximum grant for
the "underdeveloped" areas was fixed at two-thirds of the cost of
buildings and equipment in comparison to 50 percent for the rest of

----

*An interesting development has, however, taken place in recent
years as a result of increased industrialization in the western counties.
Whereas, in the 1950's, the government-assisted employment schemes
resulted in full-time farmers earning supplementary incomes from
part-time industrial employment, the current trend in many areas is
towards full-time industrial employees supplementing their incomes
by working their small holdings part-time. One of the consequences
has been an increase in the outputs of these farms and this phenomenon
is generally attributed to increased labor productivity and improved
motivation.

the country, provision for the higher rate was made in exceptional
cases outside the designated areas and the emphasis on national development, as distinct from the development of the relatively backward
areas became part of accepted government policy. Although Dublin
continued to attract the bulk of large-scale capital-intensive industries,
the new policies favored a more widespread dispersal of industrial
activities throughout the whole economy.

An exceptionally interesting experiment in regional development
was undertaken in 1959 when the Shannon Industrial Estate was built.
Located within a customs-free zone and associated with an international
airport which was in imminent danger of collapse due to the development
of jet airliners (which decreased the number of refuelling stopovers
for trans-Atlantic crossings), the Shannon Estate had the twin objectives
of providing industrial employment in an underdeveloped area and of
revitalizing a condemned airport. That the project has been an outstanding success in the short run is beyond question. A plentiful supply of
labor in the hinterland, the availability of excellent sites, the provision
of advance factories for rent, and of tax concessions and grants at
preferential rates all combined to attract a large number of foreign
industrialists to locate at the Shannon Estate. In many ways, of course,
it is unique and its special advantages could hardly be duplicated elsewhere in the country. Even if they could, it would not ensure self-
sustaining growth on a long-term basis since the individual firms are,
in general, completely divorced from the local economy, importing
their raw materials and selling their finished products abroad.* This
absence of linkage, not only with the economy in which they are located,
but also with the other firms within Shannon itself, fails to induce the
development of ancillary activities and, in effect, makes the estate a
foreign enclave within the Irish economy.

---

*At first glance this appears to call into question the conclusions
of S. Burenstam Linder (An Essay on Trade and Transformation, New
York: John Wiley, 1961) on the relationship between the exports of
industrial concerns and their total output. Linder suggests that trade
in manufactured goods depends not on the availability of the necessary
raw materials locally but rather on the preexistence of a strong home
market of which exports are then a mere extension. However, the
Shannon experience of total dependence on exports is no contradiction
of this theory since, because all the firms are branch plants of foreign-
based firms, their "exports" from Ireland are, in fact, merely exten-
sions of their domestic sales in their own home markets and form
quite a small percentage of their total sales.

In the early 1960's, further modifications in regional development policy were recommended in the interests of national growth. In 1962, the report of the Committee on Industrial Organization (CIO) suggested the abolition of the differential between the "underdeveloped" areas and the rest of the country and the substitution for it of a differential in favor of a small number of selected development centers, in the belief that overall national development would best be promoted by the concentration of investment at a few growth points. This represented a policy shift completely in line with Hirschman's general predictions. This recommendation was reiterated by the Committee on Development Centers and Industrial Estates which reported at the end of 1964 and was further endorsed by the CIO in its reports of 1965 and 1968.[10] Government commitment to regional development and official approval of the development center concept quickly gathered momentum. The second Program for Economic Expansion had provided for the preparation of a national physical planning program to provide the physical framework for national social and economic development. The Local Government (Planning and Development) Act of 1963 facilitated the implementation of the physical planning program by providing for the making of plans by each local authority in relation to future development and land use in its own area, and for the coordination of all these plans by the ministry concerned.*

The country was then divided into nine planning regions (although the basis for their delineation appears to have had all the precision normally associated with the business of pinning the tail on the donkey) and several regional studies were commissioned by the government. These included a survey of the Limerick region by Nathanial Lichfield and Associates,[11] a study of the Dublin region by Myles Wright,[12] and a survey of the remaining seven regions** by Colin Buchanan and Partners commissioned in 1966 and published in 1968.[13] Although it set out to cover only seven of the nine planning regions, in fact, because

---

*There are eighty-seven local planning authorities in the Republic: twenty-seven county (mainly rural) authorities and sixty urban authorities. The planning authority in itself has responsibility for housing, roads, water, and sewerage services, and has wide powers to engage in community development, to provide facilities for the encouragement of private investment, and even to engage directly in various forms of economic activity. The individual development plans, which by law must be kept up to date, show the policies and programs of each authority in these matters.

**The regions concerned were: Cork-Kerry, Mayo-Galway, Sligo-Leitrim, Donegal, South-East, North-East, and Midlands.

it was instructed to take account of the recommendations of the other
two regional studies, the Buchanan Report represents the most comprehensive regional survey yet undertaken in the Republic and proposes
a regional development strategy which the authors consider necessary
in order to implement the social and economic objectives of national
development. It thus deserves a correspondingly comprehensive
review.

The terms of reference instructed the team to "indicate growth
potential, identify possible development centers, establish the level
of change needed in infrastructure to facilitate growth, and make proposals for policy decisions to be taken by the Government, including
measures to implement such proposals."[14]

The report opens with a survey of the economy, together with
its problems and prospects, and includes a study of the agricultural
potential of each county. It considers that, while there is scope for
influencing agricultural and service employment on a limited scale in
certain areas, it would not be of major significance and even the expected expansion of the tourist industry could not be expected to arrest
the loss of population in declining areas since the employment created
is highly seasonal and mainly female in content. It therefore concludes
that the achievement of full employment and the reduction of emigration
to an acceptable rate by 1986[15] necessitates, on the one hand, a drop
of 180,000, or 48 percent, in the numbers employed in agriculture in
order to provide acceptable incomes in this sector and, on the other
hand, an accelerated pace of industrialization, involving concentration
at a limited number of large centers with a standard of facilities
capable of competing with those in other European cities. It recognizes
that this conflicts with the desire to spread the benefits of development
evenly over the country, and, thus, in an attempt to reconcile the economic, social, and political objectives, the report examines a number
of alternative strategies, with a view to choosing that one which seems
best able to achieve the national objectives by 1986.

In order to facilitate the selection of towns as possible growth
centers, the Buchanan team made a study of the development potential
of all urban areas, outside the three largest centers of Dublin, Cork,
and Limerick,* which had populations of 5,000 or more in 1966.**

_____

*Limerick, situated on the mouth of the river Shannon, fifteen
miles from the Shannon Airport Industrial Estate, is the third largest
city in the Republic, with a population of 58,000 in 1966.

**See Map 2.

Based upon a wide range of criteria,* against which, they claimed,
very few towns showed up well, the towns were graded in hierarchical
order.** The team then postulated five alternative strategies ranging
from extreme concentration to extreme dispersal of industrial activities.

According to the report, the first of these, the continuation of
present policies, has already proved unsatisfactory and provides no
hope of halting the decline in population in rural areas nor of eliminating
unemployment and reducing emigration to a satisfactory level. Concentration of investment in Dublin would probably lead to the fastest
overall rate of industrialization and economic growth and, thus, to
the achievement of the twin objectives relating to employment and
emigration but the accentuation of regional imbalance which would
result, would cause serious social and political problems elsewhere
in the country. The concentration of investment on Cork and the
Limerick/Shannon complex, that is, on two centers relatively far
removed from Dublin would also lead to rapid growth in industrialization,
employment, and incomes and, at the same time, offer good prospects
for full employment and the end of involuntary emigration but little
direct benefit would accrue directly to areas of the country outside
the southwest. A fourth strategy would involve the distribution of
industry over a larger but still relatively limited number of centers
in different parts of the country, namely, Dublin, Cork, and Limerick/
Shannon (the established centers), and Waterford, Galway, Dundalk,
Drogheda, Sligo, and Athlone. This would provide one growth center
for each of the nine planning regions, with two exceptions (none for
Donegal and two in the North East) and would also lead to the reduction
of unemployment and emigration, although neither as great nor as
fast as the second and third strategies. Finally, the report considers

---

*These criteria included the size and functions of towns, together
with the extent of their catchment areas, existing industry, labor
availability, infrastructure, social and shopping facilities, and communications.

**The groupings which resulted were as follows:
   Group 1 Waterford, Dundalk, Galway, and Drogheda.
   Group 2 Sligo and Tralee.
   Group 3 Wexford, Kilkenny, Athlone, Mullingar, Clonmel,
            Carlow, and Ennis.
   Group 4 Tullamore, Bray, Thurles, Monaghan, Cavan,
            Letterkenny, and Arklow.
   Group 5 Ballina, Castlebar, Enniscorthy, Cobh, Mallow,
            Portlaoise, Navan, Killarney, Ballinasloe, Dungarvan,
            and Youghal.

the alternative of an even greater emphasis than at present on the
widespread dispersal of industry and concludes that, while it might be
politically popular, the resulting increase in employment and incomes
would be less than with any of the other strategies, it would offer no
hope for a reduction in emigration, and industry would be less capable
of withstanding foreign competition.

The report considers that each of the hypothetical strategies
described has serious disadvantages, and that in order to build up a
strong and internationally competitive industrial sector while, at the
same time, attempting to spread the benefits of urban growth throughout
the country, elements of several of the strategies ought to be considered
in order to achieve a more balanced result. Accordingly, Buchanan
suggests a policy based on three tiers of growth.

The main industrial centers are to be at Dublin, Cork, Limerick/
Shannon, with the capital city growing merely by the equivalent of its
own natural increase and the other two doubling and trebling their
populations respectively as a result of an intensified industrialization
program and considerable internal migration. The report suggests
the concurrent development of six "regional" centers (Waterford,
Dundalk, Drogheda, Galway, Sligo, and Athlone) and four "local"
growth centers (Tralee, Letterkenny, Castelbar, and one for Longford,
Cavan, and Monaghan counties) in order to provide public services and
focal points for private development and to spread the benefits of
urbanization as far as possible throughout the economy.

The report later considers the economic, the physical, and the
operational feasibility of these proposals and suggests that a reorganization of local government is necessary in order to effect the implementation of the program.

The spectrum of problems identified by the Buchanan Report
and the range of questions to which it addresses itself would seem to
indicate a relatively broad approach to the spatial aspects of economic
development. However, this promise is hardly fulfilled in the policy
proposals which it finally offers. In effect, the report sets out to
determine the optimum future pattern of industrial and urban growth
in the Republic, and the physical changes, in the form of industrial
centers, roads, housing, and social facilities necessary in order to
achieve full employment in the economy by 1986. In addition, it
examines in some detail the most important activity in the economy
and assesses the agricultural potential county by county. One feels,
however, that the report fails to make adequate use of these important
data. Despite its claim that rural and urban development problems
are essentially complementary and, thus, demand an interrelated set
of corrective policies, the report in effect confines itself almost

exclusively to the search for an optimum set of urban growth centers
by examining a number of alternative urban growth strategies and
appears to suggest that the implementation of its chosen policy constitutes an adequate regional development program.

Conceding the necessity for an urban strategy along these lines
is not to admit at the same time that it is a sufficient policy for national
or regional development. The model outlined in this book claims
that a Friedmann-type package of policies is necessary, that is, one
which embraces not only an urban growth strategy but also a complementary rural strategy, involving a reorganization of all aspects of
the agricultural sector. At the same time, a set of policies must be
designed to deal with the unique difficulties of special problem areas,
such as those lying along the borders between national territories.

The shortcomings of the Buchanan Report may be due in large
part to the constraints of its terms of reference. Although the team
was fully aware of the fact that any future changes in external trading
conditions would affect industrial development and, thus, the economic
potential of the various regions in the Republic, the only "external"
factors which it was specifically instructed to take into account when
formulating policies were the recommendations of the two previous
regional studies carried out in the country by Lichfield and Wright.
Thus, the main criticism of the Buchanan exercise is its total failure--
or inability, given the present political realities--to take into consideration the plans and policies already being implemented across the
border in Northern Ireland. As already pointed out, the island forms
a spatial unit and, in addition, it is fast approaching the time when,
due to the implementation of the Anglo-Irish Free Trade Area agreement, its two economies will once again form a single trading area.
The possibility of EEC membership by both the United Kingdom and
the Republic of Ireland only adds emphasis to the need for complementary spatial policies in the two economies.

The division of a country as small as the Republic into nine
planning regions is no less odd than that of the very idea of thinking
in regional terms when applying the principles of planning to the
economic development problems of Northern Ireland. However, it
must be pointed out that in both areas the exercise has, so far, been
mainly concerned with devising a strategy of industrial growth centers.
While this is still at the blueprint stage in the Republic, the Northern
Ireland program is already underway. Its origins go back to the
Matthew Report of 1963,[16] which was concerned with the future development of the Belfast region (delimited by a line drawn through
Ballymena, Portadown, and Downpatrick). The report recommended
the establishment of a new regional center at Craigavon, a new town
to be built up by combining Lurgan and Portadown and the six-mile

corridor connecting them. The size of the designated area was considered large enough to enable it to act as a countervailing magnet to Belfast, whose growth, the report recommended, ought to be stopped. Six other large towns in addition to Craigavon and Ballymena within the Belfast region, and six others (Londonderry, Coleraine, Omagh, Dungannon, Enniskillen, and Newry) outside it were also suggested as smaller industrial growth centers. Indeed, it would be difficult to name more than six towns with population over 5,000 which were not included in this long list.

The 1964 Wilson Report[17] on the first Economic Plan for Northern Ireland supported the Matthew recommendations on growth centers and suggested further combinations of two or more towns, namely Antrim and Ballymena on the one hand, and, on the other, the Coleraine, Portrush, and Portstewart triangle. This policy, in turn, was further endorsed by the Northern Ireland Economic Council (NIEC), which arranged the growth centers in hierarchical order. Treating Belfast and the three towns immediately east of it as one complex, the NIEC names it, together with Craigavon, Antrim-Ballymena, and Londonderry, as primary growth centers, calling for massive investments of capital and involving large-scale internal migration, especially from Belfast to Craigavon and Antrim-Ballymena.* The remaining towns, Coleraine, Newry, Dungannon, Omagh, and Enniskillen, are designated secondary growth centers. Further, the NIEC tied these recommendations directly to the need to reorganize the structure of local government in Northern Ireland.

It is thus apparent that the two governments in Ireland are moving in the same direction in the field of regional development and that the island's map will undergo dramatic changes in the coming years if the policies are carried into effect. It is also apparent, however, that neither set of policies takes the other into account and that if both are implemented as they now stand, the lack of complementarity especially in the northeastern part of the island will lead to a wasteful use of

---

*It is not envisaged in the report that Londonderry will attract any net inflow of population. The loss of its natural hinterland of Donegal after the partitioning of the island in 1922, its collapse as a coal port and naval base since World War II, the decline of its shirt industry (where 95 percent of the employees are female), and its spectacularly high unemployment rate, especially among males, has created enormous social and political unrest. Its eruption into violence in 1969 directed wide attention to its economic and sectarian difficulties but, more importantly, forced the government to declare it a development area demanding immediate remedial action.

scarce resources. This will become increasingly obvious with the advent of free-trade conditions between the two economies under the Anglo-Irish Free Trade Area agreement. The suspicion that each is now merely an economic region of the larger area composed of the two neighboring islands will be confirmed if and when both the United Kingdom and Ireland become an integral part of the even-larger European trading bloc.

There is another aspect of the growth-center concept which calls for consideration. The determination of the correct number of such centers in a small island like Ireland is ultimately tied to the question of their optimum size. It is now generally agreed that the haphazard location of firms in small centers does not guarantee long-run development. The absence of linkages with other firms, of an adequate supply of skilled labor, and of transportation and other industrial amenities, including specialist services, fails to promote self-sustaining growth and necessitates continued financial and fiscal inducements to attract new firms to the center. These disadvantages can be overcome in a large center but a recent study by Economic Consultants Limited* for the Department of Economic Affairs in Great Britain concludes that the minimum size of industrial development centers is growing all the time due to the increasing complexity of modern industry. It notes that, while the minimum size needed to make the provision of a particular specialist service viable varies greatly as between one service and another, for most of them the minimum practical size is larger than that of any existing Irish centers except Dublin and Belfast. The study concedes, however, that the minimum size could be appreciably smaller than otherwise if the center was a new and well-planned one because it would then be possible to attract industries with needs in common which would make use of specialist services known to be available. The industrial mix needs to be carefully planned.** In Craigavon, for example, it

---

*Economic Consultants Limited was associated with Buchanan and Partners in drawing up the Buchanan Report. They have also carried out studies related to the planning of growth centers in northwest England and in the Atlantic Provinces of Canada.

**Industrial-complex analysis is a relatively new area of study and notable contributions have been made to it by Luttrell (of Economic Consultants Limited) and by Tosco (of Italy's Cassa per il Mezzogiorno). Both emphasize the advantages of basing an industrial complex upon a set of interrelated activities (for example, on textiles, or chemicals, or engineering trades) and using, as far as possible, available local skills and resources.

is based upon two main local resources, food, and the skills linked with textiles. As a result, the town is already building up a food-processing and packaging complex, and the new textile and clothing firms, which it is attracting, fit in well with those firms already making products ranging from knitwear to machinery.

In order to arrive at conclusions, therefore, on the appropriate number of development centers in an economy, it is necessary to consider, not only their individual sizes, but also, to some extent, their industrial composition. This, in turn, involves a consideration, not only of the trends in new and technologically advanced industries and the interrelationships within such groups, but also some research into the past behavior of communities in order to assess the way in which it has conditioned their economic activities, skills, and income levels. As D. J. Robertson[18] points out, planning can steer an economy or a community but it cannot put it into reverse. Development programs have a much greater chance of success if they do not run counter to the patterns which the development of the community has already been taking. An examination of the factors leading to industrial location in the past and of the effect which industry has had on the performance of the towns and cities in the economy is a necessary prerequisite to a fuller understanding of the present position and of the forces likely to be important in the future. The results of the writer's own research carried out in this connection for the Irish economy will be examined in the next two chapters.

NOTES

1. Gunnar Myrdal, Economic Theory and Underdeveloped Regions (London: Duckworth, 1957), Chapters 3 and 5; and Albert O. Hirschman, The Strategy of Economic Development, (New Haven: Yale University Press, 1959) Chapter 10. Myrdal's "spread" and "backwash" effects describe respectively the forces leading to or hindering the spatial transmission of growth and correspond exactly to Hirschman's "trickling-down" and "polarization" effects.

2. E. Von Boventer, "Spatial Organization Theory as a Basis for Regional Planning." Ekistics, XVIII (1964), 130-33.

3. John Friedmann, Regional Development Policy: A Case Study of Venezuela (Cambridge, Mass.: MIT Press, 1966), Chapter 1.

4. See, for example, Okun and Richardson, "Regional Income Inequality and Internal Population Migration," Economic Development and Cultural Change Vol. IX (January, 1961), who distinguish between regions on the basis of the level and trend of per capita income; and

Douglass C. North, "Location Theory and Regional Economic Growth," Journal of Political Economy, LXIII (1955), 243-58, who claims that over and beyond geographical similarities, it is the development around a common export base which gives unifying cohesion to a region and ties the fortunes of the area together.

5. The structured region concept was first suggested by François Perroux in "La Notion de Poles de Croissance," Cahiers de l'Institut de Science Economique Appliquee, 1955, and defined by him as an integrated system of relationships between economic elements woven around a growth pole or urban node. It is somewhat reminiscent of Ohlin's concept of the region (Interregional and International Trade, Cambridge, Mass.: Harvard University Press, 1935) as that area within which the factors of production are perfectly mobile.

6. The techniques of factor analysis have been applied to the problem by many writers including B. J. Berry, "A Method for Deriving Multi-factor Uniform Regions," Przeglad Geograficzny, XXXIII, 2 (1961), 263-82; M. J. Hagood, "Statistical Methods for Delineation of Regions Applied to Data on Agriculture and Population," Social Forces, XXI (March, 1943), 287-97; M. J. Hagood, N. Danlevsky, and C. O. Beum, "An Examination of the Use of Factor Analysis in the Problem of Subregional Delineation," Rural Sociology, VI (September, 1941), 216-33.

7. Hirschman, op. cit., pp. 190-95.

8. Lloyd Rodwin, "Metropolitan Policy for Developing Areas," in Walter Isard and John H. Cumberland, Regional Economic Planning (Paris: OECD, 1961), Chapter 10.

9. Charles Haar, Benjamin Higgins, and Lloyd Rodwin, "Economic and Physical Planning: Co-ordination in Developing Areas," Journal of the American Institute of Planners, XXIV, 3 (1958), 167-73.

10. Committee on Industrial Organization, Comments on Report of the Committee on Development Centers and Industrial Estates (New York, July, 1965), and Report on Industrial Adaptation and Development (New York, May, 1968).

11. Ireland, Report and Advisory Outline Plan for the Limerick Region, by Nathanial Lichfield and Associates (Dublin, Stationery Office, 1966).

12. Ireland, Advisory Regional Plan and Final Report for the Dublin Region, by Myles Wright (Dublin, Stationery Office, 1967).

13. Foras Forbartha, Regional Studies in Ireland, by Colin
Buchanan and Partners, in association with Economic Consultants Ltd.
(Dublin: Foras Forbartha, 1968). The report was commissioned by
the United Nations in response to a request by the Irish government
and the consultants were assisted by Foras Forbartha (the National
Institute for Physical Planning and Construction Research), which
had been set up in 1964 with assistance from the United Nations
Special Fund.

14. Foras Forbartha, op. cit., p. i.

15. National Industrial Economic Council, Report on Full
Employment (Dublin: Stationery Office, 1967). This report defined
the economic objectives of national policy as the reduction of unemployment to 2 percent per annum and of emigration to 5,000 per annum by
1968.

16. Northern Ireland, The Belfast Regional Plan, by Sir Robert
Matthew (Belfast: H. M. Stationery Office, 1963).

17. Northern Ireland, Economic Development in Northern
Ireland, by Professor Thomas Wilson (Belfast: H. M. Stationery
Office, 1964). One of the most significant contrasts which can be
drawn between the planning constraints operating in the Republic and
in Northern Ireland is that in the case of the former, because it is an
independent nation, investment depends to a large extent on local
savings (supplemented in the short-run by inflows of foreign capital).
In Northern Ireland, however, because it is only a region of the United
Kingdom, this factor is of only limited significance and, indeed, the
generally accepted estimate of annual budgetary support from London
(apart from government loans) is approximately £100 million.

18. D. J. Robertson, "Economists and Town Planning," Town
Planning Review, XXXIII (1962), 32-39.

4

MICRO AND MACRO
INTERRELATIONSHIPS

One of the chief concerns of regional planning is the determination of the optimum ordering of activities within supraurban space.[1] The problems associated with it are essentially macroeconomic and among its objectives is the measurement of the total effects on an area of the aggregate of location decisions, both public and private. Nevertheless, an understanding of these aggregates demands an examination, at the same time, of the factors which guide the location decisions of individual producing units. This, in turn, involves an inquiry into the forces determining industrial location.

In its early Weberian formulation,[2] location theory was essentially microeconomic in character and, therefore, of limited value in explaining regional disparities in production and incomes. The aim was to determine the optimum location of the individual firm in a geographical area in which the location of inputs, other activities, and markets were fixed. As developed by August Losch,[3] the theory was gradually extended to cover the locational patterns of systems of firms and, despite its inconsistencies,[4] it laid the foundations for the generalized models of Walter Isard and his followers,[5] who searched for patterns and regularities in such spatial relationships. The discovery of uniformities in industrial concentrations, in the hierarchy of market areas, and in the relationship between city-size distribution and economic development, provided the basis for an understanding of the laws underlying the structure of these economic relationships and, thus, for their improvement through policy interferences.

The connection between classical, and essentially micro, location theory, which concentrates on the location decisions of individual

firms, and the modern macro theory of regional economics is thus
apparent. The relationship is especially evident when studying the
problems of depressed areas. Such an area is, by definition, one in
which economic development and welfare have lagged relative to the
rest of the country, due to the tendency of the growth activities to
locate in the other regions of the economy. As John Friedmann and
William Alonso[6] point out, since the causes of the economic depression of such a region are locational in character, so, too, are the
policy solutions for its problems. If unexploited resources exist within
the area, additional investments may create attractive locations to
induce growth not only at the selected growth points but also throughout
the surrounding region. The critical investment decisions, whether of
an infrastructural or a directly productive nature, are locational in
character and are designed to alter the existing spatial pattern. But,
as already pointed out, the determination of the optimum locations,
whether for individual firms or for industry in general, is facilitated
by an examination of the forces which have in the past determined
their actual locations. However, before proceeding that far--that is,
before studying the results of the research on the locational patterns
of Irish industry--it is appropriate first to examine the forces which
are considered to be important in determining the location decisions
of producers in general.

THE LOCATION
OF ECONOMIC ACTIVITIES

Central to the causes of regional growth are the locational decisions of producers and consumers which, in turn, determine the
spatial distribution of economic activities and of population in an area.
For purposes of economic analysis, productive activities are custom-
arily classified as primary, secondary, and tertiary, which include,
respectively, the agricultural and mining sector, the manufacturing
sector, and the service sector of the economy. Just as the production
and export of primary products are determined by the resource endowment of a country, in the same way their location within the country
is constrained by the internal distribution of these resources.[7] As a
result, policy solutions to the problems associated with the primary
sector are less locational and more organizational in character and
are, thus, generally limited to such efforts as productivity improvements, the redistribution of holdings, and changes in land tenure
systems.

It is in the secondary and tertiary sectors that locations are
determined, not only by the existence of natural resources but also
by a wide variety of other factors. These are generally considered
to be mainly economic in character and specifically concerned with

cost and market considerations, however, there are also a number of noneconomic forces at work and, as we shall see later, these are often more easily manipulated by governments and other agencies and thus are more effective in guiding producers into specific areas in need of development.

In order to understand the pattern of industrial location, commodities are usually divided into three main categories: supply-oriented, market-oriented, and footloose.[8] Supply- or resource-oriented industries produce commodities which use the outputs of the primary sector as their main source of raw materials or require heavy fuel consumption in relation to the weight of the finished products. Such industries tend to be weight-losing in the course of production and, by locating them at the source of supply of the raw materials or power, transporation costs are minimized. The classic examples are iron and steel production, although technological developments in these industries, which formerly burned great quantities of coal per ton of output, have reduced the degree of their material-orientation and, thus, have made them less tied to such areas as coal mine regions. Transportation improvements, as evidenced by the successive development of canals, steamships, railways, and pipelines, have even more dramatic effects on local and international trade and, therefore, on the location of such industries.*

In contrast to the above weight-losing activities are those industries which add weight to the product in the course of production, such as mineral-water bottling and car assembling. For these industries, too, transportation costs are of paramount importance in dictating their locations. Such industries, together with those producing fragile or perishable products, are typically located at, or close to, the main centers of population. Other activities which are similarly market-oriented--but not for reasons relating to transportation costs--are those services which call for personal contact between the producer and the consumer, such as hairdressing, restaurants, and repair shops of all kinds.

Considerations other than transportation cost may be more important for other activities.[9] Industries such as textiles, which

---

*Where transportation developments lead to cost reductions which enable the raw materials to be carried cheaply over great distances, industries can be located in regions, and even countries, which entirely lack these resources. Such industries might then be called import-oriented in the area of production and are frequently located at ports in order to eliminate further (internal) transportation costs.

depend upon a plentiful and cheap supply of labor, are often called labor-oriented while those producing commodities like aluminum, which require cheap electricity, may be called power-oriented.

Industries with no strong locational preferences, and especially those which are not transport-oriented, are generally called footloose industries. The most important considerations which guide the location of such industries are the processing costs and, thus, the local rates in wages and rents are among the main determinants.* As already noted, technological progress tends to make more industries footloose. However, this does not necessarily mean that productive activities will become more dispersed. As transportation costs and other economic factors become less significant as determinants of location patterns, others, of a nonpecuniary, but not necessarily less influential character increase in importance.[10] Some of these nonpecuniary factors (for example, the existence of amenities, good schools, and personal preferences for an area) have little direct effect on industrial costs and revenues while the impact of others (such as business contacts and industrial climate[11]) cannot be easily quantified.

Analyzing the results of an investigation into the factors governing industrial locations in Michigan in 1961,[12]Eva Mueller and James Morgan distinguish between three kinds of location decision: (1) the location of new firms, (2) the decision of existing firms to stay at their present location or, alternatively, to relocate, and (3) location decisions which occur in connection with expansion of facilities. In the case of the first type of decision, the six factors rated most important by the majority of manufacturers were, in order of frequency; labor costs, proximity to markets, availability of skilled labor, industrial climate, the tax bill, and proximity to materials. In general, these are the traditionally stressed cost-and-demand factors and include only one nonpecuniary factor. However, when the discussion shifted from general locational principles to that of a particular location decision, noneconomic reasons were mentioned with more frequency. Historical accident and the personal preferences of the founder were seen

---

*It is essential for an underveloped region or country to produce at lower money wages than those prevailing in developed areas if it is to become industrialized. Even in developed countries, the tendency of trade unions to seek complete regional uniformity of wage rates may hinder the industrialization of their poorer agricultural areas. Of course, this need not mean lower real wages if prices are also relatively lower. Indeed, real wages may have to be comparable (for example between adjacent countries such as Canada and the United States, or between Ireland and Britian) if emigration is to be contained.

to play an important role, particularly in the location decisions of
small entrepreneurs for whom the choice appears to be a consumer
(or household) as well as a business decision.* One can infer from
the survey that when a number of alternative locations are feasible
for a new firm, on the basis of cost and demand considerations, the
owner's personal preferences and contacts may then be decisive in
making a selection. More than one-fourth of the manufacturers argued
that such things as community relations, a favorable industrial climate,
good schools, or adequate recreational facilities were more important
than proximity to markets and materials, leading the authors to conclude that some importance attaches to location factors which are
manmade in the sense that they can be altered by the actions of government, business, labor, and community groups.

In the case of decisions to relocate, cost factors, especially
those relating to production, such as lower wages and taxes, were
emphasized. This was in contrast to the factors regarded as important
by those planning to expand at new locations which were dominated by
considerations of demand and efficient marketing.[13] Because of the
tendency of expanding firms to seek out new customers and markets,
a high rate of growth for the economy as a whole may entail very
uneven growth rates for manufacturing industry in various regions and
localities. While this implies that declining or depressed areas cannot rely upon the development of the national economy to solve their
unemployment problems, the findings of the study indicate that a region
or a town can increase its changes of attracting new firms by providing suitable sites and advance factories, by improving the industrial
climate, and by developing the general amenities of the area.

Policy proposals designed to affect the location of economic
activities and of populations must also take into consideration the
service sector of the economy (which almost invariably is larger in
employment terms than that of manufacturing industry and which
grows in relative importance as the economy develops). For the purpose of determining which service industries might be amenable to
direct official action, T. J. Baker[14] distinguishes between those which
are autonomous from the point of view of local demand (because they
depend either upon export markets outside the area or upon externally
determined social criteria) and those which are induced (by the incomes generated in the autonomous sector). In the case of Ireland,

---

*Nonpecuniary factors are less important, not only for large-
scale businesses but also for subsidiaries (however small) of such
enterprises. This conclusion is of relevance to branch-plant economies, especially if they are also small and open. Thus, the location
decisions of local and those of foreign companies may be dictated by
rather different considerations.

tourism, horse racing, and some forms of transport serve the national or export market rather than the local market and are thus analogous to manufacturing industry, while public administration, defense, and social services, being largely determined by national decisions as to standards and availability, should also be considered as autonomous from the local viewpoint. The remaining service items, such as trading, finance, and domestic service, make up the locally induced sector, which, because its output and employment are basically determined by the size of the autonomous sector, cannot be significantly influenced by direct public intervention. Since tourists, administrative, and social services appear to be equally effective in inducing further employment and since, further, such services presently employ many more people than does manufacturing industry in the poorer counties of Ireland, Baker suggests that it may well prove more feasible to expand such services than to force manufacturing enterprises to locate in these areas.

This is in contrast to Buchanan's pessimism about the employment opportunities to be derived from such policies.[15] Undoubtedly, the employment resulting from tourist development is often small, highly seasonal, and mainly female, and thus cannot be expected to stem the population loss in declining areas. However, when he dismisses as insignificant the effects upon receiving areas of a possible decentralization of some central government departments, one feels that he has failed to appreciate the important innovatory effects which the influx of highly trained personnel can have upon provincial centers.* In general, it is in the less-developed areas, where traditional attitudes are usually most firmly entrenched, that revolutionary changes in ideas and habits are most urgently needed. Checking the "brain drain" out of such areas, and attracting into them highly skilled technicians and innovators which, in turn, depends, to a large extent, upon the creation of attractive working and social environments, would go a long way towards facilitating that revolution.

THE LOCATION OF
IRISH INDUSTRY

Purpose of the Study

An investigation into the location of Irish industry over the last forty years was carried out for both parts of the island. The level of

---

*One would suggest, however, that such transplanted departments be located not in small towns like Athlone or Castlebar as officially

disaggregation was very fine, both with respect to the classification of manufacturing activities* and, even more especially, with respect to their locations.[16] The purpose of the study was to analyze the industrial location patterns in Ireland in order to discover the underlying causal factors at work during this important period in its economic development and with the objective of assessing those factors likely to be important in the future.

In addition to examining the past locations of manufacturing and exporting industries, the study is also designed to answer some questions of specific interest to policy-makers in the field of regional planning and growth-center designation. The degree to which areas specialize and the extent to which industries are concentrated in particular cities and towns is investigated: Which industries have tended to concentrate in the main urban centers of Dublin and Belfast? Which are the most dispersed locationally? Has the degree of concentration (localization) or dispersion changed significantly over time? Which were the main growth industries at various times during the period? Were they exporting industries or those dependent in the main upon domestic demand--or did this, in turn, depend upon the stage of development? Are any trends apparent as to the distribution of growing and declining industries between growing and declining areas? Which industries have the smallest and which the largest number of production units? Where the number of production units increased over time, did the number of locations increase proportionally? The operation of various, and often conflicting forces, makes predictions difficult. On the one hand, the implementation of the government decentralization policies and the general decline in transportation costs would seem to favor increased dispersion but, on the other hand, the importance of intraindustry linkages and of external economies would strengthen the tendency towards increased concentration. It is probable that different industries will have different behavior patterns and that the stage of development of the whole economy is also of relevance in this respect.

---

mooted but in one of the larger centers such as Limerick, which has already been chosen as the site of a new college of higher education, or Galway.

*The classification of manufacturing industries was arranged so as to correspond, as far as possible, with that used in the principal tables of the Census of Industrial Production. The coverage of the study is more complete than that of the national censuses, however, because it includes even firms employing fewer than five persons.

Relating the number of establishments in each industry in the United States to the number of counties wherein they were located, E. M. Hoover[17] found a systematic tendency for the number of counties to increase proportionately less than the increase in the number of establishments, leading him to conclude that there was a systematic tendency for clustering of plants. P. Sargant Florence,[18] a pioneer in this area of study, has found opposite tendencies prevailing in the United Kingdom. The picture which emerges there is one of decreasing degrees of specialization by virtually all regions and decreasing degrees of localization in the majority of industries. This is ascribed, to some extent, to the fact that some of the industries which were most highly concentrated in particular regions (for example coalmining, shipbuilding, textiles and pottery) have been declining in relation to others that were less localized. Once again, the stage of development is probably of some relevance.

Yet another area worthy of investigation is the behavior of plant size over time both with respect to individual industries and to economic activity in general. Is there any evidence to support the view that economies of scale are of increasing importance, especially in a small, open economy? No direct data is available for Ireland but it would be helpful to look at the trends in plant size. Has the average size of plant increased over time? What relationships can be observed between localization and the size of plants, or between external agglomeration economies and economies of scale?* Florence found that the greater the localization, the larger was the size of the representative plant but that, at higher levels of localization, there was a marked concentration of industries with medium-size representative plants. External economies accrue to highly localized firms in the same industry which might well obviate the need for the internal economies of scale of the large plant. Florence also found that industries with all sizes of plant, and no representative size, tend to be footloose industries with a low degree of localization. Industries such as bakeries and the building trades will locate in areas of larger and of smaller population density and will, therefore, tend to have larger and smaller plants to serve these markets of various sizes.

Finally, throughout this study on the location of Irish industry, comparisons will be made between the various forces and trends at work in the two parts of the island.

---

*Agglomeration economies are defined as economies which accrue to firms which locate in large centers containing many industries and are to be distinguished from external economies which accrue to firms within individual industries when these firms are located close to each other.

Analysis and Implications of the Study

The Industrial Classification

The Censuses of Industrial Production divide the Irish manufacturing sector into ten broad groups, each of which is further subdivided
according to its main activities. In the most detailed published results
of the censuses, more than forty separate subdivisions are usually
distinguished but, for the purposes of this study, and particularly
with a view to facilitating comparisons between the two parts of the
island, the number of subdivisions is restricted to thirty-five. The
classifications are shown in Chart 1.

A series of tables, hundreds in number, were drawn up, showing
in detail the location of Irish industry from 1926 to 1966, classified
not only according to its main industrial groupings but also according
to each industry's individual subdivisions. It was on the basis of
these detailed data that the analysis of industrial location in Ireland
was carried out. Summaries of the data (classified by industrial
group) are contained in the tables of Appendix A.

Coverage of the study

As already noted, the data for this study were extracted from
a variety of trade directories giving the names and addresses of
manufacturers and exporters in the Republic of Ireland and in Northern
Ireland for the years 1926 to 1966. While it is felt that these were the
most complete sources of information on the location of Irish industries, complete accuracy, despite painstaking cross-checks, cannot
be guaranteed.

A comparison of the numbers of firms in each industry in the
Republic, for example, as published in the annual censuses, with the
same information, derived for the present study, discloses some important differences. In general, the census figures tend to be smaller.
This is because the principle adopted in recent years by the census
statisticians is to omit establishments which employ fewer than five
persons. But there are important instances where the census figures
are larger than those in the present study. In other words, the information given in the trade directories for certain industries is
incomplete. A case in point is the food industry, one of the subdivisions
of which is "bread, biscuits, and flour confectionery." Because the
trade directories do not list the names and addresses of local bakeries,
the number of firms in this category given in the present study falls
very short of the total given in the census results. In the other few
instances where the census figures are greater all relate to very
small establishments and occur in the earlier part of the period

CHART 1

Classification of Irish Industry

Industrial Group	Main Subdivisions
1. Food	1. Bacon 2. Biscuits and flour confectionery 3. Sugar and sugar confectionery 4. Canned and frozen foods 5. Edible oils and fats 6. Processed dairy products 7. Grain milling
2. Drink and tobacco	1. Aerated and mineral waters 2. Distilling 3. Brewing 4. Tobacco
3. Textiles	1. Cotton and linen 2. Nylon, jute, canvas, and carpets 3. Woolen and worsted 4. Hosiery and knitwear
4. Clothing and footwear	1. Clothing 2. Footwear
5. Leather	1. Fellmongery and tanning 2. Leather goods
6. Wood and furniture	1. Wood and wood products 2. Furniture and fittings 3. Brushes and brooms
7. Paper and printing	1. Printing and publishing 2. Paper and paper products
8. Chemicals	1. Chemicals and drugs 2. Soap, detergents, and candles 3. Oils, paints, inks, and polishes 4. Fertilizers
9. Clay products and cement	1. Concrete, clay, and stone products 2. Glass, china, and pottery 3. Cement
10. Engineering	1. Metal products 2. Machinery 3. Vehicles 4. Ships and boats

covered in this study. The principal industries concerned are metal
trades, printing, clothing, and timber. However, bearing in mind
these qualifications, it is felt that the data derived from the results
of the research are, in general, and especially for the latter part of
the period, reasonably accurate and complete and form a satisfactory
basis from which to analyze the location of Irish industry over the
period from 1926 to 1966.

Patterns of industrial location in Ireland, 1926-66

In examining the patterns of industrial location in Ireland from
the results of the research the picture which emerged was that of a
steady growth of industrialization and of an increased spread of industry over the island since the beginning of the period.

The total number of establishments in the Republic of Ireland
increased from 832 in 1926 to 3,095 in 1966 and in Northern Ireland
the number increased from 600 to 1, 535. While these increases
were fairly steady in both economies up to 1956, the rate of increase
started to slow down in Northern Ireland during the succeeding decade
and, in the Republic, the number of establishments both in the country
as a whole and in many individual counties and towns, actually fell
during the last decade. This was due not only to mergers and rationalization moves within Irish industry but also and most importantly,
to the disappearance of many small firms which failed to withstand
the increased competition which accompanied the reopening of the
economy.

Conceding that the process of industrialization has resulted in
a gradual and increased spread of industry over the island, it is
apparent that some areas fared less well than others and that the
disparities between areas with respect to the numbers of establishments located therein have in many cases widened since the beginning
of the period. Cases in point include Galway, Limerick, Carlow, and
Waterford counties in the Republic and County Londonderry in Northern
Ireland. Other counties, notably Longford, Leitrim, and Roscommon
in the Republic and Fermanagh in the north have been virtually bypassed by the process of industrialization. In contrast to County
Dublin's 1,533 establishments in 1966, Longford, Leitrim, and Roscommon counties had eight, thirteen, and fifteen firms, respectively,
and in contrast to County Antrim's 934 firms, County Fermanagh had
only twenty-seven in 1966. Of the 1,533 firms in County Dublin, no
fewer than 1,525 were located in Dublin City and of the 934 in County
Antrim, 765 were located in the city of Belfast. Indeed, it is apparent
that the main centers in both territories, Dublin and Belfast, have
maintained their dominant positions thoughout the period and that
Dublin's share of the Republic's manufacturing establishments has

increased steadily and significantly since 1926.   At that earlier date, the degree of concentration had been much greater in Belfast than in Dublin. In 1926, 63 percent of all manufacturing industries in Northern Ireland were located in Belfast, compared with only 39 percent of the Republic's industries located in Dublin. However, whereas in Northern Ireland the tendency in general has favored a lessening of concentration in the main center, that in the Republic has favored increased concentration. Within individual industrial groups, this tendency has been particularly strong in the important engineering and clothing divisions, which have shown an increasing propensity to locate in the capital city.

The second largest city in each area, Cork in the Republic and Londonderry in Northern Ireland, has experienced a decline with respect to the percentage of its territory's industry which is located therein. Cork's share of the Republic's establishments fell from 12 percent to 7 percent during the period while Londonderry's share of Northern Ireland's establishments declined from 10 percent to 6 percent. The net result was that by 1966, 56 percent of all manufacturing establishments in each area was concentrated in its two largest urban centers.

Accompanying the general growth of industry has been a very significant increase in the numbers of exporting firms in both economies. Once again, the dominance of the main centers, and especially that of Dublin within the Republic, is apparent. Belfast's share of Northern Ireland's exporting firms was extremely high (88 percent) in 1926 but fell to 51 percent by the end of the period. However, Dublin's share of the Republic's exporting firms, which stood at 38 percent at the beginning of the period, rose to 54 percent by 1966. Both Cork and Londonderry suffered relative declines. From 24 percent in 1926, Cork's share in the Republic fell to 6 percent by 1966 while that of Londonderry in Northern Ireland fell from 7 percent to 6 percent over the period. By 1966, therefore, 60 percent of the Republic's exporting firms, and 56 percent of Northern Ireland's exporting firms were located in their two main centers.

In Northern Ireland, despite the tendency of industry in general to be less concentrated in its main center than that of the Republic, the degree of concentration in some industries, notably in wood and furniture and in chemicals, actually rose during the period. In the Republic, where concentration of industry at the main center has increased steadily over the period, the tendency is particularly noticeable in the textiles, clothing, and engineering groups. The fact that many of the more important industries are being increasingly attracted to the main urban centers strengthens their industrial superiority over the rest of their territories. In contrast, the counties of Longford, Leitrim, and Roscommon in the Republic, and Fermanagh in Northern Ireland not only suffer from a significant lack of manufacturing industry, but among those actually located in these areas, there are very few growth industries or exporting firms.

It can be seen from Tables 38 and 40 (in Appendix A), that Dublin's share of the exporting firms in the Republic has increased to an even more significant extent than that of its share of manufacturing industry in general. Bearing in mind the importance of exports to the growth of income in a small, open economy, it is not surprising to find that the gap between the rate of growth of Dublin's income and that of the rest of the country widened during the 1960's.[19]

Breaking down the manufacturing sector into its ten industrial groups and examining the pattern of their locations over the period revealed that the most ubiquitous industries in the Republic have been food (especially processed dairy products), engineering, textiles, and wood and furniture. In Northern Ireland a fairly similar picture emerged, the most ubiquitous industries being textiles, food, clay products, and engineering. The industries with the fewest locations in both economies were leather and chemicals. However, when each industry was examined according to its main subdivisions, it was apparent that differences with respect to the number of establishments or the number of locations were frequently greater between constituent industries of a group than between the larger groups themselves. Further, in many cases, it was the behavior of one very large scattered subdivision which gave the group its dominant or ubiquitous appearance.* In terms of net output, these subdivisions are frequently not as important as their size, in terms of numbers of establishments, might seem to indicate. As can be seen from Table 17, the most important industries (measured in terms of net output) in the Republic in 1966 were machinery, brewing, vehicles, and metals; however, in terms of the number of establishments, the most important were wood products, metals, printing, and grain milling. In the more urbanized and

---

*Examples of industrial subdivisions which dominate their respective industrial groups in terms of numbers of establishments are dairy products, bread, and grain milling within the food group; mineral waters within the drink and tobacco group; hosiery and linen within the textile group; wood products within the wood and furniture group; clothing within the clothing and footwear group; printing within the paper and printing group; clay products within the clay products and cement group; and metals within the engineering group. It is also within these industrial subgroups that very small towns and villages are numerically important as locations.

industrialized economy of Northern Ireland there is a much closer
correspondence between the size of industries, in terms of the numbers of establishments which they contain and their importance in
terms of their net output.

Determinants of Industrial
Location in Ireland

One of the most contentious issues which arises during the
transition stage of economic development is that of the viability of
small-scale, rural-based industry. The migration of labor from the
countryside to the towns which accompanies and even outruns the
process of industrialization in the urban areas is seen by some as
heralding the advent of rural decay and of national cultural decline.*
As has already been seen in the theoretical model, this migration out
of agriculture in the small, open economy tends to bypass the local
towns and even the capital city, if the country's urban areas are not
comparable in size and structure with those of nearby countries. In
an attempt to contain this out-migration and, at the same time, to
prevent the capital city from garnering a disproportionate share of
the country's industry and population, the first phase of the industrialization process is generally accompanied by a scattered pattern of
industrial location. As we have already seen, this dispersion of economic activities is facilitated by the type of goods produced, the imperfections in the market and in the communications network, and by
the haphazard nature of the new tariff policy. However, when the
second phase of the industrialization process is reached, involving
the production of more difficult import substitutes, such as consumer
durables, intermediate goods, and machinery, the location pattern in
a small, open economy shifts towards a concentration at the main
center and port, through which imports of raw materials, fuel, and
capital goods arrive and out of which exports are mainly channeled.
Regional disparities, with respect to economic structure and incomes,
become increasingly wide and, unless government intervention in the
form of an active regional policy is undertaken during the transition
stage, these disparities tend to become chronic. The promotion of
regional growth centers is currently regarded as the method most
likely to succeed in activating the declining regions on the periphery.
Such a policy has been suggested for both parts of Ireland in the
reports by Matthew, Wilson, and Buchanan.

––––––––––––––––

*"Culture" is difficult to define and an attempt to do so is
hazardous. Nevertheless, the disquiet, which is legitimate, generally
springs from the observation of the gradual destruction of village
life, where local customs, traditions, and language are most firmly
entrenched.

TABLE 17

Most Important Irish Industries, 1926-66
(Measured in Terms of Value of Net Output)

Republic of Ireland

	1926	1936	1946	1956	1966
1.	Brewing	Brewing	Brewing	Brewing	Machinery
2.	Bread	Bread	Bread	Printing	Brewing
3.	Printing	Printing	Printing	Clothing	Vehicles
4.	Tobacco	Grain milling	Clothing	Bread	Metals
5.	Grain milling	Sugar and confectionery	Sugar and confectionery	Grain milling	Printing
6.	Processed milk products	Clothing	Grain milling	Vehicles	Clay products
7.	Wood and cork	Tobacco	Footwear	Sugar and confectionery	Clothing
8.	Bacon	Vehicles	Woollen and worsteds	Metals	Bread
9.	Vehicles	Bacon	Vehicles	Clay products	Canned Foods
10.	Clothing	Processed milk products	Metals	Linen, cotton, and nylon	Processed milk products

Northern Ireland

	1926	1935	1949	1956	1966
1.	Linen	Linen	Linen	Shipbuilding	Miscellaneous foods
2.	Other textiles	Shipbuilding	Shipbuilding	Linen	Other textiles
3.	Shipbuilding	Distilling and brewing	Clothing	Mechanical engineering	Linen
4.	Clothing	Other textiles	Mechanical engineering	Clothing	Mechanical engineering
5.	Mechanical engineering	Clothing	Other textiles	Other textiles	Shipbuilding
6.	Bread	Bread	Bread	Miscellaneous foods, etc.	Clothing
7.	Distilling and brewing	Mechanical engineering	Distilling and brewing	Bread	Electrical engineering
8.	Printing	Printing	Grain milling	Grain milling	Chemicals
9.	Grain milling	Grain milling	Printing	Electrical engineering	Bread
10.	Mineral waters	Mineral waters	Building materials	Milk products	Grain milling

Source: Data derived from author's research.

However, since the publication of the last report, the voices of dissent have been growing louder in the Republic. Critics of its central thesis dismiss as unrealistic the arguments of the growth-center protagonists that the benefits of industrial concentration at selected centers will spread to their surrounding hinterlands, bringing increased regional employment, reduced regional out-migration, and improved services. In general, they see only the prospect of increased local emigration and argue that the promotion of regional growth centers will speed up the decline of the smaller towns and villages and the demise of Gaelic traditions. In the opinion of these critics, what is needed in order to reverse the present trends and reduce emigration is the increased dispersal of industry among the small towns.. How justified are their fears? How legitimate is the argument in favor of small-town industry from an economic as well as from a social viewpoint? Would a policy involving the provision of a factory in every town and village be even socially justifiable? What are the economic costs of such a policy and would the community be willing to meet them?

In an attempt to answer such questions, the pattern of Irish industrial location between 1926 and 1966 was examined for evidence of increased clustering or increased dispersion.* The results of this investigation are presented in Tables 18 through 28. For manufacturing industry in general (Table 18) and for almost every separate industrial group (Tables 19 through 28), in both the Republic of Ireland and in Northern Ireland, the evidence is clearcut and consistent.

Between 1926 and 1966 the spread of industrialization throughout the island was accompanied by a tendency towards clustering of manufacturing plants, both those which manufacture for the home market and those which manufacture for export. The percentage of

---

*"Clustering" in this study is defined as the tendency of firms within the same industry to locate close to each other in a center in order to take advantage of external economies. It was chosen instead of the word "concentration," which is reserved here to describe the tendency of industry to locate in the capital cities of Dublin and Belfast. While the two phenomena are interrelated, and usually operate in the same direction, it was considered useful to distinguish between them. Clustering in this study is rather similar to the same term as used by Hoover but the basis for its calculation is different. Hoover used the county but the town is used in this study, not only because of the availability of more detailed data from the present research, but also because it was considered to be a superior basis from which to derive the necessary evidence.

TABLE 18

Number of Towns With Number of Establishments in Manufacturing
Industry in the Republic of Ireland and in Northern Ireland
in 1926, 1946, and 1966

Manufacturers

Area and year	Number of establishments						
	0-5	6-10	11-15	16-20	21-50	51-199	200 and over
Republic of Ireland							
1926	428	5	2	3	2	1	1
1946	383	33	11	4	7	2	2
1966	375	35	17	2	10	1	2
Northern Ireland							
1926	99	6	3	0	0	1	1
1946	91	8	5	4	0	1	1
1966	78	12	7	2	7	3	1

Exporters

Area and year	Number of establishments						
	0-5	6-10	11-15	16-20	21-50	51-199	200 and over
Republic of Ireland							
1926	164	2	0	0	1	1	0
1946	165	1	0	1	0	1	0
1966	153	8	5	0	0	1	1
Northern Ireland							
1926	55	1	0	0	0	1	0
1946	54	1	0	1	0	1	0
1966	45	5	2	2	2	0	1

Source: Data derived from author's research.

TABLE 19

Number of Towns With Number of Establishments in
the Food Industry in the Republic of Ireland and
in Northern Ireland in 1926, 1946, and 1966

Manufacturers

Area and year	Number of establishments						
	0-5	6-10	11-15	16-20	21-50	51-199	200 and over
Republic of Ireland							
1926	295	2	1	0	1	1	0
1946	288	6	2	2	1	1	0
1966	287	9	1	1	1	1	0
Northern Ireland							
1926	63	1	0	0	1	0	0
1946	62	1	1	0	0	1	0
1966	60	2	1	1	0	1	0

Exporters

Area and year	Number of establishments						
	0-5	6-10	11-15	16-20	21-50	51-199	200 and over
Republic of Ireland							
1926	68	1	0	0	1	0	0
1946	68	2	0	0	0	0	0
1966	68	0	1	0	0	1	0
Northern Ireland							
1926	22	1	0	0	0	0	0
1946	22	1	0	0	0	0	0
1966	22	0	0	1	1	0	0

Source: Data derived from author's research.

TABLE 20

Number of Towns With Number of Establishments in the
Drink and Tobacco Industry in the Republic of
Ireland and in Northern Ireland in 1926, 1946, and 1966

Manufacturers

Area and year	Number of establishments						
	0-5	6-10	11-15	16-20	21-50	51-199	200 and over
Republic of Ireland							
1926	71	0	1	0	1	0	0
1946	69	2	1	0	1	0	0
1966	69	2	1	0	1	0	0
Northern Ireland							
1926	15	0	0	0	1	0	0
1946	15	0	0	0	1	0	0
1966	15	0	0	0	1	0	0

Exporters

Area and year	Number of establishments						
	0-5	6-10	11-15	16-20	21-50	51-199	200 and over
Republic of Ireland							
1926	12	1	0	0	0	0	0
1946	12	1	0	0	0	0	0
1966	12	1	0	0	0	0	0
Northern Ireland							
1926	2	0	1	0	0	0	0
1946	3	0	0	0	0	0	0
1966	3	0	0	0	0	0	0

Source: Data derived from author's research.

TABLE 21

Number of Towns With Number of Establishments in
the Textile Industry in the Republic of Ireland
and in Northern Ireland in 1926, 1946, and 1966

Manufacturers

Area and year	Number of establishments						
	0-5	6-10	11-15	16-20	21-50	51-199	200 and over
Republic of Ireland							
1926	139	1	0	1	0	0	0
1946	138	1	1	0	0	1	0
1966	137	2	0	0	1	1	0
Northern Ireland							
1926	57	3	1	0	0	1	0
1946	54	7	0	0	0	1	0
1966	53	5	2	0	1	1	0

Exporters

Area and year	Number of establishments						
	0-5	6-10	11-15	16-20	21-50	51-199	200 and over
Republic of Ireland							
1926	68	1	0	0	0	0	0
1946	68	0	1	0	0	0	0
1966	67	0	0	1	0	1	0
Northern Ireland							
1926	37	0	0	0	0	1	0
1946	36	1	0	0	0	1	0
1966	35	2	0	0	0	1	0

Source: Data derived from author's research.

TABLE 22

Number of Towns With Number of Establishments in the
Clothing and Footwear Industry in the Republic
of Ireland and in Northern Ireland in 1926, 1946, and 1966

Manufacturers

Area and year	Number of establishments						
	0-5	6-10	11-15	16-20	21-50	51-199	200 and over
Republic of Ireland							
1926	76	0	2	0	0	0	0
1946	74	2	0	0	1	0	1
1966	73	3	0	0	1	0	1
Northern Ireland							
1926	38	0	0	0	1	1	0
1946	38	0	0	0	1	1	0
1966	35	3	0	0	1	1	0

Exporters

Area and year	Number of establishments						
	0-5	6-10	11-15	16-20	21-50	51-199	200 and over
Republic of Ireland							
1926	31	1	0	0	0	0	0
1946	31	1	0	0	0	0	0
1966	30	1	0	0	0	1	0
Northern Ireland							
1926	20	1	0	0	0	0	0
1946	19	0	1	1	0	0	0
1966	18	2	0	0	1	0	0

Source: Data derived from author's research.

TABLE 23

Number of Towns With Number of Establishments
in the Leather Industry in the Republic of Ireland
and in Northern Ireland in 1926, 1946 and 1966

Manufacturers

Area and Year	Number of establishments						
	0-5	6-10	11-15	16-20	21-50	51-199	200 and over
Republic of Ireland							
1926	41	0	0	1	0	0	0
1946	40	1	0	0	1	0	0
1966	41	0	0	0	1	0	0
Northern Ireland							
1926	9	1	0	0	0	0	0
1946	9	0	0	1	0	0	0
1966	9	0	1	0	0	0	0

Exporters

Area and Year	Number of establishments						
	0-5	6-10	11-15	16-20	21-50	51-199	200 and over
Republic of Ireland							
1926	16	0	0	0	0	0	0
1946	16	0	0	0	0	0	0
1966	16	0	0	0	0	0	0
Northern Ireland							
1926	2	0	0	0	0	0	0
1946	2	0	0	0	0	0	0
1966	2	0	0	0	0	0	0

Source: Data derived from author's research.

TABLE 24

Number of Towns with Number of Establishments in the
Wood and Furniture Industry in the Republic of
Ireland and in Northern Ireland in 1926, 1946, and 1966

Manufacturers

Area and year	Number of establishments						
	0–5	6–10	11–15	16–20	21–50	51–199	200 and over
Republic of Ireland							
1926	130	1	1	0	0	1	0
1946	124	5	2	0	1	1	0
1966	127	2	2	0	1	1	0
Northern Ireland							
1926	30	1	0	1	0	0	0
1946	30	1	0	0	0	1	0
1966	27	4	0	0	1	0	0

Exporters

Area and year	Number of establishments						
	0–5	6–10	11–15	16–20	21–50	51–199	200 and over
Republic of Ireland							
1926	22	1	0	0	0	0	0
1946	23	0	0	0	0	0	0
1966	22	0	0	0	1	0	0
Northern Ireland							
1926	10	0	0	0	0	0	0
1946	10	0	0	0	0	0	0
1966	9	1	0	0	0	0	0

Source: Data derived from author's research.

TABLE 25

Number of Towns With Number of Establishments in the
Paper and Printing Industry in the Republic of
Ireland and in Northern Ireland in 1926, 1946, and 1966

Manufacturers

Area and year	Number of establishments						
	0-5	6-10	11-15	16-20	21-50	51-199	200 and over
Republic of Ireland							
1926	83	1	0	0	1	0	0
1946	79	4	0	1	0	1	0
1966	80	3	1	0	0	1	0
Northern Ireland							
1926	38	0	0	0	1	0	0
1946	36	1	0	1	0	1	0
1966	34	4	0	0	0	1	0

Exporters

Area and year	Number of establishments						
	0-5	6-10	11-15	16-20	21-50	51-199	200 and over
Republic of Ireland							
1926	11	1	0	0	0	0	0
1946	12	0	0	0	0	0	0
1966	11	0	0	0	1	0	0
Northern Ireland							
1926	11	0	0	0	0	0	0
1946	11	0	0	0	0	0	0
1966	10	0	1	0	0	0	0

Source: Data derived from author's research.

TABLE 26

Number of Towns with Number of Establishments in
the Chemical Industry in the Republic of Ireland
and in Northern Ireland in 1926, 1946, and 1966

Manufacturers

Area and year	Number of establishments						
	0-5	6-10	11-15	16-20	21-50	51-199	200 and over
Republic of Ireland							
1926	49	1	0	0	1	0	0
1946	49	0	1	0	0	1	0
1966	49	0	0	1	0	1	0
Northern Ireland							
1926	12	0	0	1	0	0	0
1946	12	0	0	0	1	0	0
1966	11	1	0	0	1	0	0

Exporters

Area and year	Number of establishments						
	0-5	6-10	11-15	16-20	21-50	51-199	200 and over
Republic of Ireland							
1926	13	0	1	0	0	0	0
1946	13	1	0	0	0	0	0
1966	13	0	0	0	1	0	0
Northern Ireland							
1926	3	0	0	0	0	0	0
1946	3	0	0	0	0	0	0
1966	3	0	0	0	0	0	0

Source: Data derived from author's research.

95

TABLE 27

Number of Towns With Number of Establishments in the
Clay Products and Cement Industry in the Republic
of Ireland and in Northern Ireland in 1926, 1946, and 1966

Manufacturers

Area and year	Number of establishments						
	0-5	6-10	11-15	16-20	21-50	51-199	200 and over
Republic of Ireland							
1926	99	1	0	0	0	0	0
1946	98	0	1	0	0	1	0
1966	98	1	0	0	0	1	0
Northern Ireland							
1926	41	0	0	1	0	0	0
1946	41	0	0	0	1	0	0
1966	38	2	1	0	1	0	0

Exporters

Area and year	Number of establishments						
	0-5	6-10	11-15	16-20	21-50	51-199	200 and over
Republic of Ireland							
1926	25	0	0	0	0	0	0
1946	25	0	0	0	0	0	0
1966	24	0	0	0	1	0	0
Northern Ireland							
1926	9	0	0	0	0	0	0
1946	8	1	0	0	0	0	0
1966	8	1	0	0	0	0	0

Source: Data derived from author's research.

TABLE 28

Number of Towns With Number of Establishments in
the Engineering Industry in the Republic of Ireland
and in Northern Ireland in 1926, 1946, and 1966

Manufacturers

Area and year	Number of establishments						
	0-5	6-10	11-15	16-20	21-50	51-199	200 and over
Republic of Ireland							
1926	130	0	1	0	1	0	0
1946	126	2	1	1	1	1	0
1966	126	4	0	0	1	0	1
Northern Ireland							
1926	39	0	0	0	1	0	0
1946	39	0	0	0	1	0	0
1966	33	5	1	0	0	1	0

Exporters

Area and year	Number of establishments						
	0-5	6-10	11-15	16-20	21-50	51-199	200 and over
Republic of Ireland							
1926	46	1	0	0	0	0	0
1946	47	0	0	0	0	0	0
1966	44	2	0	0	0	1	0
Northern Ireland							
1926	25	0	0	0	0	0	0
1946	24	1	0	0	0	0	0
1966	22	2	0	0	1	0	0

Source: Date derived from author's research.

establishments located in small centers has decreased and the percentage located in the larger centers has gone up significantly over the period. The tendency towards clustering of plants is weak in a few industries, notably in the drink and tobacco group and in the leather industry, but in the more important industries, especially those in the engineering and textile groups, which are "leading" industries with respect to the growth of net output, the tendency towards clustering is particularly noticeable.

In some instances, the increases in clustering which occurred between 1946 and 1966, while real are not immediately apparent from an examination of the tables. The original data need to be consulted. The clustering phenomenon, in these cases, is masked by the fact that the shifts which took place between the classes were not always as great as the changes which occurred within the individual classes themselves. Examples of such industries are food, clothing and footwear, wood and furniture, paper and printing, and clay products. Within these industries, the increased clustering is mainly the result of increased concentration at the main centers, and especially at Dublin, but there are also instances, for example, in the cases of furniture, processed foods, and footwear, where the increases are also a reflection of increased cluster at other important one-industry or "specializing" centers.

For firms which export, the tendency towards clustering is much more clear cut; it continued strongly throughout the whole period from 1926 to 1966, for manufacturing industry as a whole and for almost every individual industrial group. The only case where increased clustering was not apparent among exporting firms was in the drink and tobacco group, an industry which had, even in 1926, already reached a high level of locational concentration.

Thus, it is apparent that, in both parts of Ireland, despite the operation of government policies favoring a dispersal of industry (see pages 58 - 68), the general reaction of industrialists has been to cluster together, not only within industrial groups but also within large centers of population. Were they justified in doing so? Are there special advantages to be gained by industrialists who cluster in groups and are there agglomeration economies available for firms locating in large industrial centers?

To answer these questions, further investigations were carried out. These investigations all related to the behavior of establishments within manufacturing industry in Ireland during the twenty-year period from 1946 to 1966. They set out to determine whether firms which located in clusters or in large centers had a relatively higher chance of survival or a relatively greater tendency to attract new industry than firms which located singly or in smaller centers.

1946 was chosen as the base year for three reasons: first, because the industrialization process had hardly taken root in the Republic before that date, and thus, a sufficient number of observations within each industrial group could only then be obtained; second, it avoided the disruptive effects of the war years; and third, the twenty-year span between 1946 and 1966 was considered to be sufficiently long to test the survival rates of firms within industries as well as the ability of towns to attract new industries.

In order to examine the relationship, if any, between clustering and failure rates within Irish industry, an investigation was conducted into apparent failure rates,* within each industrial group, in towns classified according to the number of establishments contained therein at the beginning of the period.

Three classes of towns are distinguished: towns containing one firm in an industry, towns containing two to five firms in an industry, and towns containing six firms or more within an industry.

The results of the investigation are presented in Table 29. For both the Republic of Ireland and for Northern Ireland, and in the case of every individual industrial group, the evidence suggests that lower failure rates are associated with clustering within industrial groups. The apparent failure rates of industries in the one-firm towns are very high, and, for five of the ten industrial groups, are 50 percent or more in Northern Ireland. In contrast to this, the apparent failure rates fall sharply when there are six or more firms within the same industry located in a town. In many cases, the apparent failure rates in these towns fall significantly below 5 percent.

Among the more important industries (importance being measured in terms of net output) such as engineering, textiles, and food processing, the apparent failure rates declined steadily as the number of firms

---

*The apparent failue rate is defined as the percentage fall in the number of establishments within an industry between 1946 and 1966 in towns classified according to the number of establishments contained therein in 1946. For example, if there were six establishments in six one-firm towns within a particular industry in 1946, and if there were only three establishments in these same six towns in 1966, then the apparent failure rate of establishments in one-firm towns within this industry is 50 percent. The rate is called apparent because there is no way of ascertaining from the data in the detailed tables (unpublished) whether the remaining three establishments are three of the original six, or whether all six failed and three new firms were established, or whether nine new firms were established and twelve failed, and so on, during the period.

TABLE 29

Apparent Failure Rates of Establishments in Each Industry,
1946-66, in Towns Classified According to the Number of
Establishments Contained Therein in 1946

Republic of Ireland

Number of establishments in towns in 1946	1	2 - 5	6 and over
Industry	Apparent failure rate	Apparent failure rate	Apparent failure rate
All industries	42	23	5
Food	26	22	9
Drink and tobacco	13	18	10
Textiles	40	32	5
Clothing and footwear	17	32	5
Leather	43	63	17
Wood and furniture	38	45	6
Paper and printing	21	46	10
Chemicals	18	50	0
Clay products	50	59	1
Engineering	35	31	7

Northern Ireland

Number of establishments in towns in 1946	1	2 - 5	6 and over
Industry	Apparent failure rate	Apparent failure rate	Apparent failure rate
All industries	29	16	1
Food	50	25	11
Drink and tobacco	25	0	32
Textiles	20	33	17
Clothing and footwear	40	18	5
Leather	100	67	18
Wood and furniture	50	33	2
Paper and printing	50	9	6
Chemicals	80	40	0
Clay products	0	0	0
Engineering	0	0	0

Source: Data derived from author's research.

within the group increased in a town. Indeed, in Northern Ireland, this steady fall in the apparent failure rates with increased cluster was the general rule. In the case of the Republic, however, an economy which is less advanced, both with respect to industrialization and urbanization, the apparent failure rate was higher in seven out of the ten industrial groups in the two-to-five-firm towns than it was in the one-firm towns.

It was felt that a major part of the explanation for the relatively poor performance of firms in the one-firm and in the two-to-five firm towns in the Republic of Ireland might lie in the smaller scale of industry and the smaller size of the average firm in the Republic relative to that in Northern Ireland.

In a study conducted into the size (measured in terms of numbers of persons per establishment) of industrial establishments in the Republic for 1958, T. P. Linehan[20] concluded that, while establishments in the Republic compare reasonably well, in this respect, with those in other European countries, they are generally smaller than establishments in Northern Ireland. While no direct data is available on internal economies of scale in industry in the Republic of Ireland, it is instructive to examine the behavior of plant size over time. The average size of plant in manufacturing industry as a whole increased from thirty-two to fifty-five between 1929 and 1963. In addition, the number of firms employing more than five hundred persons increased from nine to forty-five over the same period. Significantly enough, most of these have been located in Dublin city and county while, in contrast, there is a great concentration of very small firms in the relatively underdeveloped counties of the provinces of Connacht and Ulster (three counties). The vast majority of firms still employ fewer than ten persons and while this is still, in most cases, the most representative size class, there have been important shifts during the period, notably within the textile and engineering groups and in the printing industry. Further, the proportion of firms now employing more than fifty persons has increased in almost all industrial groups, the most notable increase being in textiles, clothing, wood and furniture, and clay products, the very industries which showed the greatest tendencies towards clustering of plants during the 1946-66 period, and the industries within which are to be found the lowest failure rates in the manufacturing sector. Thus, the phenomenon which Florence observed in the United Kingdom, that of increased localization being associated with increasing size of plant, appears to operate in the Republic also.

Although industry in the Republic was still mainly serving the domestic market in 1946, some manufacturing firms were already exporting goods abroad at that date (as they were in Northern Ireland) and, thus, it was considered useful to measure separately the apparent failure rates within these firms in order to see whether firms exposed

TABLE 30

Apparent Failure Rates of Exporting Establishments in Each
Industry, 1946-66, in Towns Classified According to the
Number of Establishments Contained Therein in 1946

Republic of Ireland

Number of establishments in towns in 1946	1	2 - 5	6 and over
Industry	Apparent failure rate	Apparent failure rate	Apparent failure rate
All industries	40	12	0
Food	64	42	0
Drink and tobacco	50	25	0
Textiles	44	20	0
Clothing and footwear	0	-	0
Leather	-	-	-
Wood and furniture	20	0	-
Paper and printing	0	0	-
Chemicals	0	-	0
Clay products	25	0	-
Engineering	0	0	-

Northern Ireland

Number of establishments in towns in 1946	1	2 - 5	6 and over
Industry	Apparent failure rate	Apparent failure rate	Apparent failure rate
All industries	16	0	0
Food	50	17	0
Drink and tobacco	0	20	-
Textiles	13	29	0
Clothing and footwear	0	0	6
Leather	-	0	-
Wood and furniture	0	0	-
Paper and printing	-	0	-
Chemicals	0	0	-
Clay products	0	-	0
Engineering	0	-	0

Note: A dash (-) in the table indicates that there were no firms within the particular class in 1946.

Source: Data derived from author's research.

102

to a wider market (and, therefore, assumed to be benefiting from internal economies of scale) fared better in the smaller centers than firms in these towns which served the local market only. It was also considered useful to ascertain whether exporting firms benefit, in general, from clustering in groups.

From the results presented in Table 30 it is clear that for industry as a whole and for most of the individual industrial groups the apparent failure rates among exporting firms are significantly lower than those for manufacturers in general, suggesting, perhaps, that internal economies of scale may operate for firms in one- and few-firm towns when the market which they serve is the wider international market. However, exceptions to this general rule occur in the Republic within the food, drink and tobacco, and textile industries in the one-firm and in the two-to-five-firm towns. Nevertheless, the value of net output and the value of exports in these industries increased steadily and significantly between 1946 and 1966. Thus, the high apparent failure rates experienced by exporting firms in these industries in the one-firm and in the two-to-five-firm towns in the Republic would appear to be due more to inefficiency and/or locational disadvantages.*

As regards the relatively poor performance of firms within many industrial groups in the two-to-five-firm towns in the Republic in comparison to the performance of firms in the one-firm towns, the explanation is not immediately obvious. It may be that where there is only one firm in a town, special economies may accrue to an industrialist because of his monopsonistic position in the labor market, in comparison to that of the industrialist competing for labor in the town containing two to five firms. Another point worth noting is that the success of small-scale industry in small centers is often closely associated with the degree of local financial participation in the venture. Such financial support may be more forthcoming in a very small center, lacking employment opportunities and anxious to attract industry, than in slightly larger centers already possessing some industry, where the local businessmen often fear the advent of wage increases following upon increased competition for labor within the town.**

---

*Mergers can be ruled out as an important source of decrease in the numbers of manufacturing establishments between 1946 and 1966, as they were not significant during this period. Similarly, tariff reductions, especially those associated with the implementation of the Anglo-Irish Free Trade Area agreement of 1965, only began to take effect in the late 1960's.

**There is a fairly close association between the number of firms in towns in the Republic and the size of towns measured in terms of their populations. See also the second asterisk on page 115.

The relatively poor performance of exporting firms within the textile industry in Northern Ireland was caused by the decline of the linen industry during the period. Belfast, which contained more than one hundred exporting firms within the industry in 1946, succeeded in making a shift into the production of manmade fibers, but many of the smaller towns, especially those containing two to five firms within the industry, failed to make the necessary transformation and, thus, failed to maintain their export markets.

Thus, for both the Republic of Ireland and for Northern Ireland, the evidence relating to the behavior of exporting firms supports the findings of the investigation covering all manufacturing firms. Advantages appear to accrue to exporters who cluster together in groups. The high apparent failure rates, where they occur, are associated with the one-firm and the two-to-five firm towns, while in those centers containing six or more within an industry there was apparently only one industry where failures among exporting firms occurred. These apparent failures took place within the clothing industry in Londonderry, an industry whose most important product in that city was shirts and whose production declined drastically during the period.

It has been shown that manufacturing firms in Ireland, whether they serve the local or the international market, tend to cluster together. This pattern of industrial location is beneficial to industrialists because the apparent failure rates within industries tend to decline as the number of firms within a cluster increases. While the size of the individual establishments is not ruled out as a factor contributing to their success or failure, it is, nevertheless, clear that the benefits to be derived from a trained labor pool or from the existence of services unique to particular industries, such as special commercial, technical, or educational facilities, play an important role in promoting the success of firms locating close to others within the same industry.

A clustered pattern of industrial location evidently promotes the chances of success within existing industry in both parts of Ireland. Is it not logical to conclude, therefore, that new industry would be attracted to existing clusters? If not, what consequences would the dispersion of new industry have for economic development? Do towns that contain clusters of firms within a particular industry generate more new firms within that industry than towns containing only one or a few such firms?

To answer these questions, the increases* which took place between 1946 and 1966 in the number of firms within each industrial

---

*Just as in the case of failure (see note on page 99), the estimation of the number of new firms generated within towns between

group were calculated and an investigation was then conducted into the way in which these increases were distributed between towns, classified according to the number of establishments contained therein in 1946. The investigation also included an examination of exporting firms and the results are presented in Tables 31 and 32.

For industry in general and for almost every individual industrial group, in both the Republic of Ireland and in Northern Ireland, the greater proportion of the increase in the number of firms was recorded in centers containing more than six establishments. Such centers obviously tend to generate new industry to a much more important extent than do the towns containing one or a few firms. The only exception to this general rule in the Republic was in the case of leather, an industry whose locational pattern favored one-firm towns almost exclusively in 1946. A similarly ubiquitous pattern of location operates in the food, clothing, and clay products industries in Northern Ireland, which helps to explain the attraction of its smaller centers for new firms within these footloose industries. It should be noted, however, that, in general, industry in the more industrialized and urbanized economy of Northern Ireland, even where it is dispersed, tends to locate in centers which are relatively large in comparison to those in the Republic. In both areas, the vast majority of firms within industry as a whole in 1946 (82 percent in the Republic and 92 percent in Northern Ireland) were located in centers containing six or more firms. Only 4 percent of Northern Ireland's manufacturing establishments were located in one-firm towns in 1946 (compared with 6 percent in the Republic); in absolute terms the number of firms involved in some industries was very insignificant.

In six out of the ten industrial groups in the Republic of Ireland and in four out of the ten groups in Northern Ireland, the percentage of the increase in the number of establishments which was generated within towns containing two to five firms was lower than that generated in the one-firm towns. This can be compared with the relatively high

---

1946 and 1966 was made on a net basis. Industry was also attracted during the period to towns which contained no industry in 1946. Among the towns in the Republic of Ireland, for example, which lacked any industry in 1946, fifty had attracted between them fifty-five new firms by 1956. There were only thirty-four firms in these same towns in 1966. The apparent failure rate among these firms was 53 percent (higher than that experienced in any other category of town). The net increase in these towns which had no industry in 1946 was only eight firms during the 1956-66 decade. The performance of industry in this category of town in Northern Ireland was only slightly better.

TABLE 31

Distribution of Increase in the Number of Establishments Within
Each Industry, 1946-66, Between Towns Classified According
to the Number of Establishments Contained Therein in 1946

Republic of Ireland

Number of establishments in towns in 1946	1	2 - 5	6 and over
Industry	Percent of increase	Percent of increase	Percent of increase
All industries	6	10	84
Food	22	26	52
Drink and tobacco	30	30	40
Textiles	29	18	53
Clothing and footwear	6	3	91
Leather	100	0	0
Wood and furniture	45	7	48
Paper and printing	15	15	70
Chemicals	14	0	86
Clay products	32	0	68
Engineering	8	6	86

Northern Ireland

Number of establishments in towns in 1946	1	2 - 5	6 and over
Industry	Percent of increase	Percent of increase	Percent of increase
All industries	12	11	77
Food	47	47	6
Drink and tobacco	0	0	0
Textiles	24	22	54
Clothing and footwear	48	52	0
Leather	0	0	0
Wood and furniture	18	15	67
Paper and printing	18	15	67
Chemicals	4	22	74
Clay products	35	55	10
Engineering	12	19	69

Source: Data derived from author's research.

TABLE 32

Distribution of Increase in the Number of Exporting
Establishments Within Each Industry, 1946-66, Between
Towns Classified According to the Number of
Establishments Contained Therein in 1946

Republic of Ireland

Number of establishments in towns in 1946 Industry	1 Percent of increase	2 - 5 Percent of increase	6 and over Percent of increase
All industries	8	8	84
Food	7	2	91
Drink and tobacco	0	0	100
Textiles	7	20	73
Clothing and footwear	7	-	93
Leather	-	-	-
Wood and furniture	18	82	-
Paper and printing	5	95	-
Chemicals	9	-	91
Clay products	0	100	-
Engineering	0	100	-

Northern Ireland

Number of establishments in towns in 1946 Industry	1 Percent of increase	2 - 5 Percent of increase	6 and over Percent of increase
All industries	24	28	48
Food	8	8	92
Drink and tobacco	0	0	-
Textiles	21	27	52
Clothing and footwear	17	0	83
Leather	-	0	-
Wood and furniture	20	80	-
Paper and printing	-	100	-
Chemicals	0	100	-
Clay products	0	-	100
Engineering	18	-	82

Note: A dash (-) in the table indicates that there were no firms within the particular class in 1946.

Source: Data derived from the author's research.

107

apparent failure rates of industry in many of the two-to-five-firm towns as against those experienced in the one-firm towns. Again it is suggested that the extent of local financial support and involvement in new enterprises may be a contributory factor.

In the case of exporting firms, as Table 32 shows, the greater proportion of the increase in the number of such firms was generated in centers which already contained more than one exporting firm in 1946. Within those industries which contained clusters of six or more exporting firms at that date, it is apparent that most of the new firms were generated within these same clusters.

The combination of low apparent failure rates and of high rates of increase in the number of establishments within industries which are located in clusters of six or more firms has meant that, in the case of most industries, the numbers of firms in these clusters increased absolutely between 1946 and 1966. The ratios of the number of firms in 1966 to the number of firms in 1946 in Irish towns (classified according to the number of establishments contained therein in 1946) are shown in Tables 33 and 34. For all manufacturing industries in the Republic of Ireland, the ratios are significantly higher for towns containing six or more firms within an industry than they are for towns containing one or two to five firms. For exporting firms, the ratios rise steadily as the number of firms within a center increases, but for manufacturing industry generally the ratios for the two-to-five-firm centers are more often lower than those in the one-firm towns. These ratios, of course, reflect the ability of a town to maintain or to generate industry and, once again, it is suggested that the towns containing more than one firm within an industry--but lacking a cluster of such firms--may be subject to special disadvantages.

In Northern Ireland, the ratio of the number of firms in 1966 to the number in 1946, within industry in general, in centers containing more than six establishments, demonstrates the success of these centers in maintaining and attracting industry.

Within some industries (food, drink and tobacco, textiles, clothing and footwear, and leather), however, values of less than 100 for the ratio reflect the relatively high apparent failure rates and the relatively low increases in the number of establishments which were experienced within these industries. In the case of textiles, the main cause for the low value of the ratio appears to be a high apparent failure rate but, in the case of the remaining four industries, the low ratio results from a combination of high apparent failure rates and low rates of increase in the number of establishments. In the case of most industries, the ratios for the towns containing clusters of six or more firms within an industry compare unfavorably with the ratios

TABLE 33

Ratio of Number of Establishments in 1966 to Number of
Establishments in 1946 in Towns Classified According
to the Number of Establishments Contained Therein in 1946

Republic of Ireland

Number of establishments in towns in 1946			
	1	2 - 5	6 and over
Industry	Ratio	Ratio	Ratio
All industries	85	100	121
Food	91	100	113
Drink and tobacco	107	100	104
Textiles	84	84	123
Clothing and footwear	104	86	151
Leather	70	36	83
Wood and furniture	90	60	103
Paper and printing	88	61	101
Chemicals	155	50	134
Clay products	63	41	117
Engineering	92	84	162

Northern Ireland

Number of establishments in towns in 1946			
	1	2 - 5	6 and over
Industry	Ratio	Ratio	Ratio
All industries	208	184	132
Food	113	122	91
Drink and tobacco	75	-	68
Textiles	135	108	93
Clothing and footwear	300	200	95
Leather	0	33	82
Wood and furniture	100	133	120
Paper and printing	121	111	125
Chemicals	40	160	165
Clay products	275	320	106
Engineering	320	270	240

Note: A dash (-) in the table indicates that there were no firms within the particular class in 1946.

Source: Data derived from author's research.

109

TABLE 34

Ratio of Number of Exporting Establishments in 1966 to Number of
Exporting Establishments in 1946 in Towns Classified According
to the Number of Establishments Contained Therein in 1946

Republic of Ireland

Number of establishments in towns in 1946 Industry	1 Ratio	2 - 5 Ratio	6 and over Ratio
All industries	180	233	680
Food	52	63	453
Drink and tobacco	50	75	117
Textiles	111	360	533
Clothing and footwear	550	-	2,150
Leather	-	-	-
Wood and furniture	200	750	-
Paper and printing	200	1,000	-
Chemicals	250	-	567
Clay products	75	1,200	-
Engineering	100	860	-

Northern Ireland

Number of establishments in towns in 1946 Industry	1 Ratio	2 - 5 Ratio	6 and over Ratio
All industries	337	362	150
Food	63	100	211
Drink and tobacco	100	80	-
Textiles	175	135	116
Clothing and footwear	150	100	109
Leather	-	100	-
Wood and furniture	150	233	-
Paper and printing	-	500	-
Chemicals	100	200	-
Clay products	100	-	117
Engineering	800	-	430

Note: A dash (-) in the table indicates that there were no firms in the particular class in 1946.

Source: Data derived from author's research.

for towns containing one firm or two to five firms. Again it must be
pointed out that only 4 percent of all firms in Northern Ireland in
1946 were located in one-firm and also in two-to-five-firm towns,
and a comparison of the ratios for these classes shows that, in most
cases, and especially for exporting firms, the towns containing two
to five firms within an industry have higher ratios than those containing only one firm.

The evidence suggests that ability of all types of firms to survive and ability of towns to generate new industry are closely associated
with an industrial location pattern involving the clustering of firms
together within industrial groups. Indeed, the benefits associated with
clustering within industrial groups follow from clustering of firms in
general, whether within the same industry or not. In other words, in
addition to the advantages which accrue to firms which cluster together
in homogeneous groups, there is also strong evidence to suggest that
additional and very important benefits are also available to firms
which locate in heterogeneous clusters within large industrial centers.
These "agglomeration economies" (as distinct from the aforementioned
external economies) are associated with the existence of a large labor
pool, endowed with a wide range of skills, superior social overhead
capital, a larger market, and, generally, a more favorable industrial
climate. Indeed, the results of the investigation into the behavior of
industry in Irish towns, containing various numbers of firms of all
types, suggest that agglomeration economies are even more important
in the promotion of industrial success and exercise an even stronger
locational pull on industry in general than do the external economies
already discussed.

In searching for the existence of agglomeration economies, an
investigation was conducted into the apparent failure rates of firms
within industry as a whole between 1946 and 1966. For this investigation, the classification of the towns was changed. When the investigations were concerned with the search for external economies, three
classes of towns--one-firm, two-to-five-firm, and towns containing
six firms and more--were considered sufficient, since most towns
contained fewer than six manufacturing firms within any given industry.
This was particularly so in the case of exporting firms. Now, however, since the investigation covers the whole of manufacturing industry, the number of firms in many towns will be much greater than six.
For this reason, the six-and-over group has been replaced by the
following classes: six to ten, eleven to fifteen, sixteen to twenty,
twenty-one to fifty-one, fifty-two to one hundred and ninety-nine, and
two hundred and over.

An examination of Table 35, which shows the apparent failure
rates of firms within the manufacturing sector as a whole, reveals

that these rates, which again are very high in the one-firm towns, fall significantly as the number of firms of all types increases within a center.

In Northern Ireland, the apparent failure rate falls steadily as the number of firms within centers increases. In the Republic the economies of agglomeration are obviously very high in towns which contain over two hundred firms.* However, a startling and significant exception to the general case of increasing agglomeration economies occurs in the Republic's medium-sized towns. In the 2 classes of twenty-one-to-fifty-one-firm towns and fifty-two-to-one hundred and ninety-nine-firm towns, the apparent failure rate rises again. The towns involved are Sligo, Galway, Tralee, Waterford, Wexford, Dundalk, Drogheda, and Clonmel in the twenty-one-to-fifty-one range, and Limerick in the fifty-two-to-one hundred and ninety-nine range. The populations of these towns in 1966 ranged from 11,000 in Clonmel to 58,000 in Limerick.

It will be remembered that Limerick (in conjunction with Shannon) has been recommended by Buchanan as a primary growth center in the Republic, that five of the first group (Sligo, Galway, Waterford, Dundalk, and Drogheda) have been suggested as "regional" growth centers, and that Tralee has been named as a possible "local" center of growth. However, in these towns, there appear to be important diseconomies at work.

Table 36, showing the distribution by towns (classified according to the number of establishments contained therein in 1946) of the increase in the number of firms within manufacturing industry between 1946 and 1966, makes clear, once again, that the largest industrial centers in the Republic of Ireland (Dublin and Cork) generated an extremely high percentage of the new establishments.

The medium-size towns again show up badly. It is probably safe to say that the diseconomies ultimately associated with inadequate infrastructural facilities in medium-size towns put a brake on the agglomeration economies which such centers may offer.

The industrial "mix" and the presence or absence of interfirm or interindustry linkages (through the purchase of each other's outputs)

---

*There are only three such towns in the whole island: Dublin (1,065 firms in 1946 and 1,525 in 1966), and Cork (234 firms in 1946 and 224 in 1966) in the Republic, and Belfast (693 firms in 1946 and 760 in 1966) in Nothern Ireland.

TABLE 35

Apparent Failure Rates of Establishments in Manufacturing
Industry in the Republic of Ireland and in Northern
Ireland, 1946-66, in Towns Classified According to the
Number of Establishments Contained Therein in 1946

Number of establishments in towns in 1946	Republic of Ireland Apparent failure rate	Northern Ireland Apparent failure rate
1	42	29
2 - 5	23	16
6 - 10	8	3
11 - 15	5	3
16 - 20	5	0
21 - 51	16	-
52 - 199	22	0
200 and over	1	0

Note: A dash (-) in the table indicates that there were no towns
within the particular class in 1946.

Source: Data derived from author's research.

TABLE 36

Distribution of Increase in the Number of Establishments
Within Manufacturing Industry, 1946-66, Between
Towns Classified According to the Number
of Establishments Contained Therein in 1946

Number of establishments in towns in 1946	Republic of Ireland Percent of increase	Northern Ireland Percent of increase
1	6	12
2 - 5	10	12
6 - 10	8	13
11 - 15	3	18
16 - 20	3	28
21 - 51	0	-
52 - 199	0	0
200 and over	70	17

Note: A dash (-) in the table indicates that there were no towns within the particular class in 1946.

Source: Data derived from author's research.

would be expected to play an important part in the fate of industrial establishments located in towns containing several types of industry. However, the absence of such information for Irish towns precludes an investigation into this question.

In Northern Ireland, the ability of towns to generate new industry appears to rise steadily as the number of establishments located therein increases. The major exception to this general rule is Londonderry, a city already defined as a downward-transitional industrial area. Belfast, too, compares unfavorably with some smaller centers (and also with Dublin) in attracting new industry. This may be explained by the fact that it forms the nucleus of a relatively highly industrialized and urbanized area, and the new industries, where they failed to go to Belfast, generally located in the other industrial centers contiguous to it.

The results of an inquiry conducted by the Buchanan team into the factors limiting the expansion of industrial firms in the Republic are summarized in Table 37. They show that for Irish firms, which are predominantly oriented towards the home market, the most limiting factor was the small size of the Irish market.

For overseas firms, which are, for the most part, export-oriented, the chief constraint was overseas marketing problems and (probably reflecting the use of a more advanced technology) the shortage of skilled labor.*

Of more immediate significance to the present discussion, however, is the fact that for all industrialists, both domestic and foreign, the general impression conveyed was that most would prefer to locate in larger centers than their actual ones. Thirty-two percent of the industrialists interviewed (accounting for 46 percent of industrial employment) put the optimum size of town at 20,000 population and over.**

---

*The lowering of Irish tariffs on imports and the drive for increased exports by Irish firms, since the advent of the third phase of the industrialization program, probably accounts for the importance of competition in the Irish market and overseas marketing problems as other serious constraints limiting the expansion of the local firms.

**In the Republic of Ireland, there is a fairly close association between the size of towns, measured in terms of their populations, and the number of manufacturing firms which they contain. Outside Dublin and Cork, which each had populations exceeding 100,000 in

TABLE 37

Factors Limiting Expansion of Irish Firms and
Overseas Firms in Survey Sample

Irish Firms

Factor	Frequency factor* mentioned (Percent)	Proportion of firms mentioning factor (Percent)	Proportion of firms giving factor as most important (Percent)
1. Size of Irish market	21.8	71.6	27.1
2. Competion in Irish market	14.5	55.8	11.8
3. Overseas marketing problems	11.5	49.7	8.8
4. Cost of labor	10.8	44.7	8.8
5. Shortage of skilled labor	7.5	34.5	7.5
6. Difficulties with supplies	6.5	23.9	11.0
7. Capacity of existing plant	6.4	26.4	7.0
8. Lack of long-term capital	5.9	26.4	5.7
9. General shortage of labor	4.5	24.9	3.9
10. Difficulties with transport	3.8	19.3	3.5
11. Size of existing site	2.6	16.2	1.3
12. Lack of short-term credit	2.4	13.7	1.8
13. Difficulties with services	1.8	11.2	1.8
Total	100		100

Overseas Firms

Factor	Frequency factor* mentioned (Percent)	Proportion of firms mentioning factor (Percent)	Proportion of firms giving factor as most important (Percent)
1. Overseas marketing problems	14.7	42.9	15.0
2. Shortage of skilled labor	12.4	38.8	13.3
3. Capacity of existing plant	11.3	32.6	11.7
4. Cost of labor	10.6	36.7	8.3
5. Size of Irish market	10.6	32.6	11.7
6. Difficulties in transport	7.8	28.6	8.3
7. General shortage of labor	7.8	22.4	11.7
8. Competition in Irish market	5.5	20.4	5.0
9. Lack of long-term capital	5.5	14.3	6.7
10. Difficulties with supplies	5.1	22.4	3.3
11. Lack of short-term credit	4.6	18.4	3.3
12. Difficulties with services	3.2	18.4	1.7
13. Size of existing site	0.9	6.1	–
Total	100		100

*The weighted number of times factor cited as limiting expansion as a percentage of weighted total of all mentions of all factors.

Weighting: 4 for each time factor cited as most important one, 3 for each time cited as second most important, 2 for third, and 1 for fourth and lesser importance.

Source: Foras Forbartha, Regional Studies in Ireland, by Colin Buchanan and Partners, in association with Economic Consultants Ltd. (Vol 1: Dublin: Foras Forbartha, 1968), Technical Appendix.

An additional 29 percent (accounting for 22 percent of industrial employment) favored a place between 10,000 and 20,000 population. Only 18 percent (10 percent of industrial employment) favored a place below 5,000, and none at all a place below 1,000.

Implications of the study

It has been shown that during the last forty years--a period which covers the transition stage of economic development in the Republic of Ireland--the process of industrialization has been accompanied by a systematic tendency towards the clustering of plants. This tendency operates, not only within the industrial sector as a whole, but also within most of the individual industrial groups.

It has also been shown that industrialists in both parts of Ireland are correct in pursuing this pattern of industrial location, since there are important economies to be derived from it. External economies, associated with the clustering of plants within the same industrial group, become very significant for firms which locate in towns containing six or more establishments within the same industry, as is suggested by the low apparent failure rates in such firms and the superior ability of the towns which contain them to attract new industry. Agglomeration economies, on the other hand, which are associated with the clustering of plants of all types together in large industrial centers, and which also rise steadily as the number of firms in a town increases, only become significant in towns containing more than two hundred firms in the Republic.

The proposition that the two types of clustering might be advantageously combined seems inescapable. In other words, it is suggested that the process of industrialization, in an economy like that of Ireland, and, thus, the process of economic development itself in such a country, would be more assured of success if industrial establishments were arranged in groups of similar or related firms, located within the large industrial clusters of the urban agglomerations.

1966 and which each contained over two hundred manufacturing establishments, there were only four other towns in the Republic at that date with populations greater than 20,000. These were Limerick (58,000), Waterford (29,000), Galway (26,000), and Dundalk (21,600). They contained sixty-one, forty, thirty, and forty-three firms, respectively. There were eight towns with populations ranging between 10,000 and 20,000 and the number of firms which these towns contained ranged from eleven to thirty-seven.

Most towns in the Republic, with the obvious exceptions of Dublin and Cork, are not large enough to guarantee a high survival rate in industry. Further, despite the argument advanced by many economists that very large cities experience diseconomies of agglomeration, due to congestion and high costs, no Irish city has yet attained the scale of agglomeration where such diseconomies might become serious constraints on industrial growth. The economic case for containing the growth of Ireland's main centers on the grounds that they are inefficient locations remains to be proved.

The policy of industrial dispersal, advocated by many sociologists as an antidote to rural decay, carries a high economic cost. The apparent failure rate of firms in one-firm towns is high. Unless the community in general is prepared to meet this high cost--that is, unless the taxpayers in the country are prepared to replace industries in these small towns at a high, and indeed increasing,* rate, in order to maintain industrial employment in these centers--the only sound policy of industrial location is one based upon selected centers, small in number and large in size.

NOTES

1. John Friedmann, "Regional Planning as a Field of Study," Journal of the American Institute of Planners, Vol. XXIX, (August, 1963).

2. Alfred Weber, Theory of the Location of Industries (English translation; Chicago: University of Chicago Press, 1928).

3. August Losch, The Economics of Location (New Haven: Yale University Press, 1954).

4. Losch argues that, in a system characterized by a perfectly homogeneous population and income distribution and with perfectly appropriate transportation facilities, different types of economic activities would be distributed so that each producer would be at the center of a regular hexagon. This he considered to be "the most economical shape for trading areas" ("The Nature of Economic Regions," Southern Economic Journal, Vol. XXIX, August, 1963) because, unlike the circle, no gaps remained in the system when the regional and, more especially, the whole national market is considered. It

*The apparent failure rate of industry in small centers in Ireland was greater in the 1956-66 decade than it had been in the 1946-66 period.

is difficult, however, to fit the whole variety of economic activities
into one or other of the categories of national, regional, and local
markets, because differences in transportation costs for particular
products will affect the size of the hexagons which are likely to be of
different sizes for each product. Thus the assumptions of the theory
impose constraints upon its application in practice.

5. Walter Isard, Location and Space Economy (New York:
the Technology Press and John Wiley and Sons, 1956). See also
Walter Isard et al., Methods of Regional Analysis (Cambridge, Mass.:
Harvard University Press, 1960).

6. John Friedmann and William Alonso, eds., Regional Development and Planning: A Reader (Cambridge, Mass.: MIT Press,
1964), p. 76.

7. The first model of a rational spatial order for agricultural
production was presented in Johann von Thunen's Der Isolierte Staat,
in 1826. In an attempt to determine the optimum arrangement of
various agricultural products, von Thunen assumes a very large city
in the center of a fertile plain and concludes that the products will
be located in successive circles emanating from the city according
to the degree of their perishability and the cost of transporting them
to the urban population. The habit of using circles to delimit market
areas and regions, which can, thus, be traced back to von Thunen,
and which may well be more traditional than useful, has been criti-
cized by Christaller (Das Grundgerust der raumlichen Ordnung in
Europa, Frankfurt am Main, 1950) and Losch (see footnote 4, this
chapter), whose systems of central places or cities are located in
hexagonal arrangements.

8. C. P. Kindleberger, International Economics, (rev. ed.;
Homewood, Ill., Irwin, 1958), Chapter 8.

9. William Alonso, "Location Theory," in John Friedmann
and William Alonso, eds., Regional Development and Planning: A
Reader, op. cit., Chapter 4.

10. Eva Mueller and James Morgan, "Location Decisions of
Manufacturers," American Economic Review, LII (May, 1962), 204-17.

11. Defined as "attitudes of the state or community towards
industry," in Mueller and Morgan, op. cit., 207.

12. Eva Mueller, Arnold Wilken, and Margaret Wood, Location
Decisions and Industrial Mobility in Michigan, 1961 (Ann Arbor:
Survey Research Center, University of Michigan, January, 1962).

The study was based on personal interviews with top executives of
two hundred and thirty-nine Michigan manufacturing plants, in Spring,
1961.

13. Analyzing the causes of industrial relocation in the United
Kingdom since World War II, R. S. Howard (The Movement of Manufacturing Industry in the U.K. 1945-65, Board of Trade, 1968, cited
in A.J. Brown, "Surveys of Applied Economics: Regional Economics
with special reference to the U.K.," Economic Journal, LXXIX, 316,
[December, 1969], 759-96) distinguishes between two classes of moves:
those which are accompanied by net movements of population (the
dispersions from the big conurbations into surrounding areas and
into the southwest and East Anglia) and those which run counter to
net population movements (broadly the movement of industry from
the southwest and Midlands to Wales and the north). While the former
is a "colonization" of open country by population and capital, the
latter constitutes part of a mutual adjustment between the regions
where population increases faster than jobs and those where jobs
increase faster than population. The net number of jobs shifted
northwards and westwards in this adjustment appears on average to
have been only half that of the movement of population in the opposite
direction. Brown concludes that, despite the common assertion that
regional policy aims at moving the work to the worker, it is the
movement of workers to the work that predominates in the United
Kingdom.

14. T. J. Baker, Regional Employment Patterns in the Republic
of Ireland, Paper No. 32 (Dublin: Economic and Social Research
Institute, August, 1966).

15. Foras Forbartha, Regional Studies in Ireland, by Colin
Buchanan and Partners, in association with Economic Consultants
Ltd. (Dublin: Foras Forbartha, 1968), p. 92.

16. The industries were located by towns. Since no such data
were already available for centers other than the large cities, the
information had to be derived from a variety of basic sources,
principally the annual trade directories, which give the names and
addresses of manufacturers and exporters in both parts of the island.
The principal sources were: Thom's Trade Directory, 1926 through
1966 (which covered the location of manufacturers in the Republic
from 1926 to 1966 and in Northern Ireland from 1926 to 1956), Who
Makes What in Northern Ireland, 1966 (which covered the final year
for that area), Kelly's Directory of Manufacturers and Merchants,
1926 through 1966, and The Irish Export Directory 1966 (both of
which covered the location of exporters for the period).

17. E.M. Hoover, Industrial Location and National Resources (Washington, D.C.: Government Printing Office, 1943), Chapter 14.

18. P. Sargant Florence, Industrial Location and Size of Plants (Cambridge: NIESR, 1948), and Post-war Industrial Location and Size of Plant (Cambridge: Cambridge University Press, 1962).

19. Data contained in the preliminary results of a survey by Michael Ross (of the Economic and Social Research Institute in Dublin).

20. T. P. Linehan, "The Structure of Irish Industry," Journal of the Statistical and Social Inquiry Society of Ireland (1961-62), 220-53.

21. Foras Forbartha, op. cit., Technical Appendix, Vol. 1, pp. 97-102.

URBANIZATION AND SOCIAL CHANGE

The process of economic development involves both an economic and a social restructuring of society; an industrial revolution is necessary to implement the economic transformation, and urbanization is needed to effect the social change.

We have already seen from the model, as well as from its application to Ireland, that these twin processes are closely interrelated. Industry is typically an urban activity and, in turn, it promotes urban growth. However, it is also evident that a smooth and steady advance along both fronts is by no means inevitable. Imbalances may appear between urban growth and the growth of industry. In the early period of the transition stage of development, the drift of population from the rural areas to the towns will probably outrun the growth of industry in the receiving areas. The transforming economy, at this stage, may be "overurbanized" in relation to its development and stage of industrialization. Disguised rural unemployment, or underemployment, becomes overt urban unemployment and the growth of slums and shanty-towns become the physical witnesses of the failure of economic achievements to match the rising expectations of the majority of the population in the short run.

The process of urbanization speeds up as industrialization gathers momentum and the urban areas improve their ability to absorb effectively the rural exodus. Areas of the country which had hitherto remained outside any urban influence increasingly participate in the urban way of life and, according to Friedmann,[1] this leads to changes in the social order, to the disruption of accustomed patterns of behavior, and to their reintegration around new value principles. Indeed,

123

the failure of these social changes to occur, or the failure of the growth of social overhead capital to keep pace with the growth of cities, produces urban problems and imperfections. However, as Leonard Reissman[2] points out, the "evils" which many associate with cities are less a consequence of industrialization than of attempts to preserve pre-industrial ways of life in an alien society.* Cities are natural growths and the argument frequently advanced that people want to live in small communities and to get back to nature remains to be proved.[3]

Cities are the nuclei of social and economic change, the centers from which innovatory waves emanate in a transforming society and, thus, an examination of the forces behind the interrelated processes of urbanization and industrialization helps to explain, in large part, the process of economic development itself.

URBAN CENTERS AND THEIR DISTRIBUTION

According to Walter Christaller,[4] the ideal umland, or hinterland, of a city is bounded by a circular line. The sum of the distances of all points in the hinterland to the center thus represents a minimum. If, however, the circular umland touches the umlands of the neighboring cities, a hexagon becomes the most favorable boundary.[5] From these ideas originated the theory of central places. Christaller defines a central place as a city or settlement which functions as an economic or social center for a larger or smaller hinterland and central place activities as those which serve the local market. Central-place theory seeks to determine the optimum distribution of these settlements in space. The ideal pattern is considered to be an evenly spaced distribution over an entire area, in order to minimize the number of centers while, at the same time, furnishing the area with goods and services in the most efficient manner. These central places are said to form a hierarchic system from the smallest rural centers up to the largest urban ones and with central places of equal order in the hierarchy evenly spaced apart.

In contrast to central-place theory, the theory of industrial location, which was dealt with in the previous chapter, considers the distribution of activities which serve the wider regional and national markets. As Morrill[6] points out, these are of even greater importance than central-place activities as support for urban populations. They thus call for more careful consideration when examining the forces

---

*As Reissman explains, child labor is generally acceptable on farms but considered a social evil in factories.

underlying urbanization and the causes of urban growth. In the present
study on Ireland, the emphasis is placed on the role of manufacturing
industry in the growth process. Christaller[7] examines the influence
of industry on the system of central places and observes that industry
either settles in the central places, thus increasing their importance,
or close to raw-material bases, or along favorable traffic routes. He
concludes that these developments modify the system of central places.

According to Buchanan,[8] the hierarchy of urban centers in the
Republic of Ireland is unusual in that there are few medium-size towns.
One hundred years ago there was a fairly even distribution, with small
towns about seven to ten miles apart and larger towns about twenty to
twenty-five miles apart. In other countries, the report claims, many
towns have developed to a greater or lesser extent as manufacturing
centers, but in Ireland this has been infrequent. The only town in the
Republic which has managed to sustain a pull on other parts of the
country is Dublin, now more than five times the size of its nearest
rival, Cork. The third largest city is Limerick (with a population of
slightly less than 60,000), followed by Waterford (approximately
30,000), Galway (26,000), Dundalk (20,000), and Drogheda (18,000).
There are very few towns in the 50,000-150,000 range, and none of the
above group of towns is in the northwestern part of the country. Galway, in the middle of the western coast, experienced a serious population decline after the great famine of the 1840's but has recently re-
covered and is now a center of increasing importance. Buchanan claims
that one consequence of the general absence of industrialization is that
relatively small towns* such as Galway (26,000), Tralee (12,000), and
Longford (4,000) have much larger shopping catchment areas and are
more important as local commercial centers than towns of comparable
size would be in othern western European countries. Friedmann[9] would
comment that such an urban hierarchy is to be expected. In the early
stages of development, he argues, significant gaps exist in the hierarchical structure, with a few cities growing disproportionately to the
rest of the economy and with vast areas remaining largely outside the
sphere of any urban influence. Development induces the spread of the
urban way of life to all regions. While this is conceded, the model in
the present study claims that in a small, open economy the dominant
position of the main center, established in the preindustrial era, will
not lessen, but rather grow in the industrial period unless positive
steps are taken to build up additional large centers during the transitional stage.

---

*In the Irish context, the grouping of such a disparate trio of towns
together, with all defined as relatively small, is considered to be rather
too generalized by the winter.

The findings of Brian J. L. Berry[10] are relevant to the model. City-size distributions are usually classfied into two types: <u>rank-size</u>, according to which the distribution of cities by population size class within countries is truncated lognormal; and <u>primate</u>, whereby a stratum of small towns and cities is dominated by one or more very large cities and there are deficiencies in numbers of cities of intermediate size. As Berry points out, rank-size regularities had hitherto been associated with the existence of integrated systems of cities in economically advanced countries, whereas primate-type distributions had been associated with overurbanization and superimposed colonial economies in underdeveloped countries. Questioning these convictions, Berry conducted a detailed investigation into the whole relationship between city-size distribution and economic development in thirty-eight countries. He concluded that there is no connection between the type of city-size distribution and either relative economic development or the degree of urbanization of countries although, of course, urbanization and economic development are themselves highly associated. There appears to be a scale from primate to lognormal distributions which is somehow tied to the number and complexity of forces affecting the urban structure of countries, such that when few strong forces obtain primacy results and when many forces act in many ways with none predominant, a lognormal city-size distribution is found. Of the fifteen countries with primate city-size distributions in his sample, lognormally distributed lesser city sizes are followed by a gap (either because cities of intermediate size are absent or in short supply) and then by a rapid cumulation to one or several primate cities. Of immediate relevance is the fact that all fifteen countries are small. They range from underdeveloped Thailand through countries with dual and peasant economies, to Denmark and the Netherlands, with highly specialized agricultural economies. Although Ireland is not included in the study, its city-size distribution would seem to display a high degree of primacy. Berry's conclusions suggest that this structure can continue even when the country reaches an advanced stage of economic development. It thus lends support to the model proposed in the present study.

INDUSTRY AND URBAN GROWTH

Once it is accepted that the processes of industrialization and urbanization are closely interrelated aspects of the development process, it then follows that an important aspect of economic planning involves an efficient spatial ordering of the economy and that the promotion of certain urban centers can be used as an important means of promoting economic growth.

We have already seen that industry has a greater chance of success in large centers which provide external economies and economies of agglomeration to activities located in them. This provides the rationale for the growth-center approach. The promotion of industrialization, which is essential to development, is aided by an efficient locational pattern. Thus, in a transitional economy, it is claimed that the imperfections and inefficiencies normally associated with industrial location decisions can be minimized by directing the greater part of new industry to a small number of carefully chosen urban centers which are then expected to act as nuclei of growth, not only for their own regions but also for the national economy.

In a small, open economy, with a primate-type city-size distribution involving a single dominant center, the model and the available evidence suggest that the promotion of other large urban centers is necessary if spatial imbalance is considered undesirable and capable of being overcome. It has also been suggested that the smaller the country, the smaller is the number of such growth centers which the economy will be capable of sustaining. In a very small economy this number may well be limited to one or two. Growth centers may also be chosen to act not merely as countermagnets to the dominant center but also as positive activators of peripheral regions. The functions are distinct and should be distinguished one from the other. A given center may fulfill both functions but a center may justify substantial investment in it by virtue of providing only one of these functions.

If we accept these conclusions, then the choice of growth centers is facilitated by the establishment of the causes of urban growth. If it is to succeed in its role, the chosen center must, by definition, grow. The question then, stated simply, is: What makes towns grow?

It has already been suggested that manufacturing industry plays a crucial role. It has, further, been suggested that certain types of manufacturing industry may be more important as growth generators than others and that the industrial mix of a town should be carefully considered. This provides the core of industrial complex analysis. How important are intraindustry and interindustry linkages? Exports are generally assumed to be an important motor of growth in a small, open economy. Indeed, the smaller the area the greater is their growth impact presumed to be. Is it not then reasonable to assume that the presence of export industries in a town will have a particularly important impact on its growth? Baker[11] has suggested that certain service industries, such as tourism, horse-racing, and public administration, which are autonomous in the regional sense, may provide significant amounts of induced employment in underdeveloped regions. Might they not then be even more important at the town level? Finally, is size important? Do big towns grow faster than small ones, or would a relatively small center, carefully planned, have an equally good chance of success as a large one? Would the growth-center strategy tend to preempt all growth to the chosen few or does growth trickle down from large urban centers to smaller ones in the hinterland? Does the level of urbanization in an area affect the rate of growth of its small towns?

Many of these questions have been the subject of theoretical inquiry on the part of economists and geographers in the past. In particular, the role of exports in urban growth has been investigated at length, not only at the theoretical, but also at the empirical level. This discussion has centered on the relationship between those activities whose products are sold outside the town (and thus bring money into it) and those activities which produce goods and services principally for the local population (and thus result in an exchange of that money which the exports brought in). The former are called basic and the latter nonbasic activities.* M. Aurousseau[12] pioneered the investigation; later John W. Alexander[13] and Gunnar Alexandersson,[14] among others, explored the concept of the basic-nonbasic employment ratio as a method of classifying cities. Although generally considered to be a useful approach in this respect, Victor Roterus and Wesley Calef[15] rightly point out that the concept remains essentially a descriptive tool which highlights certain limited aspects of the economic functioning of a city or region but that the collection of elaborate data for the purpose of quantifying the ratio gives, in their opinion, a false certitude to the results. It is now generally agreed that the really important element of the concept is the notion of the growth-inducing influence of basic (exporting) industry because, essentially, the concept is a modified form of the multiplier. It is, thus, often useful to look for sources of instability in an area in the behavior of the basic activities. As Charles M. Tiebout[16] points out, local recessions do not start because of layoffs in the retail sector but usually because of downturns in manufacturing industry. Thus, although the approach has its limitations, it has had the beneficial effect of highlighting the important role of exports in the growth of towns.

As an aid to the determination of the choice of growth centers in Ireland, further investigations were undertaken by the writer into the performance of Irish cities and towns since the 1920's. An economic profile of each center in the island was drawn up, showing its level of population, industrial structure, and employment breakdown at various dates throughout the period. A few examples of such profiles are

---

*Different terminologies are employed by different authors: basic activities have also been called primary, urban growth, external, or supporting; while nonbasic are also referred to as secondary, service, or internal.

presented in Appendix B. The purpose of the study was to provide a picture of the urban pattern in the island and, more importantly, to try to uncover the causes of urban growth in Ireland over the period so as to help plan the future urban strategy in the island. Specifically, information was sought on the relative importance of each of the possible causes of urban growth mentioned earlier in this section and, while many of the conclusions are not clearcut, some important aspects of the urban growth process in Ireland are disclosed.

THE CAUSES OF URBAN GROWTH IN IRELAND

The causes of urban growth in any developing country are a complex combination of many factors, both economic and noneconomic. Rural-urban migration and the natural increase in the population cause the urban areas to grow in size. Behind these phenomena, in turn, lie the "push" factors driving the rural population to the cities (such as the lack of employment opportunities and low incomes in the agricultural sector, outmoded land tenure systems, and a general lack of social overhead capital), and the "pull" factors attracting the migrants (such as increased employment opportunities and higher money incomes in the growing industrial sector, and the superior social overhead capital of the urban areas).

In both parts of Ireland, with long traditions of emigration, the push factors, while important in reducing the rural population, do not automatically lead to corresponding increases in the populations of the urban areas in the island. This is particularly so in the Republic of Ireland, where unemployment and other welfare benefits compare unfavorably with those in Great Britain.* Those leaving the land in the Republic of Ireland who either fail or feel they will fail to obtain industrial employment in Irish towns tend to emigrate abroad. Thus, apart from the natural increase, the main cause of urban growth in Ireland, and especially in the Republic of Ireland, centers on the ability of Irish towns to attract or pull the rural population to them by increasing the employment opportunities which they can offer in the nonagricultural sector. Since employment in the service sector is

---

*Unemployment in Northern Ireland, on the other hand, whether in rural or in urban areas, is cushioned by welfare payments which are equal to those in Great Britain. This helps to explain the lower rate of emigration from Northern Ireland (and especially from very underdeveloped areas such as County Fermanagh) to Britain, despite the fact that its unemployment rate is generally higher than that in the Republic of Ireland.

mainly induced as a result of increased employment in the secondary
sector, it is the role of manufacturing industry which is considered
crucial in the urban growth process. Hence the emphasis which is
placed on this sector in this study.

Yet, focusing attention on one sector does not remove the complexity. Individual industries may have different effects on the urban
growth process by differing in their ability to create employment
opportunities. Indeed, any given industry may offer radically different
employment opportunities at various stages of the development process,
depending upon whether it is a growing or a declining industry, whether
it exports goods abroad, and whether it provides linkages with other
industries within the manufacturing sector. Thus, the impact of
manufacturing industry on the growth of urban centers will depend upon
the interplay of all these factors. In addition, the growth of individual
centers may depend upon their size, their location in relation to the
large agglomerations, and the level of urbanization in the economy as
a whole. In examining the causes of urban growth in Ireland, therefore,
the complexity and interrelatedness of the forces involved are recog-
nized, and the limitations of the present study are fully acknowledged.

As already pointed out, economic profiles of all the towns in
Ireland were drawn up for the purpose of providing a picture of the
pattern of urban growth in the island since the 1920's. Each center,
down to the smallest village which contained industry, was included
in the study. A total of two hundred and sixty-six centers in the
Republic of Ireland and one hundred and one in Northern Ireland were
examined. However, since employment data at the town level are
available in the Republic only for centers with populations above 1,500,
and since this type of data is not available at all for Northern Ireland,
the analysis of urban growth focuses mainly on the growth experiences
of the ninety-six towns in the Republic that have populations above
1,500 and twenty-six of the Northern Ireland towns that have populations
above this figure. While the emphasis in the following discussion will
be on the behavior of these one hundred and twenty-two towns, the
performance and prospects of the remaining two hundred and forty-five
small centers will also be examined.

Each of the profiles provided information on the population and
on the structure of the manufacturing sector of a town in Ireland. In
addition, the section on the Republic of Ireland included detailed data
on the sectoral and industrial breakdown of the labor force in the towns.*
The tables thus provided a description of the demographic behavior

---

*The employment figures in the Republic of Ireland tables (where

and the industrial structure of each town and as useful a tool, it is hoped, as the basic-nonbasic employment ratio for assessing their prospects and providing a basis for choosing an urban strategy suitable for the next stage of Ireland's economic development.

The causes of urban growth are many and the interrelationships between them are complex but a number of possibilities were investigated and a discussion on each of them is now presented under separate headings.*

Size

Both parts of Ireland are economies which have long been dominated, from a demographic viewpoint, by their capital cities. In 1966, Dublin and Belfast each contained over 500,000 inhabitants while Cork and Londonderry, the second-largest cities in each economy, contained only 125,000 and 55,000, respectively. There were about ten towns in each area with populations between 10,000 and 50,000 but the vast majority of centers, especially in the Republic, contained fewer than 5,000 inhabitants.

Efforts on the part of both governments to encourage the growth of urban areas outside the main centers through policies designed to disperse industry have been largely unsuccessful. This is borne out by a comparison of the rankings of Irish towns by population in 1946 (1951 in the case of Northern Ireland) with similar rankings in 1966. The rank correlation coefficient[17] in the case of the ninety-six towns in the Republic of Ireland sample is 0.96; in the case of the twenty-six towns in the Northern Ireland sample the coefficient is 0.97. Even when the large Republic of Ireland sample is subdivided into groups of towns according to population size, the coefficients remain very close to 1 in all cases.

---

available) are classified by occupations from 1926 up to, and including, 1946. Only a limited population census was taken in 1956 and no data on employment at the town level are, therefore, available for that year. The employment figures for 1966 in the tables are classified by industry. Thus, no comparisons can be made between the employment figures for 1946 and those for 1966 in the tables in Appendix B.

*The investigation into the causes of urban growth in the Republic of Ireland is confined to the 1946-66 period in order to relate this investigation to those carried out in Chapter 4. The period covered in the case of Northern Ireland is 1951-66, since no census was taken in that area between 1937 and 1951.

Correlating the populations of the urban centers at the beginning of the period with the increases which took place in these centers during the period under review gives the initial impression that there is very little relationship between the size of centers and their ability to grow. The rank correlation coefficient between the populations of the ninety-six towns in the Republic of Ireland sample and their actual increases in population between 1946 and 1966 is only 0.36. However, breaking up the sample into groups of towns shows that the low coefficient is caused by the erratic behavior of certain groups of towns in the sample--in particular, those towns with populations below 5,000.

The rank correlation coefficient for the towns with populations greater than 90,000 is 1; for towns between 10,000 and 50,000 the coefficient is 0.3;* for towns between 5,000 and 10,000 the coefficient is 0.5; and for towns with populations below 5,000 the coefficient is -0.01.**

Thus it is apparent that in the Republic of Ireland the relationship between size and growth is very high in the case of the very large centers and very low in the case of small-size and medium-size centers. Indeed, it is interesting to note that the relevant correlation coefficient is lower in the case of the medium-size centers, with populations between 10,000 and 50,000, than it is in the case of all the towns in the sample. It will be recalled from Chapter 4 that these medium-size towns experienced high apparent failure rates within industry and seemed to offer no significant agglomeration economies to firms which located in them.

It was apparent from an examination of the profiles of the towns that the very large centers in the Republic of Ireland are the only ones which are capable of sustaining growth over a long period. Of the ninety-six towns in the sample, only fifty-six experienced any growth between 1946 and 1966. Of the fifty-three towns which experienced growth between 1946 and 1956, only thirty-nine continued to grow during the succeeding decade. In other words, only thirty-nine towns out of ninety-six experienced sustained growth during the twenty-year period. Indeed, the town which grew the fastest between 1946 and 1956, Clara, actually suffered a population decline between 1956 and 1966.

---

*There were no towns in the Republic of Ireland with populations between 50,000 and 90,000 in 1946.

**In Northern Ireland, the relationship between size and growth appears to be relatively close. The rank correlation coefficient for the 26 towns in the Northern Ireland sample is 0.67.

Very few towns succeeded in maintaining a high rate of growth throughout the whole period. The exceptions were Dublin, Cork, Limerick,
and Galway, and a number of towns close to the capital city.

    Between 1946 and 1966, Dublin, Cork, and Limerick grew by
33.5 percent, 39.4 percent, and 35.1 percent, respectively, and these
were the highest percentage increases in population experienced by
towns in the Republic of Ireland, with the exceptions of Tramore, a
small holiday resort which grew by 37.5 percent, and Clara and
Letterkenny, which grew by 48.3 percent and 59 percent, respectively.
However, in these last two towns growth was not sustained. Indeed,
in terms of absolute numbers, Dublin added more than twice as many
to its populations as all the other ninety-five towns together and Cork
added almost as many as did the ninety-four towns smaller than it in
the sample.

    Although average rates of increase may not be a very useful
measure of growth, it is often instructive to measure such rates for
groups of towns and to compare the results. Taking the percentage
changes (both increases and decreases) in the populations of the
ninety-six towns in the Republic of Ireland sample, the average
increase in the populations of the ninety-six towns between 1946 and
1966 was 4.4 percent. The average increase in the populations of the
fifty-six towns which actually grew was 15.4 percent and the average
decrease in those which declined was 11.2 percent.

    Once again the nine medium-size towns with populations in the
10,000-50,000 range, taken as a group, do not show up particularly
well. Two of them, Wexford and Kilkenny, suffered from population
declines while the remaining seven towns experienced an average
growth of 15 percent, which is not significantly different from the
14.6 percent average growth experienced by all towns outside Dublin
and Cork which had positive growth during the period. Indeed, if
Limerick and Galway, which grew very fast, are omitted from the
group, the average growth of towns in the 10,000-50,000 range was
only 9 percent. The evidence, therefore, suggests that size and sustained growth appear to be significantly related only in the case of
the very large centers in the Republic of Ireland.

    A comparison of the growth of urban centers in the Republic of
Ireland with that in Northern Ireland discloses some important
differences. Of the twenty-six towns in the Northern Ireland sample,
only one, Newry, experienced a population decline between 1951 and
1966. The average growth of the remaining 25 towns was 31 percent
during the fifteen-year period. In other words, almost all of Northern
Ireland's urban centers grew during the period and, in addition, the
average growth was greater than that experienced in towns in the

Republic of Ireland. One small town, Antrim, with a population of 1,600 in 1951, grew exceptionally fast and more than doubled its size during the period but the average growth of the remaining twenty-four towns was still high at 23 percent. Belfast and Londonderry added more in terms of actual numbers than did all the other towns together but their percentage increases were well below the average at 9.4 percent and 11.2 percent, respectively. The policy of growth curtailment being applied in Belfast appears to be having some effect and the impression conveyed is that the other urban centers in Northern Ireland are growing at the expense of the capital city.

Proximity to a Very Large Center

The growth experiences of small centers were examined in order to see whether relatively small centers which are situated near very large ones benefit from a trickling down or "spread" of growth from the large centers.

The growth of towns in Dublin, Kildare, Meath, and Wicklow counties was measured in order to determine whether they grew faster on average than towns assumed to be outside the sphere of influence of Dublin City. All ten towns in these counties in the sample experienced population growth between 1946 and 1966. Their average growth at 17 percent was significantly higher than that of the remaining small towns in the country. Indeed, the spread effects from Dublin would appear to emanate out as far as Drogheda.

While towns located within the sphere of influence of Dublin appear to benefit from growth at the main center, no such effects are evident in the cases of towns in close proximity to either Cork or Limerick. The behavior of the towns in County Cork is particularly erratic. The average growth of the towns of Midleton, Youghal, Cobh, Passage-West, and Kinsale, all situated very close to Cork City, was less than 1 percent over the period, which was less than the average of all towns in the country outside Dublin, Cork, and Limerick. Indeed, County Cork towns, as a group, showed a poor growth record overall. It is interesting to note that the two fastest-growing towns in the county were Charleville and Mitchelstown, which are located farthest away from Cork City.

The third-largest city in the Republic, Limerick, would also appear to be too small to influence significantly the growth of towns in its vicinity. The towns of Ennis, Kilrush, Rathkeale, and Nenagh experienced an average decline in population of 4.3 percent over the period. Despite the fact that the towns close to Cork and Limerick are bigger on average (3,500 and 3,800, respectively) than those located close to Dublin (3,000), their growth records are much poorer.

In the case of Northern Ireland, spread effects do not appear to operate significantly in the growth process of small centers. The average growth of the eleven towns in the Belfast region* was 40 percent, but if Antrim is omitted from this group, the average growth of the remaining ten towns was only 21 percent, which is slightly less than the average growth of all twenty-four towns outside Belfast and Antrim. The explanation is probably to be found in the relatively slow growth of the capital city itself which is the result of conscious government policy. Belfast grew by only 9.4 percent between 1951 and 1966 while the remaining twenty-five towns in Northern Ireland grew by 30 percent. Rather than inducing growth in the neighboring towns by virtue of its own growth, it would appear that the low growth of Belfast is merely facilitating the growth of the other towns close to it or, in other words, as already suggested, that the towns close to Belfast are growing at the expense of the capital city. If this conclusion is correct, then it follows that for spread effects to be significant, the city must not only be very large but must also be growing at a substantial rate. In addition, it suggests that if the growth of a capital city or other large agglomeration is deliberately curtailed by government policy the result will be a compensatory growth of the towns in its vicinity rather than the automatic inducement of growth in other urban areas relatively far removed from the main center. This outcome is particularly likely when the large agglomeration is the center of a highly urbanized and industrialized complex of towns such as the Belfast region. The curtailment of the growth of Dublin or that of any large city in a small, open economy which is conveniently located with respect to its export market would probably have this same effect on the pattern of urban growth in the economy.

Degree of Urbanization

Northern Ireland is much more urbanized than the Republic and this appears to have an effect upon the growth of its small towns and villages. Although the population of the Republic, at slightly less than 3 million, is almost twice that of Northern Ireland, it contains the same number of towns with populations above 10,000. Each area contains one city with a population greater than 500,000, six towns with populations above 20,000, and thirteen towns with populations above 10,000. Indeed, with twenty towns containing populations above

---

*The Matthew Report of 1963 delimited the Belfast "region" by a line drawn through Ballymena, Portadown, and Downpatrick.

5,000, Northern Ireland has only nine fewer than the Republic even
in this category. While most of these towns in the Republic experienced
population growth during the 1946-66 period, almost half of the fifty-
eight towns with populations between 1,500 and 5,000 experienced
population declines. In contrast, all the towns in Northern Ireland
with populations above 1,500, with the sole exception of Newry, experienced population growth between 1951 and 1966.

The higher degree of urbanization in Northern Ireland appears
also to have favored the growth of its very small towns and villages.
Out of seventy-five centers in Northern Ireland with populations
between 200 and 1,500 which are included in the present study, only
16 percent experienced population declines between 1951 and 1966.
In contrast, 26 percent of the one hundred and seventy centers within
this size category which are included in the Republic of Ireland section
of the study suffered from population decreases between 1946 and
1966.

The Role of Manufacturing Industry

The growth of a town, in the final analysis, depends upon the
number of jobs which it can provide for its actual and potential labor
force. This, in turn, depends upon the growth of industries producing
goods and services, either for sale within the town or for export
outside it. While the service sector undoubtedly provides a significant
amount of the employment opportunities in any center, many of these
jobs are induced by activities within manufacturing industry and it is,
therefore, this latter sector which may be considered crucial in the
urban growth process.

The rate at which a town will grow will depend, first, upon the
rate at which it attracts industries; second, upon the extent to which
these industries induce the growth of linked industrial activities,
either in a backward or a forward direction; and third, upon the size
of its wages bill which, in turn, will induce the production and exchange
of nonbasic goods and services. For this reason, it is generally
acknowledged that towns which contain growth industries should grow
faster than towns not similarly endowed. In both parts of Ireland,
certain subsections of the textile, engineering, chemical, and food
industries have been growing faster than all others during the last
twenty years. In particular, the production of manmade fibers, of
machinery, and of processed food has increased very substantially
over the period. Thus it would be reasonable to assume that towns
which contained these industries in 1946 should have grown faster
than the average during the period up to 1966.

Most of the forty towns in the Republic of Ireland whose populations fell between 1946 and 1966 had very little manufacturing industry
in 1946 and attracted very few manufacturing firms during the period.
The towns which suffered the most severe decreases in population were
those towns which experienced the greatest decreases in manufacturing
employment. However, there appears to be very little relationship
between the presence of growth industries in these smaller towns and
the growth of such towns in terms of population. Admittedly, most of
the firms within the growth industries were located in Dublin in 1946,
and that center showed a very strong tendency towards sustained and
 substantial growth during the succeeding twenty years. Nevertheless,
for smaller centers, the mere presence of growth industries does not
appear to have offered any guarantee of urban growth.

The explanation is to be found in the high apparent failure rates
of firms in all towns in Ireland outside the very large centers. As
Table 29 showed, these high apparent failure rates operate with equal
force within growth industries as within industry in general. In the
one-firm towns, textiles, engineering, food, and chemicals rank third,
fifth, sixth, and eighth, respectively, as regards apparent failures.
In two-to-five-firm towns they rank sixth, eighth, ninth, and third,
respectively. It is only in towns that contain over six firms in a
given industry that one of them, chemicals, emerges with a zero
apparent failure rate. The conclusion, therefore, is obvious. In a
country where the majority of towns are too small to produce significant agglomeration economies and where, therefore, the apparent
failure rate among industries, regardless of their nature or of their
national rate of growth, is high, then there is no guarantee that the
presence of a growth industry will ensure the growth of the center
because there is no high probability that the industry itself will be a
success. The fact that many small towns which grew during the
period can be seen to have had a high percentage of their labor force
employed in these growth industries is generally due to the fact that
these industries in these particular towns succeeded. Perhaps the
firms had superior management; perhaps the towns had a favorable
industrial climate. Many explanations are possible. But, taking
industry as a whole, the high apparent failure rates among all types
of manufacturing activities in small and medium-size centers and
their relatively high rates of success in very large centers help to
explain the contrasts between the growth experiences of the very
large and those of the small-size and medium-size centers in the
Republic of Ireland.

The existence of linkages between productive activities has
also been suggested as a factor favoring the growth prospects of
urban centers. They are considered to be important not only because

they increase the chances of survival for every firm forming part of
the "chain" but also because, in the event of a failure, the chances of
the redundant labor force being reabsorbed locally is normally rather
high. Perhaps one should distinguish between linkages within industrial
groups and linkages between groups. The former, what might be called
intraindustry linkages, exist between firms within a given industry
which exchange goods and services with each other. An example would
be the sales which take place between metal fabricating firms and
machinery-producing firms within the engineering industry. Interindustry linkages, on the other hand, exist between different but related industries, such as textiles and clothing, or between packaging and food
processing. Despite the wealth of data available from the present study,
it was not possible to be specific about the existence of linkages within
Irish industry at the town level. The determination of their importance
would necessitate a separate and more detailed investigation.

One point which does emerge from an examination of the data
on the location of the individual subsections of Irish industry is that
there has been a significant increase in diversification within many
large firms in some Irish centers. Within the engineering industry
this applies in the case of most towns in Northern Ireland and in the
case of the very large centers in the Republic. Within the chemical
industry, most firms in most towns tend to specialize in the production
of a single chemical product, with the notable exceptions of Dublin,
Cork, Belfast, and Londonderry, where considerable internal diversification exists within many large firms. As might be expected, these
cities, which contain such large diversified establishments within
certain industries, tend to attract a very high proportion of the new
firms within those industries to them.

Because theory tells us that exports are an important motor of
growth in small areas, we would expect that the existence of exporting
firms in a town should enhance its prospects of growth. Unfortunately,
it was not possible to examine the impact of such firms upon the
growth of Irish towns between 1946 and 1966 because relatively few
towns, outside the very large centers, had any exporting firms in
1946. The growth of the manufacturing sector in the Republic of Ireland
during the transition stage was largely a function of domestic demand
reflecting the import-substitution bias of the industrialization policy.
An examination of the composition of its exports at the beginning of
the 1970's, however, shows that over 50 percent of the value of all
exports now comes from the industrial sector. Thus, assuming that
the existence of exporting activities is conducive to urban growth, we
can expect that Irish towns which contain exporting firms will benefit
from them increasingly in the future. Of course it is important to
bear in mind the fact that such benefits may be less significant in the
case of foreign-owned firms which remit profits abroad and/or make
relatively little use of local raw materials and intermediate products

as inputs. It is also relevant to note that the proportion of total exporting firms in the Republic of Ireland which are located in Dublin increased from 37 percent to 54 percent between 1946 and 1966 and thus that it is likely that the greater part of the initial benefits from the future growth of exports will flow to the main center.

The conclusions which emerge are thus consistent with the model and with the findings in Chapter 4. Urban growth is a function of many interrelated factors. Size, proximity to a large center, degree of urbanization, and the presence of growth industries, of exporting firms, and of linked industrial activities can all be expected to play their part in the process to a greater or lesser extent. While the results of this study do not detract from the importance of any of these factors, it is apparent that in the Irish context size is the truly dominant consideration. If the minimum necessary size is not attained in a center, none of the other factors can compensate for its absence and no guarantee of sustained and substantial growth can be made.

In the case of small towns, proximity to a very large center is an advantage even if they contain no industry. If, however, a small town is located outside the sphere of influence of a very large center, even the presence of growth industries and of exporting firms offers no guarantee of sustained growth because of the high failure rate of industry in such small towns.* The trickling down of growth from large to small centers occurs in Ireland only in the case of towns located close to Dublin. The promotion of very large centers should be expected to have a similar growth-inducing effect upon the smaller towns within their spheres of influence. Thus, a growth-center policy, involving the promotion of only one or two centers, need not be inimical to the development prospects of small towns. The concentration of investment at a few centers does not necessarily preempt all growth to these chosen few. Indeed, it probably enhances the growth prospects of smaller towns--not only those which are located close to the growth centers but also many of those situated outside their immediate spheres of influence because these too should benefit from the improved level of development and the increasing urbanization of the economy as a whole. The growth-center policy is a sound urban strategy for a small,

---

*In many cases the presence of an industry in a small center may even indirectly promote out-migration. Labor may be "trained for emigration" in the sense that young people often spend a short time only in the local firm and, when trained, they then tend to leave the town, better equipped to take advantage of the more attractive economic or social opportunities available in larger centers in Ireland or abroad.

open economy, but it must be stressed that, since the minimum size
of a growth center appears to be relatively large, the number of such
centers in a very small country must consequently be few if sustained
and substantial growth is to be assured.

NOTES

1.   John Friedmann, "Cities in Social Transformation," Comparative Studies in Society and History, 1V (July, 1961), reprinted in
Friedmann and Alonso, eds., Regional Development and Planning:
A Reader (Cambridge, Mass.: MIT Press, 1964), pp. 343-60.

2.   Leonard Reissman, The Urban Process (New York: Free
Press, 1964), p. 174.

3.   Reissman, op. cit., Chapter 3.

4.   Walter Christaller, "The Advantages of a Space-economical
Theory for the Practice of Regional Planning," Ekistics, 20, 119
(October, 1965), 223-27.

5.   cf. Footnote 7, Chapter 4.

6.   Richard Morrill, "The Development of Spatial Distributions
of Towns in Sweden: An Historical-predictive Approach," Annals of
the Association of American Geographers, LIII (March, 1963), reprinted
in Friedmann and Alonso, op. cit., pp. 173-86.

7.   Christaller, op. cit., 224.

8.   Foras Forbartha, Regional Studies in Ireland, by Colin
Buchanan and Partners, in association with Economic Consultants Ltd.
(Dublin: Foras Forbartha, 1968), p. 5.

9.   John Friedmann, "Cities in Social Transformation," op. cit.,
p. 349. In common with many writers, Friedmann argues that the
rise and growth of cities is linked to innovations in agriculture and
that the lack of an agricultural surplus is one of the main constraints
to the growth of cities. This argument would appear to confuse cause
and effect. More recent opinion holds that it is, in fact, the growth of
cities which provides the spur for increased productivity in agriculture
and not the reverse. (See, for example, Jane Jacobs, The Economy
of Cities, London, Jonathan Cape, 1970.) The demand for food to
feed the growing urban populations, the spread of technological progress
(which originates in cities) to the agricultural sector, and the "demonstration effect" of higher living standards in cities, induces the

transformation of agriculture and of the rural areas and facilitates the spread of the benefits of economic development to all parts of an economy.

10. Brian J. L. Berry, "City Size Distributions and Economic Development", Economic Development and Cultural Change, IX, 4 (July, 1961), 573-87.

11. T. J. Baker, Regional Employment Patterns in the Republic of Ireland, Paper No. 32 (Dublin: Economic and Social Research Institute, August, 1966).

12. M. Aurousseau, "The Distribution of Population: A Constructive Problem," Geographical Review, X1 (1921), 563-92, and "Recent Contributions to Urban Geography," Geographical Review, XXVI (1936), 620-39.

13. John W. Alexander, "The Basic-nonbasic Concept of Urban Economic Functions," Economic Geography, XXX (July, 1954), 246-61.

14. Gunnar Alexandersson, "City-forming and City-serving Production," Industrial Structure of American Cities (Lincoln: University of Nebraska Press, 1956), pp. 14-20.

15. Victor Roterus and Wesley Calef, "Notes on the Basic-nonbasic Employment Ratio," Economic Geography, XXXI (January, 1955), 17-20.

16. Charles M. Tiebout, "The Urban Base Reconsidered," Land Economics, XXXII (February, 1956), 95-99.

17. Spearman's rank correlation coefficient was used to measure the correlation between the paired observations. The coefficient was calculated on the basis of the ranks of the towns' populations at the beginning and at the end of the period

The formula is $$r' = 1 - \frac{6(\Sigma\ d_i^2)}{n(n^2 - 1)}$$

where d_i stands for the differences between the ranks of the corresponding populations of the towns at the beginning and at the end of the period, n is the size of the sample, and r' is the coefficient of rank correlation.

TOWARD A SPATIAL POLICY
FOR ECONOMIC DEVELOPMENT
IN IRELAND

REGIONS WITHIN SYSTEMS OF REGIONS

The main objectives of economic policy in both parts of Ireland, the raising of per capita incomes and the reduction of emigration, have already met with a significant degree of success and, in the Republic, the population has recently begun to increase after more than a century of steady decline. Nevertheless, the agricultural sector, especially in the Republic, lags behind industry with respect to the growth both of output and of incomes. The coming decades will, therefore, witness a continuing transfer of labor out of poor rural areas into the growing urban industrial centers.

For historical and economic reasons the main urban centers and focal points of growth in Ireland have been situated along the east coast, close to the center (Great Britain), and conveniently located for the exchange of goods and services between the two islands. Further, we have already seen that, far from decreasing, this polarization of growth on the east, and especially around Dublin and Belfast, has tended to increase steadily with the continued progress of the two economies. In both parts of the island this polarization is considered to be undersirable on social and political grounds. Consequently, with a view to correcting the resulting spatial imbalances while, at the same time, attempting to spread the benefits of urbanization more evenly throughout the island, the two Irish governments have recently begun to think and to plan in spatial terms.

Officially, if somewhat mysteriously, the Republic of Ireland has been divided into nine regions for planning purposes. Unofficially, the country had long been thought to consist of two regions--the underdeveloped poor counties west of the River Shannon and the relatively developed and well off counties to the east of it. Even in Northern

Ireland, with a total area of approximately 5,500 square miles, there
is a tendency to discuss development in regional terms and the list
of proposed growth centers for the area is even longer than that suggested for the Republic.

For such a small island, Ireland's "regions" seem to be un-
realistically large in number. If they were to be regarded merely as
short-term survey areas no great harm would be done, but the growth-
center strategies already proposed would appear to lend the divisions
a spurious authenticity by assigning to each of them at least one, and
in some cases more than one, focal point of growth. In any event,
regional boundaries shift over time as a result of development and of
changes in trading relationships. In the Republic, the rapid growth
experienced during the 1960's has already caused the traditional "east
and west of the Shannon" division to become outmoded. According to
T.J. Baker and M. Ross,[1] some of the counties to the northwest of
the river are now more developed and richer than some of the counties
to the southeast of it. When tariff barriers between the Republic and
Northern Ireland disappear with the completion of the Anglo-Irish
Free Trade Area, other and perhaps more significant regional shifts
will occur.

In considering the spatial aspects of Ireland's economic development, therefore, it is important to bear in mind the essential unity
of the island. The changes in trading relationships, both internal and
external, which are expected to take place in the future, will only
serve to underline this sense of spatial cohesion. In general, therefore, it seems wise to avoid any arbitrary division of the island into
regions on the basis of level and trend of development because of the
danger of their becoming entrenched in the minds of the planners in
the long run.

On the other hand, it might be useful, in the short run, to attempt
to apply, on an island-wide basis, Friedmann's regional classification
(see pages 58-61). At this point in time, the only core regions of the
first rank in Ireland are Dublin and Belfast. Other smaller urban
centers with good growth potential, such as Cork, Limerick, and
Galway in the Republic, and Craigavon, Antrim, and many of the towns
close to Belfast in Northern Ireland, could be described as core regions
of lesser rank according to Friedmann's terminology. The upward-
transitional areas in the island are those areas contiguous to the core
regions which are capable of more intensified development and which
could be expected to benefit from any major future injections of investment. The major upward-transitional area in the island at this
juncture is that embracing the counties adjoining Dublin. Ireland
contains no resource frontier regions and only one urban area,
Londonderry in Northern Ireland, which might be classified as

downward-transitional. The greater part of the former congested districts along the western seaboard, together with Leitrim, Roscommon
and Longford counties in the Republic and Fermanagh in Northern Ireland could be described as rural downward-transitional, being areas
of heavy out-migration and poor agricultural potential. Indeed, the
extreme western fringes of the island, together with Cavan and
Monaghan counties in the Republic and Fermanagh in Northern Ireland
(which lie along the border between the two political units), constitute
special problem areas calling for correspondingly special treatment.
Many of these areas may be suitable only for the intensive development
of tourism.

Despite the fact that the lists of growth centers already proposed
for each part of the island have been graded into "national," "regional,"
and "local" centers, it is the opinion of the writer that the designation
of a host of such primary, secondary, and tertiary growth poles is
unrealistic on the one hand and, on the other, even if they were to be
implemented, likely to perpetuate the very problems which they are
designed to correct. In addition, there is strong evidence to suggest
that such a spatial spread of investment might seriously jeopardize
the overall national development plans in the island. Change is needed.
Spatial imbalance exists. But the regional problems of a small, open
economy must be examined with the cold eye of realism--which means
keeping the other eye trained on the international scene.

Whether considered as two separate political entities or as a
single spatial unit, Ireland is a small, open economy and its traditional
dependence on international trade may be expected to continue in the
long run because of its relatively meager endowment of natural
resources and its commitment to policies of industrial growth and
economic and social transformation. Regional development problems
in Ireland must be viewed within the context of national development
problems and the island itself, even when considered as a unit, must
be seen as forming part of the international economy. Local plans
must be consistent with the national plan which constrains them; the
national plan, in turn, must take account of exogenous factors on the
international front which, in a small, open economy, are largely outside its control.

Economically, both parts of Ireland are closely dependent on
Great Britain and it on them through the exchanges of goods and
services and of the factors of production. Indeed, taking the two
islands as a unit, Ireland may be usefully regarded as an economic
region of the whole. This interdependence may be expected to increase
in the 1970's with the complete implementation of the Anglo-Irish
Free Trade Area agreement. Internally, the advent of free trade between the Republic and Northern Ireland may also be expected to
produce change and to alter existing spatial relationships.

Londonderry (in Northern Ireland) will recapture its natural hinterland of County Donegal in the Republic, and the increase in trade and traffic between many towns close to the border will automatically rearrange many important trading relationships and thus may be expected to affect the impact of the individual growth-center policies which, especially for those areas close to the border, will then be seen to be largely competitive in nature.

The enlargement of the European Economic Community and the admission into it of the two islands of Ireland and Great Britain, which may take place before 1975, might well lead to additional changes and necessitate the formulation of spatial policies that take cognizance of such a contingency. From Ireland's point of view, the center of gravity would then shift even further eastward, where the new markets will be located and the polarization of economic activity around Dublin and Belfast should be expected to increase. Within this enlarged free-trade area Ireland would appear as a rapidly developing but still largely agriculture-based region on the western periphery. The importance of maximizing the growth and development of the whole island and of building up a few strong urban centers, comparable in size and economic structure to many of those in Europe, would then become critical. Internal imbalances, now classified as regional problems, would then be seen as local in the European context and their solution would depend to a large extent upon policies determined in Brussels and not in Dublin or Belfast. Polarization of development around the capital cities, agricultural poverty and the absence of a strong urban center on the west, the industrial decline of Londonderry, and the special problems of the border areas will continue to occupy the energies of planners in Ireland but may well appear peripheral to planners in Brussels, Rome, and Paris. For this reason it is essential for the Irish planners now to view their regions and their regional problems in proper perspective, to establish a set of economic priorities, to isolate the crucial spatial problems, and to concentrate on correcting these before entering Europe.

THE THESIS RESTATED

In order to help explain the course of economic development in a small, open economy like that of Ireland and to isolate the main factors considered to be important in that process, a stages model of development was outlined. This model leaned heavily upon Structuralist writings, in particular those of Dudley Seers, and incorporated, to an equally important extent, the ideas of John Friedmann and other regional scientists. The central themes of the Structuralist school, the concern with local historical experience and with its relevance to the present social and economic structure of a developing area, the role of the large international corporation in contemporary economic development, and the center-periphery interpretation of current international flows of goods and factors were all emphasized in the model.

Four stages of development were proposed; the agrarian economy, the transitional economy, the urbanized industrial economy, and the urbanized service economy. The first describes the behavior of a colonial or neocolonial type economy, on the periphery of a free-trade system where the greater part of the labor force is employed in the primary sector, whose output is geared in the main to the needs of importers at the center. While the operation of international free trade brings benefits to the primary sector, in general it is seen to militate against the development of local manufacturing industry. The level and rate of urbanization are both low and, although the tendency of the main city and port to dominate the economy is apparent, the low level of communications and the prevalence of imperfect competition within existing local industries permit the spatial dispersion of economic activities and the growth of other, smaller centers, relatively far removed from the capital city. Because there is nothing endogenous to the system which might induce structural transformation, an exogenous shock in the form of political independence, war, or a world slump is needed to disturb the status quo.

Once this has occurred, the process of deliberate industrialization and guided economic development begins. Protection is progressively increased to help foster infant industries, and the economy tends to become isolated from external competition. As the country moves through the transitional stage, urbanization speeds up, facilitated by the drift from the land and the improvement in the absorptive capacities of the industrializing urban centers. The polarization of industry and of wealth at the main center becomes more pronounced as the economic structure becomes increasingly sophisticated and the economy progresses from the stage of producing simple consumer goods to replace imports on the home market to that of manufacturing intermediate goods, household durables, and machinery which, in a small economy, requires substantial amounts of imported capital equipment, raw materials, and technical skills. The need to export industrial products in order to take advantage of economies of scale eventually necessitates dismantling the high tariff barriers in return for reciprocal concessions from trading partners; this leads to the reopening of the economy, which usually extends to an increase in direct foreign investment. Many small local firms, catering exclusively to the home market and located at scattered points throughout the country, fail to survive in the increasingly competitive conditions, while the growth industries and exporting firms tend to cluster at the main city and port. Just as in the earlier stages of development it was the poor level of internal communications and the general

imperfection of the market which permitted the growth of smaller
urban centers on the periphery, so it is the improvement in communications and in the operation of the market mechanism which, in the
later stages, proves inimical to the continued growth of many of these
smaller centers, and, at the same time, facilitates and even promotes
the dominance of the main city. The process of polarization at the
center is, therefore, not self-correcting. Neither is it, in general,
considered desirable on social and political grounds, and government
intervention is necessary in order to prevent the resulting regional
imbalances from becoming entrenched in the long run. This intervention should be undertaken during the transitional stage and before the
economy completes the process of urbanization so that eventually,
when it becomes an urbanized, service-oriented economy, all parts
of the country and all sections of the population can participate with
equal opportunity in the transformed and, it is hoped, improved living
conditions.

The form which government intervention should take has been
the subject of considerable debate. On one side of the fence stand the
so-called rural mythologists, whom we might usefully describe as
Dispersionists, defenders of the countryside and of local culture and
traditions, who tend to see the presence of a factory in every town
and village as the answer to rural decay and as a means of distributing
the benefits of development more equitably throughout the country.
On the other side are ranged the growth-center protagonists, or what
we might call the Centralists, who tend to emphasize the benefits to
be derived from increasing total national wealth which, they claim,
is more likely to be maximized if investment is concentrated at a
small number of carefully selected and relatively large urban centers,
where external economies and the economies of agglomeration will
help to ensure the success of industrial activities. The population
shifts which such a policy calls for are decried by the first group
but justified by the second on the grounds that, provided the growth
centers are carefully sited on the basis of strict social and economic
criteria, they should substitute intraregional for interregional and
international labor movements.

The a priori argument in favor of growth centers is certainly
very strong, especially in a small, open economy such as that of
Ireland, whose experience was found to fit very well into the model,
and where, despite the fact that it has already arrived at the end of
the transition stage of development, industry is still to a large extent
internationally uncompetitive and the problems of unemployment and
underemployment are still being disguised by large annual outflows
of emigrants. Notwithstanding the fact that the governments in both
parts of Ireland have publicly endorsed the growth-center strategy
as a means of maximizing overall national growth, the government

in the Republic would presently appear to be sitting on the fence between
the rival factions of Dispersionists and Centralists with respect to
the implementation of its spatial policy. Committed to a program of
industrialization and rapid economic development, and apparently
convinced by the arguments in favor of spatially concentrated investment, it nevertheless appears to be reluctant to offend the traditional-
ists and fearful of alienating that large section of the electorate which
presently lives in areas outside those already recommended as growth
centers in official reports.

This book maintains that the government of the Republic is
correct in its misgivings--but, unfortunately, for the wrong reasons.
The growth-center package proposed by Buchanan is considered likely
to perpetuate the very problems it is designed to correct and the combined policies of both governments in Ireland are considered inimical
to the future economic and spatial development of the island in so far
as they lack complementarity and ignore the essential spatial unity
of the area.

IMPLICATIONS OF THE RESEARCH

In an attempt to compare the merits of the separate arguments
of the Dispersionists and the Centralists, an investigation was conducted into the location and behavior of manufacturing industry in
Ireland during the forty-year period from 1926 to 1966. In particular,
the viability of enterprises in small towns was compared with that of
industries located in large centers.

High failure rates were apparent for industries in one-firm
towns and these rates tended to decrease, in general, as the number
of establishments in a center increased. Surprisingly, however, they
were found to rise again significantly for industries located in medium-
size towns with populations between 10,000 and 50,000, and the sug-
gestion was put forward that in such centers diseconomies in the form
of infrastructural inadequacies might be tending to outweigh the economies of agglomeration.

While the process of industrialization resulted in an increased
spread of industry over the island during the transition stage of
development, its dispersion was not uniform, and some areas on both
sides of the border were virtually bypassed by the process of industrialization. At the same time, polarization of industry at the main
centers, and particularly at Dublin, increased significantly. A systematic tendency towards the clustering of plants was evident in both the
Republic of Ireland and in Northern Ireland for manufacturing industry
in general and for almost every individual industrial group, and

manufacturers were considered to be correct in pursuing this policy
of location because of the external economies and economies of agglomeration to be derived from it. These economies, however, in the
case of towns in the Republic, were seen to be really significant only
in the case of very large centers and this, together with the related
fact that industries in such centers have a very high survival rate as
well as a strong tendency to attract other related activities, suggests
that large industrial centers are needed at this stage in Ireland's
economic development in order to ensure that level of industrial
success, without which the economy could not hope to compete in conditions of international free trade. Since Ireland is now facing increasingly competitive trading conditions externally, and since, internally, the polarization of growth on the east is becoming progressively more serious, a few large countermagnets of growth, preferably
located relatively far removed from Dublin and Belfast, are now seen
to be necessary if the objectives of maximum national growth and
minimum spatial imbalance are to be reconciled. However, since the
objectives and constraints of the three levels of planning--national,
regional, and city--are often mutually competitive, priorities need
to be established and the primary objectives of economic policy at
this stage in Ireland's development involve ensuring the international
competitiveness of industry and laying the foundations of a spatial
distribution of economic activities and of population designed to achieve
this aim. At the same time, the social objectives, concerned with
achieving the maximum possible internal spread of the benefits of
industrialization and of urbanization, consistent with the principal
objectives, are acknowledged.

Assuming that the growth-center approach is, thus, justified
for Ireland on theoretical and empirical grounds, the next step involves
choosing locations. An investigation was conducted into the causes
of urban growth in the island between 1946 and 1966 in order to facilitate this choice. Many possible causes of urban growth were considered, including the presence of growth industries, of exporting
firms, and of linked industrial activities, and while each was acknowledged to be important, it was apparent that in the Irish context the
size of the center proved to be the one really significant factor. Thus,
in order to ensure the sustained and substantial growth of both industry and industrial centers and to maximize the spread effects on
surrounding areas, it seemed doubly clear that only large centers
would prove feasible. In a small, open economy these would have to
be very few in number and planned carefully if the main spatial problems, common to both parts of the country, the polarization of growth
on the east, the relative decline over time of the second-largest urban
center in each area, and the low incomes on the western periphery
are to be solved.

Many other problems would still remain in the short run, not
the least of which is that of placating the very real fears of the Dispersionists on the fate of the declining rural areas and of those towns
not chosen as growth centers. The difficulty of building up important
urban centers in areas of poor agricultural potential is generally
acknowledged. It is, therefore, necessary to plan equally carefully
for growth in these areas where it it possible and for decrease in
population where this is inevitable. The rural areas must be defended
and developed through improvements in the organization and productivity of agriculture and the village, which should not be regarded as
a miniature industrial center, has an important part to play in this
process. The spatial aspects of economic development should not be
artificially divided into urban and rural, and both the Dispersionists
and the Centralists would benefit from considering the economy as
a rural-urban continuum involving an interdependence of the two
sectors.

Assuming that growth centers need to be large, is there any way
of determining for a given country an optimum size which will minimize
the costs of industrial production and of infrastructural facilities
while at the same time maximizing external economies, the economies
of agglomeration, and the spread effects to surrounding areas? Perhaps it would be wiser to concentrate on the question of the minimum
feasible size, and while the judicious choice of the centers and the
careful planning of their industrial composition would undoubtedly
reduce this, certain indications may be obtained from examining the
past performance of a country's urban centers and of the industries
located in them. In the case of the Republic of Ireland, as the results
of the research have shown, it is only in centers of approximately
100,000 and over that the economies of agglomeration become significant and the survival rates of industrial establishments have reached
satisfactory levels. In Dublin, for example, with a population of 550,000
in 1946 and containing over 1,000 establishments in manufacturing
industry, four hundred and sixty net new establishments were generated
between 1946 and 1966; in Cork, with a population of approximately
90,000 in 1946 and two hundred and thirty-four establishments in
manufacturing industry, a relatively low industrial failure rate of 4
percent was experienced. In addition, both centers enjoyed substantial
population growth during the period. In contrast, the eight medium-
size towns of Clonmel, Wexford, Tralee, Dundalk, Drogheda, Sligo,
Waterford, and Galway, with populations in 1946 ranging from 10,000
to 28,000, and containing between twenty and fifty industrial establishments each, experienced, on average, very high industrial failure
rates and generated relatively few new firms during the period.
Further, with the notable exception of Galway, their population growth
records were also generally rather poor.

Thus, the implications of the research are that, in a small, open economy like Ireland, a growth-center strategy of economic development is justified, but the size of chosen centers must be large and, therefore, their number small, and their composition may have to be carefully planned in order to ensure self-generating growth in the long run and the international competitiveness of the industries located in them. Government intervention is seen to be necessary for the implementation of such a policy.

LIMITS TO GOVERNMENT INTERVENTION

In the early 1950's, the idea of widespread government intervention in the economy of the Republic of Ireland was abhorrent to most sections of the population--including government officials. However, the long-run inefficiency of the earlier protectionist policies of industrial promotion was already apparent by the mid-1950's, when the economy had obviously arrived at a stage of virtual stagnation and emigration was the only economic indicator showing steady growth. In order to prevent the catchphrase "the vanishing Irish" from becoming an imminent reality, the government initiated a series of economic reforms which culminated in the publication in 1958 of the first Program for Economic Expansion. The success of this first plan and the spirit of national self-confidence which it engendered were largely responsible for the gradual erosion of opposition to large-scale government intervention in the economy. Social and physical planning legislation complemented planning on the economic front and, by the end of the 1960's, concern with spatially unbalanced growth had resulted in the division of the country into nine planning "regions" and in proposals by a government-sponsored team for the promotion of a host of primary, secondary, and tertiary growth centers to help solve this problem.

While such suggestions would have been condemned on the grounds of undue interference in the 1950's, today they are rejected by many sections of the population because it is felt that they do not go far enough. It would seem that every town in the country wants to be designated as a growth center and the obvious contradictions contained in such a policy are indicative not only of the general lack of understanding of basic economic principles but also of the widespread belief that it is now the government's function to dictate solutions to all the economy's problems. It is apparently not realized that such demands are inconsistent with the desire to maintain a democratic political structure involving a strong private sector and rights to private property, only lately won and still jealously guarded. In such an economy there is need for a proper balance to be maintained between the actions of the public and those of the private sector.

One of the assumptions of this book is that the scarcest factor
of production in a developing economy is enterprise, or, to put it in
Hirschman's terminology, the ability to make investment decisions.
It probably matters little to total economic welfare which sector
provides the greater part of this factor. In the early stages of development, it may well be the public sector; in the later stages, if democracy
prevails, the private sector will probably provide most of the entrepreneurs. At all stages, the government's role should include the
encouragement of enterprise but the task is a delicate one and too
much intervention may stifle the very factor it is attempting to promote.

Hirschman's solution is to create deliberate imbalance, as between, for example, social overhead capital and directly productive
activities, as a means of inducing decisions regarding either of these
two types of investment. The principle may apply equally well to the
spatial aspects of economic development. Where imbalance exists
it might be corrected by the creation of countervailing imbalances
elsewhere. Instead of designating a large town in every so-called
region as a growth center and sharing out the available resources
between them, the Irish government would be better advised to concentrate initially on the promotion of only a few centers, creating
new disequilibria and thereby inducing the remainder to provide for
themselves the conditions necessary to attract industry to them.
Government advice and encouragement are still needed and these
centers should not be discriminated against, but the success of many
relatively small centers in the past demonstrates an important lesson
in the value of self-help.

CONCLUSIONS AND RECOMMENDATIONS

Ireland has now arrived at the beginning of the urban-industrial
stage of its development. In many respects, however, it is still relatively underdeveloped in comparison to some of the other western
European countries with which, in the future, it will most likely become
more closely associated. Therefore, the main objectives of Irish
economic policy, the raising of per capita income, the reduction of
unemployment and emigration, and the achievement of an international
level of efficiency in the economy, are perfectly justified at this point
in time. The spatial problems--the polarization of growth in the east,
the relative industrial decline of the second cities in each part of the
island, and the low level of development in the west, must be examined
and can only be effectively solved within the context of these aims.
Bearing this in mind, the following recommendations are suggested
as a means of promoting an optimum spatial ordering of the Irish
economy.

The Choice of Growth Centers

The main core regions in Ireland and the only cities where self-sustained growth on a large scale has been experienced in the past are Dublin and Belfast. These are also the only centers in the island which compare favorably in size and structure with the large cities in other parts of Europe, and especially in Great Britain, to which many of Ireland's unemployed emigrate. It is only in these two centers that the labor-absorption mechanism operates to any important extent and succeeds in effectively absorbing a significant proportion of the rural outflow. Therefore, as long as emigration remains a problem in the island, it is imperative to ensure the continued growth of such centers which are capable of competing as points of attraction with centers in nearby countries. The growth of Dublin and Belfast should not, therefore, be discouraged or contained. While their behavior in the past does not suggest that there is any necessity to actively promote their growth, it is suggested that no restrictions should be imposed on them at present and that their development, while calling for careful internal planning, should be allowed to continue unimpeded in the interests of national growth and the international efficiency of the economy.

Such a policy, although considered conducive to the maximization of national growth and the reduction of emigration, does nothing to solve, and indeed actively promotes, the spatial imbalance arising from the polarization of growth on the east. To solve this problem, it is suggested that large countermagnets of growth be established at Cork and Londonderry, the second-largest cities in each part of the island. The results of the research have shown that, in the Republic of Ireland, it is only in centers of 100,000 and over that the economies of agglomeration become significant. Although it is acknowledged that careful planning of the industrial mix might reduce the minimum size of a growth center below this figure, it is clear that Cork, with a population of 125,000, containing more than two hundred industrial establishments and with a reasonable if unspectacular record of growth, is the obvious choice for the countermagnet to Dublin in the Republic. The agricultural potential of the surrounding area, particularly to the north and east, is high and the area, being relatively densely populated, can provide a labor pool to fill the needs of an expanding industrial sector. Further, the inhabitants of County Cork are well known for their energy and entrepreneurial ability, no small advantage in an area facing rapid growth and structural transformation. The port at Cobh handles large trans-Atlantic liners, and that at nearby Bantry accommodates the world's largest oil tankers. The fact that Cork is relatively far removed from the main center, Dublin, being located on the western half of the south coast and having a hinterland which is well endowed with small towns, many of which

contain industrial establishments, suggests that a large-scale investment program in Cork could transform it into a very important core
region and absorptive cell capable of producing spread effects important enough to promote the growth of neighboring towns.

The Buchanan Report, which recommends Cork as one of two
"national" growth centers (Limerick being the other), proposes a
steady build-up of the city to a peak of about 250,000 by 1986. It also
envisages that the 1961-66 rate of growth in Dublin, which, if allowed
to continue, would produce a 1986 population of 1.2 million, will be
curtailed by government intervention, so that the population at that
date will be somewhat lower at 1.125 million. Since this study stresses
the importance of maintaining the growth of Dublin, and since, moreover, the government policies envisaged by Buchanan have, thus far,
not been effected, it is suggested that the 250,000 target for Cork
should be considered not as a peak but as a minimum. The present
ratio of Dublin's population to that of Cork is six to one and its reduction in 1986 to slightly less than five to one (assuming no curtailment of growth in Dublin) might not be sufficient to enable Cork to
fulfil its main function as the major countermagnet of growth in the
economy.

Londonderry, the second-largest city in Northern Ireland, and,
like Cork a university town and a large port, is in many respects a
less obvious choice for promotion as a large-scale growth center.
The loss of its natural hinterland of County Donegal as a result of the
partitioning of the island in 1922, its collapse as a coal port and naval
base since World War II, the decline of its shirt industry, and its
spectacularly high unemployment rate, especially among males, have
created large-scale unrest in this religiously divided city. There are,
nevertheless, powerful arguments to support the choice of Londonderry
as a major growth center and not the least of these is the seriousness
of its social and economic problems. The Wilson Report recommended
that the city should be one of more than a dozen growth centers in
Northern Ireland but this study suggests that, with the exception of
Craigavon, whose development has probably already gone too far ahead
to be economically abandoned, all other growth-center proposals for
Northern Ireland should be dropped and the greater part of the large-
scale investment planned for these centers should be concentrated in
Londonderry in order to solve at one stroke the two spatial problems
of Northern Ireland: the polarization of growth on the east and the
downward transition of its second city.

Given the social and religious discrimination existing in Northern
Ireland, the choice of Londonderry as a growth center (where the
majority of the population is Catholic) would be politically unpopular
with large sections of the community. However, if it were pointed out

to them that the full implementation of the Anglo-Irish Free Trade
Area agreement will remove trade restrictions between Northern
Ireland and the Republic and that this, in turn, should mean the re-
capturing by Londonderry of its natural hinterland of County Donegal
in the Republic, the redevelopment of the city as a major center and
port might then receive the approval of the majority. Another point
is that it is not outside the bounds of possibility that the wall of
economic protection between the two parts of the island is not the only
one which will fall in the years to come. It seems reasonable to assume
that one day the island will somehow be politically reunited. The
Northern Ireland Protestant majority may require practical assurances
from the Catholic government in the Republic that, within such a unit,
it would itself not be subjected to the type of discrimination which it
has long practiced against its own Catholic minority. It is therefore
suggested that Buchanan's proposal to develop small growth centers in
County Donegal and the counties bordering on Northern Ireland should
be dropped also and that Londonderry should be allowed to act as the
focal point of growth for the whole northwestern part of the island.
A quid pro quo of this nature may appear to be politically impractical
today, requiring, as it would, close and trusting cooperation between
the two governments, but it makes sound political and economic sense
in the long run. It is suggested that a really massive investment
program be launched in Londonderry so that by the end of the century,
when political reunification might be feasible, the city would match
the size of Cork and would exert the same countermagnetic pull on
the north as Cork is intended to exercise on the south.

The other major spatial problem in Ireland, the relative poverty
of the western counties in the Republic, is seen to require agricultural
reorganization and the development of a major urban center in that
downward-transitional region. Two existing cities, Limerick (with
a population of 58,000 in 1966) and Galway (with a population of 26,000),
are the only candidates to be seriously considered as possible growth
centers. The Buchanan Report has recommended both for development,
the first (in conjunction with Shannon) as a "national" center and the
second as a "regional" one. From an industrial viewpoint, Limerick's
qualifications and experience are certainly superior. Compared with
its manufacturing base of sixty-one firms employing more than 5,700
persons in 1966, Galway's thirty firms employing approximately 1,600
appears small. Viewed in relation to Dublin's 1,500 firms and 80,000
industrial employees, however, the contrasts are not so obvious, and
when Galway's location in the middle of the west coast is taken into
consideration, the arguments in favor of promoting the smaller city
become stronger. It also has a large port, a thriving university, and
excellent amenities to cater to the rapidly expanding tourist industry
which is the backbone of the region's economy. Undoubtedly, Buchanan's
choice of Limerick was prompted by the proximity to it of the Shannon

Industrial Estate which, it is conceded, has been an outstanding
success in the short run. It is felt, however, that the development of
Shannon was a long-run mistake and that its industries ought to have
been located at Limerick, where external economies and economies
of agglomeration could have been created on a large scale. The
transport of goods between the airport and Limerick which this would
have entailed would have been preferable to the present transportation
pattern which involves the large-scale daily commuting of workers.
The failure of Shannon, so far, to develop as a community and as a
town capable of attracting permanent residents demonstrates the
importance of amenities and of pleasant living conditions in the promotion of growth centers.

Such amenities are present on a large scale in Galway, which
also possesses an abundant labor supply in its hinterland, located as
it is in the heart of the so-called former congested districts, containing
some of the most densely populated and poorest counties in the country.
Galway is also the center of the Gaeltacht district, where the Irish
language and traditions form an integral part of the daily lives of
many people. It is not, therefore, only on the basis of need or only
as a means whereby an underdeveloped region can be "activated,"
that Galway is chosen as the Republic's second growth center. The
city has many positive points in its favor, and while it is not envisaged
that it will rival Cork or Londonderry in size and structure in the
foreseeable future, it is suggested that it should be promoted on a
scale large enough to enable it to become the Republic's third city
and a center capable of absorbing a large part of the rural outflow
from its own region.

Thus, based upon the findings of the research on the forces
operating in Ireland to promote both industrialization and urbanization,
and upon the supposed functions of growth centers, a small group of
such centers has been proposed for the island in the belief that they
will help solve its principal spatial problems while, at the same time,
proving consistent with the primary objectives of economic policy in
both parts of the island. The proposals are also seen as a means
whereby the foundations of a spatial distribution of population and
economic activities can be laid which will facilitate the reunification
of the island in the future.

While the Wilson and Buchanan reports each recommended a
set of secondary and tertiary centers in addition to "national" growth
centers, this book makes no such recommendations. Dublin and
Belfast, together with Cork, Londonderry, and Galway form a well-
spaced ring around the island's perimeter, close to which the vast
majority of the population already lives. The spatial disequilibria,
which the implementation of these proposals would create elsewhere

in the economy, might well be conducive to the fostering of a spirit of
dissatisfaction and, thus, of self-help amongst the remainder and
induce them to provide for themselves the conditions necessary for
their growth and development.

The Composition of the Growth Centers

In a small, open economy, which relies on foreign capital for
the greater part of its investment funds for industry, it is difficult to
plan for the promotion of specific activities at specific locations.
The fact that foreign capital has to be enticed, very often in competition with other areas offering similar types of inducements, reduces
the amount of control which a government can exercise over its use
and location. Thus, it is difficult to plan the composition of growth
centers in any detail.

Both parts of Ireland rely upon external capital to an important
extent although, of course, since Northern Ireland is an integral part
of the United Kingdom, British capital really represents internal,
although not local, finance in that part of the island. Nevertheless, it
remains true that neither government can exercise that degree of
control over the location of industry which is necessary if growth
centers are to be developed around a particular industrial mix.
Industrial-complex analysts have pointed to the advantages of a
strategy based upon the concentration in one center of a group of
economic activities which are interrelated through direct interfirm
transactions, their joint demand for goods and services, and the
factors of production. Industries such as engineering and chemicals,
within which firms today increasingly tend to specialize in one or a
few specific activities and thus require, in many cases, the presence
of others, within the same group, as support units, are considered to
be a sound basis upon which to build up an industrial complex within
a growth center. Complexes may also be built on a foundation of food
production, textiles, or on many other light industries.

While conceding the advantages which the industrial complex
approach undoubtedly confers, one must, nevertheless, acknowledge
the obvious constraints which would be encountered in a small, open
economy in seeking to employ such a strategy. Because large capital
resources are needed and because in a small, open economy this often
necessitates inflows of foreign capital, the aforementioned lack of
control over the location of foreign firms must be considered the
principal constraint. In addition, there are also the more general
problems relating to the need, within a complex, for superior management, technical skills and services, and large-scale infrastructural
facilities, which are typically in short supply in a developing country,

and the concentration of which on a narrow range of activities may
result in an excessively concentrated industrial structure. In Ireland's
case, as the results of the research have shown,* the presence in the
center of one or two large diversified establishments tends to attract
a large number of small related firms to the same center. Thus,
provided the central government invests large sums in social overhead
capital, if a few large-scale, capital-intensive firms within growth
industries could be persuaded to locate in the chosen growth centers,
it is highly probable that the small-scale support units would follow,
without costly inducements being necessary for their attraction. As
far as possible, local resources and skills should be utilized so that
each growth center can become a motor of development for its surrounding region.

Finally, in so far as the composition of growth centers can be
influenced, they should be planned with the probable long-term trends
of the economy in mind. Industries which are not considered viable
in the long run should be eschewed, regardless of their short-term
benefits either to the economy as a whole or to particular regions.
The total economic and social environment of the country should come
first. If an economy is endowed with a small but quickly exhausted
supply of ores, for example, it would probably be preferable, in the
interests of long-run development, to export them unprocessed, thus
depriving the economy of a smelting plant, than to invest large supplies
of scarce capital in a short-term project which is likely to result in
unusable excess capacity in the near future.

Dublin and Belfast, the established core regions in Ireland, do
not call for any special planning efforts in relation to their industrial
composition. Both cities tend to attract, without offering any special
inducements, the bulk of the large-scale, capital-intensive projects
which are set up within the island. There is, however, one important
constraint operating in these two centers, and especially in the case
of Dublin. We have already seen from the model that the small size
of the domestic market, and, to a lesser extent, the lack of local raw
materials, precludes the development in a small, open economy of
certain large-scale intermediate and capital-goods industries. Therefore, Irish planners should avoid setting up certain types of activities,
as for example, steel mills and automobile plants, even in Dublin,
because such industries would not be viable in the long run in the
Irish economy.

Some planning of industrial composition may be called for in
the cases of Cork and Londonderry. The former city, with a population

---

*Cf. p. 138

of well over 100,000 and a relatively wide range of industrial activities and skills, already provides significant external economies and
economies of agglomeration for industry but it will be necessary for
the central government to invest heavily in new industrial and social
infrastructure in order to attract sufficient new industries to enable
the city to fulfil its functions as a major growth center. In particular,
Cork's physical problems are such as to make imperative the careful
internal planning of the city. A determined effort must be made to
attract a number of large-scale, capital-intensive firms within such
growth industries as engineering. Firms producing components and
standardized parts could then be expected to follow in order to take
advantage of the external economies, and many of these could also be
expected to locate in nearby towns where an abundant supply of labor
and some engineering skills are available. The university should be
encouraged to promote research into the region's special problems.

     Londonderry's problems are not only economic and social but
also political and sectarian and, thus, massive investments in social
overhead capital are needed initially to transform its environment.
Despite its decline as an industrial center and port, the city in recent
years has succeeded in attracting a number of large-scale, capital-
intensive industries which now form the nucleus of an industrial
complex composed of a large power station, an acetylene plant, and
firms producing synthetic rubber and manmade fibers. It is suggested
that other smaller firms locating in Londonderry could be greatly
increased in number if the social and industrial climate of the city
were transformed.

     It is considered that the development of a relatively small city
like Galway into a large growth center requires careful planning and
that an industrial complex approach might be useful. It is not envisaged
that the city will become a center of heavy industry; indeed, it is
suggested that since Galway lies in the heart of Connemara, potentially
one of Europe's great tourist attractions, the city should deliberately
be preserved from the pollution-inducing types of industrial production
and encouraged to specialize in activities which will not detract from
the amenities while, at the same time, fitting in with the agricultural
possibilities of the region and the special skills and traditions with
which the area is endowed. Although the industrial base of the city
is small, it possesses a range of skills suitable for the production of
food, clothing, textiles, printed products, and light engineering goods.
The surrounding region, which is the center of Gaelic traditions in
the island, contains, especially in the west, relatively poor land and
its agricultural production is organized on the basis of very small
farming units. It is suggested that these factors, long considered as
problems, should be regarded in a positive fashion and that the
industries to be promoted in the growth center be chosen so as to
stimulate the agriculture of the region.

A complex of light industries should be established at Galway, based primarily upon the production of income-elastic goods and services such as tourism, luxury foods, flowers, tweeds, high-class clothing, household and personal ornaments, and the reproduction of old Gaelic manuscripts. Some market gardening is already carried on in east Galway but this activity should be promoted right across the region. The relatively densely populated agricultural sector with its small holdings is ideally suited to this type of production and together with the output of the fishing industry, which, it is suggested, should concentrate on the lucrative shellfish catch, would provide the raw materials for a specialized food processing industry in the growth center. The packaging industry should benefit considerably and the related printing skills could also be used in the reproduction of ancient manuscripts. The production of the kind of textiles and clothing which are income-elastic and the production of toys and of decorative goods in general demands a level and originality of design which should be fostered locally but which, in the initial stages, may have to be imported. Large investments in research and in design would be paid for in the long run by increased exports.

Implementation of the Policy

As regards the implementation of the proposed growth-center strategy, it is suggested that the two governments must provide the social overhead capital considered necessary to create a favorable industrial and social climate in the chosen centers. They should also attempt to guide to Cork, Londonderry, and, to a lesser extent, to Galway, a minimum number of large-scale firms around which others will then cluster.

Much controversy surrounds the question of whether differential grants and tax concessions ought to be given to industrialists to locate in the growth centers. It is suggested that such policies ought not to be employed because of the implied discrimination against other centers. It is felt that the large-scale investments in social overhead capital which the governments should make and the designation of the chosen cities as growth centers ought to be a sufficient inducement to manufacturers to locate in them. Other industrialists who might prefer smaller centers, and it is envisaged that many such cases will arise, would not then be penalized for locating in towns in other parts of the country.

Because of the controversial nature of the recommendations, close cooperation will be needed between the two governments in Ireland. They and the community in general must be persuaded to see the island as a spatial unit, demanding a single integrated policy on the lines suggested in this book. It is felt that these

recommendations should promote the island's growth and development while at the sane time helping to redress its more obvious
spatial imbalances. Eventually, although certainly not in the immediate
future, the benefits of urbanization should be spread fairly evenly
over the island.

The recommendations are based upon the nature of the main
immediate problems facing Ireland and upon the conclusions reached
from the research. They may appear radical. It may even be suggested that they would be politically impossible to implement. But
alternative strategies produce high economic costs and, thus, the
issues should presented to the electorate in simple terms. Economic
planning is for people and the final decision must, therefore, rest with
an informed community.

NOTE

1. T. J. Baker and M. Ross, ''The Changing Regional Pattern
in Ireland,'' Economic and Social Review, I, 2 (January, 1970).

A

SUMMARY OF DATA
ON THE LOCATION
OF MANUFACTURERS
AND OF EXPORTERS
(BY INDUSTRIAL GROUP)
IN THE REPUBLIC OF IRELAND
AND
IN NORTHERN IRELAND

TABLE 38

Summary of Data on the Location of Manufacturers
In the Republic of Ireland, 1926-66

Industrial group	1926	1936	1946	1956	1966
Food Industry					
Number of counties	20	25	25	26	26
Number of towns	76	203	208	226	218
Number of establishments	216	526	552	660	637
Percent of establishments located in Dublin	26	19	22	24	28
Percent of establishments located in Cork	11	11	9	7	7
Percent of establishments located in Dublin and Cork	37	30	31	31	35
Drink and Tobacco					
Number of counties	18	21	22	23	23
Number of towns	28	43	47	56	61
Number of establishments	77	116	120	149	144
Percent of establishments located in Dublin	38	28	29	25	30
Percent of establishments located in Cork	17	11	11	10	9
Percent of establishments located in Dublin and Cork	55	39	40	35	39
Textiles					
Number of counties	21	21	23	24	24
Number of towns	55	68	82	99	92
Number of establishments	88	158	206	268	253
Percent of establishments located in Dublin	19	34	34	34	34
Percent of establishments located in Cork	9	9	7	9	10
Percent of establishments located in Dublin and Cork	28	43	41	43	44
Clothing and Footwear					
Number of counties	14	21	23	23	23
Number of towns	20	41	62	62	67
Number of establishments	51	242	327	472	466
Percent of establishments located in Dublin	29	62	62	71	73
Percent of establishments located in Cork	27	11	10	7	5
Percent of establishments located in Dublin and Cork	56	73	72	78	78
Leather and Leather Goods					
Number of counties	10	14	16	19	17
Number of towns	14	23	29	32	24
Number of establishments	33	56	70	96	56
Percent of establishments located in Dublin	55	39	40	40	50
Percent of establishments located in Cork	6	11	11	16	4
Percent of establishments located in Dublin and Cork	61	50	51	56	54
Wood and Furniture					
Number of counties	17	26	26	26	26
Number of towns	23	54	104	102	90
Number of establishmnets	107	255	358	459	357
Percent of establishments located in Dublin	49	48	40	42	42
Percent of establishment located in Cork	13	11	9	10	11
Percent of establishment located in Dublin and Cork	62	59	49	52	53

Industrial group	1926	1936	1946	1956	1966
Paper and Printed Products					
Number of counties	14	26	26	26	26
Number of towns	14	57	70	77	72
Number of establishments	72	209	282	372	266
Percent of establishments located in Dublin	65	42	45	50	55
Percent of establishments located in Cork	8	9	7	8	6
Percent of establishments located in Dublin and Cork	73	51	52	58	61
Chemicals					
Number of counties	10	11	10	16	18
Number of towns	11	16	16	34	39
Number of establishments	65	129	165	217	243
Percent of establishments located in Dublin	75	72	79	69	73
Percent of establishments located in Cork	3	2	1	1	0
Percent of establishments located in Dublin and Cork	78	74	80	70	73
Clay Products and Cement					
Number of counties	10	22	23	23	25
Number of towns	11	54	53	60	58
Number of establishments	20	146	142	176	157
Percent of establishments located in Dublin	50	37	43	43	40
Percent of establishments located in Cork	5	9	8	5	6
Percent of establishments located in Dublin and Cork	55	46	51	48	46
Engineering Products					
Number of counties	18	24	25	26	26
Number of towns	24	62	85	107	92
Number of establishments	103	262	349	439	516
Percent of establishments located in Dublin	47	44	44	42	60
Percent of establishments located in Cork	13	14	12	11	7
Percent of establishments located in Dublin and Cork	60	58	56	53	67
All Industries					
Total number of establishments	832	2,099	2,571	3,308	3,095
Percent located in Dublin	39	39	41	43	49
Percent located in Cork	12	11	9	9	7
Percent located in Dublin and Cork	51	50	50	52	56

Source: Data derived from author's research.

167

TABLE 39

Summary of Data on the Location of Manufacturers
In Northern Ireland, 1926-66

Industrial Group	1926	1936	1946	1956	1966
Food Industry					
Number of counties	6	6	6	6	6
Number of towns	17	32	40	41	48
Number of establishments	60	94	149	191	179
Percent of establishments located in Belfast	47	36	48	45	35
Percent of establishments located in Londonderry	16	11	9	7	9
Percent of establishments located in Belfast and Londonderry	63	47	57	52	44
Drink and Tobacco					
Number of counties	4	4	4	5	5
Number of towns	6	6	5	15	13
Number of establishments	31	29	41	60	43
Percent of establishments located in Belfast	81	80	90	58	58
Percent of establishments located in Londonderry	3	3	0	3	5
Percent of establishments located in Belfast and Londonderry	84	83	90	61	63
Textiles					
Number of counties	6	6	6	6	6
Number of towns	38	36	37	52	49
Number of establishments	201	201	291	423	309
Percent of establishments located in Belfast	55	55	66	59	50
Percent of establishments located in Londonderry	2	3	2	1	2
Percent of establishments located in Belfast and Londonderry	57	58	68	60	52
Clothing and Footwear					
Number of counties	5	6	6	6	6
Number of towns	10	11	11	28	33
Number of establishments	93	101	145	233	198
Percent of establishments located in Belfast	60	59	66	61	48
Percent of establishments located in Londonderry	28	27	23	18	14
Percent of establishments located in Belfast and Londonderry	88	86	89	79	62
Leather and Leather Goods					
Number of counties	2	2	4	3	3
Number of towns	3	3	5	5	5
Number of establishments	12	9	23	25	19
Percent of establishments located in Belfast	75	77	74	76	74
Percent of establishments located in Londonderry	16	11	13	12	6
Percent of establishments located in Belfast and Londonderry	91	88	87	88	80

Industrial group	1926	1936	1946	1956	1966
Wood and Furniture					
Number of counties	5	5	5	6	6
Number of towns	13	13	14	19	24
Number of establishments	50	49	97	142	148
Number of establishments located in Belfast	16	63	75	68	62
Number of establishments located in Londonderry	12	12	8	7	4
Number of establishments located in Belfast and Londonderry	28	75	83	75	66
Paper and Printed Products					
Number of counties	2	6	6	6	6
Number of towns	3	29	32	28	31
Number of establishments	49	112	182	217	230
Percent of establishments located in Belfast	87	38	46	61	60
Percent of establishments located in Londonderry	12	14	9	6	4
Percent of establishments located in Belfast and Londonderry	99	52	55	67	64
Chemicals					
Number of counties	4	4	4	4	4
Number of towns	6	6	8	9	8
Number of establishments	24	26	36	56	58
Percent of establishments located in Belfast	67	65	71	78	74
Percent of establishments located in Londonderry	8	8	6	6	12
Percent of establishments located in Belfast and Londonderry	75	73	77	84	86
Clay Products and Cement					
Number of counties	4	4	4	6	6
Number of towns	6	6	8	21	40
Number of establishments	21	23	42	69	130
Number of establishments in Belfast	76	78	76	58	26
Number of establishments located in Londonderry	0	0	0	6	5
Number of establishments located in Belfast and Londonderry	76	78	76	64	31
Engineering Products					
Number of counties	4	4	5	6	6
Number of towns	12	12	9	16	37
Number of establishments	59	54	60	104	221
Percent of establishments located in Belfast	75	72	75	67	49
Percent of establishments located in Londonderry	7	7	7	5	2
Percent of establishments located in Belfast and Londonderry	82	79	82	72	51
All Industries					
Total number of establishments	600	698	1,066	1,520	1,535
Percent located in Belfast	63	55	65	60	50
Percent located in Londonderry	10	10	9	6	6
Percent located in Belfast and Londonderry	73	65	74	66	56

Source: Data derived from author's research.

169

TABLE 40

Summary of Data on the Location of Exporters in
The Republic of Ireland, 1926-66

Industrial group	1926	1936	1946	1956	1966
Food Industry					
Number of counties	12	13	13	13	19
Number of towns	24	36	34	37	39
Number of establishments	60	80	59	71	119
Percent of establishments located in Dublin	7	9	14	30	47
Percent of establishments located in Cork	34	26	12	10	10
Percent of establishments located in Dublin and Cork	41	35	26	40	57
Drink and Tobacco					
Number of counties	8	9	7	5	8
Number of towns	9	9	7	5	8
Number of establishments	21	15	14	11	15
Percent of establishments located in Dublin	43	33	42	45	47
Percent of establishments located in Cork	19	13	14	18	7
Percent of establishments located in Dublin and Cork	62	46	56	63	54
Textiles					
Number of counties	9	10	10	12	22
Number of towns	11	12	12	18	63
Number of establishments	19	22	26	47	170
Percent of establishments located in Dublin	35	39	46	57	38
Percent of establishments located in Cork	20	17	12	4	10
Percent of establishments located in Dublin and Cork	55	56	58	61	48
Clothing and Footwear					
Number of counties	3	2	3	4	16
Number of towns	3	2	3	4	32
Number of establishments	9	7	8	24	185
Percent of establishments located in Dublin	66	86	75	88	69
Percent of establishments located in Cork	22	0	13	4	5
Percent of establishments located in Dublin and Cork	88	86	88	92	74
Leather and Leather Goods					
Number of counties	1	1	0	6	13
Number of towns	1	1	0	6	14
Number of establishments	1	1	0	8	17
Percent of establishments located in Dublin	0	0	0	38	24
Percent of establishments located in Cork	0	0	0	12	0
Percent of establishments located in Dublin and Cork	0	0	0	50	24

170

Industrial group	1926	1936	1946	1956	1966
Wood and Furniture					
Number of counties	2	1	5	4	18
Number of towns	2	1	6	5	22
Number of establishments	8	5	9	14	58
Percent of establishments located in Dublin	75	100	44	71	52
Percent of establishments located in Cork	25	0	11	7	3
Percent of establishments located in Dublin and Cork	100	100	55	78	55
Paper and Printed Products					
Number of counties	2	1	3	2	10
Number of towns	2	1	3	2	11
Number of establishments	9	5	6	5	54
Percent of establishments located in Dublin	89	100	66	80	76
Percent of establishments located in Cork	11	0	16	0	2
Percent of establishments located in Dublin and Cork	100	100	82	80	78
Chemicals					
Number of counties	3	3	3	4	12
Number of towns	3	3	3	4	15
Number of establishments	15	14	11	14	67
Percent of establishments located in Dublin	80	79	82	71	75
Percent of establishments located in Cork	13	14	9	14	6
Percent of establishments located in Dublin and Cork	93	93	91	85	81
Clay Products and Cement					
Number of counties	2	2	4	6	17
Number of towns	2	2	5	7	24
Number of establishments	2	2	6	9	50
Percent of establishments located in Dublin	50	50	32	22	48
Percent of establishments located in Cork	0	0	0	0	2
Percent of establishments located in Dublin and Cork	50	50	32	22	50
Engineering Products					
Number of counties	4	3	4	4	22
Number of towns	4	3	4	5	47
Number of establishments	12	10	11	19	156
Number of establishments located in Dublin	56	60	45	63	49
Number of establishments located in Cork	8	10	27	11	5
Number of establishments located in Dublin and Cork	64	70	72	74	54
All Industries					
Total number of establishments	156	161	150	222	891
Percent located in Dublin	38	34	37	52	54
Percent located in Cork	24	19	13	8	6
Percent located in Dublin and Cork	62	53	50	60	60

Source: Data derived from author's research.

171

TABLE 41

Summary of Data on the Location of Exporters
In Northern Ireland, 1926-66

Industrial group	1926	1936	1946	1956	1966
Food Industry					
Number of counties	3	6	4	5	6
Number of towns	3	10	11	9	18
Number of establishments	10	20	23	16	45
Percent of establishments located in Belfast	60	40	39	31	42
Percent of establishments located in Londonderry	30	15	17	6	7
Percent of establishments located in Belfast and Londonderry	90	55	56	37	49
Drink and Tobacco					
Number of counties	1	1	1	1	1
Number of towns	2	2	2	2	3
Number of establishments	12	7	6	6	6
Percent of establishments located in Belfast	92	86	83	83	67
Percent of establishments located in Londonderry	0	0	0	0	0
Percent of establishments located in Belfast and Londonderry	92	86	83	83	67
Textiles					
Number of counties	5	5	5	6	6
Number of towns	13	12	15	17	33
Number of establishments	116	125	128	161	187
Percent of establishments located in Belfast	84	82	77	76	60
Percent of establishments located in Londonderry	3	2	2	2	1
Percent of establishments located in Belfast and Londonderry	87	84	79	78	61
Clothing (no footwear exports)					
Number of counties	2	4	3	5	5
Number of towns	2	4	5	8	20
Number of establishments	11	37	35	37	62
Percent of establishments located in Belfast	64	57	54	59	39
Percent of establishments located in Londonderry	36	38	34	24	16
Percent of establishments located in Belfast and Londonderry	100	95	88	83	55
Leather and Leather goods					
Number of counties	1	1	1	2	2
Number of towns	1	1	1	2	2
Number of establishments	1	2	3	4	4
Percent of establishments located in Belfast	100	100	100	75	75
Percent of establishments located in Londonderry	0	0	0	25	25
Percent of establishments located in Belfast and Londonderry	100	100	100	100	100
Wood and Furniture					
Number of counties	0	0	2	3	5
Number of towns	0	0	3	4	10
Number of establishments	0	0	5	6	19
Percent of establishments located in Belfast	0	0	60	33	37
Percent of establishments located in Londonderry	0	0	0	0	0
Percent of establishments located in Belfast and Londonderry	0	0	60	33	37

Industrial group	1926	1936	1946	1956	1966
Paper and Printed Products					
Number of counties	1	1	1	1	5
Number of towns	1	1	1	1	11
Number of establishments	3	2	3	6	27
Percent of establishments located in Belfast	100	100	100	100	56
Percent of establishments located in Londonderry	0	0	0	0	7
Percent of establishments located in Belfast and Londonderry	100	100	100	100	63
Chemicals					
Number of counties	1	1	1	1	2
Number of towns	1	1	2	2	3
Number of establishments	2	2	3	3	7
Percent of establishments located in Belfast	100	100	66	66	56
Percent of establishments located in Londonderry	0	0	0	0	28
Percent of establishments located in Belfast and Londonderry	100	100	66	66	84
Clay Products and Cements					
Number of counties	1	1	2	2	4
Number of towns	1	1	3	2	9
Number of establishments	1	1	8	7	18
Percent of establishments located in Belfast	0	0	75	84	39
Percent of establishments located in Londonderry	0	0	0	0	0
Percent of establishments located in Belfast and Londonderry	0	0	75	84	39
Engineering Products					
Number of counties	1	1	2	5	6
Number of towns	1	1	2	7	24
Number of establishments	5	10	11	25	94
Percent of establishments located in Belfast	100	100	91	76	46
Percent of establishments located in Londonderry	0	0	0	4	2
Percent of establishments located in Belfast and Londonderry	100	100	91	80	48
All Industries					
Total number of establishments	161	206	226	271	469
Percent located in Belfast	83	74	71	71	51
Percent located in Londonderry	6	10	8	6	5
Percent located in Belfast and Londonderry	89	84	79	77	56

Source: Data derived from author's research.

B

**ECONOMIC PROFILES
OF SELECTED TOWNS
IN THE REPUBLIC OF IRELAND
AND
IN NORTHERN IRELAND**

TABLE 42

Dublin

	1926	1936	1946	1956	1966
Population	443,259	512,697	550,725	650,375	734,967
intercensal percent change		+15.7	+7.4	+18.1	+13.5
Percent change 1946-66					+33.5
Total employed	160,550	200,844	236,851	n.a.	285,917
Percent in each sector:					
Agriculture and mining	0.7	0.8	1.6		1.0
Manufacturing (incl. misc.)	24.1	26.2	19.5		29.7*
Building and construction	5.8	6.5	5.1		8.1
Services (incl. public utilities)	69.4	66.5	73.8		61.2
Structure of manufacturing sector					
Food: Number of firms	57	97	122	156	178
Number of export firms	4	7	8	21	56
Employment	7,067	8,159	3,979	n.a.	12,747
Drink and tobacco: Number of firms	23	26	29	31	37
Number of export firms	9	5	6	5	7
Employment	6,577	5,606	987	n.a.	6,619
Textiles: Number of firms	17	54	71	91	86
Number of export firms	7	9	12	27	64
Employment	1,004	1,225	1,308	n.a.	4,558
Clothing and footwear: Number of firms	15	149	201	333	340
Number of export firms	6	6	6	21	129
Employment	7,249	13,308	13,429	n.a.	13,660
Leather: Number of firms	18	22	28	40	28
Number of export firms	0	0	0	3	4
Employment	344	499	712	n.a.	3,884
Wood and furniture: Number of firms	52	122	143	195	149
Number of export firms	6	5	4	10	30
Employment	2,465	3,709	6,807	n.a.	638
Paper and Printing: Number of firms	47	88	127	185	146
Number of export firms	8	5	4	4	41
Employment	4,798	6,267	4,263	n.a.	11,127
Chemicals: Number of firms	49	93	131	148	178
Number of export firms	12	11	9	10	51
Employment	1,420	2,288	412	n.a.	5,385
Clay Products: Number of firms	10	54	61	76	74
Number of export firms	1	1	2	2	24
Employment	381	620	303	n.a.	2,343
Engineering: Number of firms	48	114	152	182	309
Number of export firms	7	6	5	12	76
Employment	6,454	8,677	12,255	n.a.	19,913
Summary: Total firms	336	819	1,065	1,437	1,525
Total export firms	60	55	56	115	482
Total employment (excl. misc.)	37,759	50,358	44,455	n.a.	80,874

*See Footnote 19, Chapter 5.

Source: Data derived from author's research.

TABLE 43

Cork

	1926	1936	1946	1956	1966
Population	78,490	80,765	89,877	114,428	125,283
intercensal percent change		+2.8	+11.3	+27.3	+9.5
Percent change 1946-66					+39.4
Total employed	27,862	29,058	36,811	n.a.	44,011
Percent in each sector:					
Agriculture and mining	0.7	0.6	1.9		1.3
Manufacturing (incl. misc.)	25.3	28.9	19.8		32.8*
Building and construction	4.3	5.6	4.5		8.2
Services (incl. public utilities)	69.7	64.9	73.8		57.7
Structure of manufacturing sector					
Food: Number of firms	23	57	49	46	42
Number of export firms	21	19	7	7	12
Employment	1,458	1,758	793	n.a.	2,225
Drink and Tobacco: Number of firms	13	13	13	15	13
Number of export firms	4	2	2	2	1
Employment	588	497	96	n.a.	816
Textiles: Number of firms	8	14	14	25	25
Number of export firms	4	4	3	2	17
Employment	212	216	809	n.a.	2,723
Clothing and Footwear: Number of firms	14	26	31	35	24
Number of export firms	2	0	1	1	10
Employment	1,643	2,655	1,902	n.a.	1,380
Leather: Number of firms	2	6	8	15	2
Number of export firms	0	0	0	1	0
Employment	81	64	83	n.a.	33
Wood and Furniture: Number of firms	14	29	32	45	39
Number of export firms	2	0	1	1	2
Employment	492	529	882	n.a.	593
Paper and Printing: Number of firms	6	19	20	29	15
Number of export firms	1	0	1	0	1
Employment	526	700	462	n.a.	1,072
Chemicals: No of firms	6	14	15	21	18
Number of export firms	2	2	1	2	4
Employment	349	414	65	n.a.	1,033
Clay Products: Number of firms	1	13	11	9	10
Number of export firms	0	0	0	0	1
Employment	19	29	n.a.	n.a.	192
Engineering: Number of firms	13	36	41	48	35
Number of export firms	1	1	3	2	8
Employment	1,576	1,055	1,649	n.a.	2,288
Summary: Total firms	100	227	234	289	223
Total export firms	37	28	19	18	56
Total employment (excl. misc.)	6,944	7,917	6,741	n.a.	12,355

*See Footnote 19, Chapter 5.

Source: Data derived from author's research.

TABLE 44

Limerick

	1926	1936	1946	1956	1966
Population	39,448	41,061	42,987	51,666	58,082
intercensal percent change		+4.9	+4.7	+20.2	+12.4
Percent change 1946-66					+35.1
Total employed	14,526	13,381	16,340	n.a.	19,655
Percent in each sector:					
Agriculture and mining	2.0	1.7	1.8		1.5
Manufacturing (incl. misc.)	23.8	27.5	19.0		29.3*
Building and construction	9.2	6.5	7.4		7.1
Services (incl. public utilities)	65.0	64.3	71.8		62.1
Structure of manufacturing sector					
Food: Number of firms	13	16	16	17	17
Number of export firms	6	5	5	5	3
Employment	1,748	1,518	568	n.a.	1,705
Drink and tobacco: Number of firms	5	7	8	8	3
Number of export firms	0	0	0	0	0
Employment	176	211	73	n.a.	128
Textiles: Number of firms	1	1	1	2	1
Number of export firms	0	0	0	0	0
Employment	52	13	23	n.a.	337
Clothing and footwear: Number of firms	1	3	3	5	6
Number of export firms	0	0	0	0	4
Employment	648	935	779	n.a.	985
Leather: Number of firms	2	3	4	2	2
Number of export firms	1	1	0	0	1
Employment	56	98	70	n.a.	53
Wood and furniture: Number of firms	7	14	12	21	12
Number of export firms	0	0	0	0	2
Employment	321	282	542	n.a.	251
Paper and Printing: Number of firms	4	10	10	13	6
Number of export firms	0	0	0	0	1
Employment	139	152	117	n.a.	220
Chemicals: Number of firms	1	1	2	2	2
Number of export firms	0	0	0	0	0
Employment	6	6	2	n.a.	79
Clay Products: Number of firms	1	7	5	5	1
Number of export firms	0	0	0	0	0
Employment	3	6	n.a.	n.a.	329
Engineering: Number of firms	5	8	15	16	10
Number of export firms	0	0	0	0	3
Employment	290	398	852	n.a.	1,484
Summary: Total firms	40	70	76	91	61
Total export firms	7	6	5	5	14
Total employment (excl. misc.)	3,439	3,619	3,026	n.a.	5,571

*See Footnote 19, Chapter 5.

*Source: Data derived from author's research.

TABLE 45

Waterford

	1926	1936	1946	1956	1966
Population	26,647	27,968	28,269	28,878	29,842
intercensal percent change		+4.9	+1.1	+2.2	+3.3
Percent change 1946-66					+5.6
Total employed	9,404	9,041	10,199	n.a.	10,934
Percent in each sector:					
Agriculture and mining	2.0	1.2	2.8		1.4
Manufacturing (incl. misc.)	20.0	22.6	17.1		38.3*
Building and construction	5.6	6.8	5.6		6.1
Services (incl. public utilities)	72.4	69.4	74.5		54.2
Structure of manufacturing sector					
Food: Number of firms	10	16	13	14	9
Number of export firms	4	4	3	1	3
Employment	609	655	348	n.a.	889
Drink: Number of firms	2	5	4	4	2
Number of export firms	1	1	1	0	0
Employment	155	97	9	n.a.	121
Textiles: Number of firms	1	3	4	3	3
Number of export firms	0	0	0	0	1
Employment	90	245	54	n.a.	608
Clothing and footwear: Number of firms	2	1	1	2	1
Number of export firms	1	0	0	1	0
Employment	450	366	380	n.a.	73
Leather: Number of firms	1	1	1	1	1
Number of export firms	0	0	0	0	0
Employment	12	18	12	n.a.	16
Wood and furniture: Number of firms	2	4	6	7	6
Number of export firms	0	0	1	1	3
Employment	171	233	221	n.a.	194
Paper and Printing: Number of firms	3	7	7	9	5
Number of export firms	0	0	0	0	0
Employment	190	203	111	n.a.	465
Chemicals: Number of firms	1	2	1	4	4
Number of export firms	0	0	0	0	1
Employment	11	27	3	n.a.	115
Clay Products: Number of firms	1	4	4	5	3
Number of export firms	0	0	1	2	1
Employment	8	14	n.a.	n.a.	806
Engineering: Number of firms	2	5	6	12	6
Number of export firms	0	0	0	0	3
Employment	170	159	567	n.a.	790
Summary: Total firms	25	48	57	61	40
Total export firms	6	5	6	5	13
Total employment (excl. misc.)	1,866	2,017	1,705	n.a.	4,077

*See Footnote 19, Chapter 5.

Source: Data derived from author's research.

TABLE 46

Galway

	1926	1936	1946	1956	1966
Population	14,227	18,294	20,370	21,219	24,597
intercensal percent change		+28.5	+11.3	+4.2	+15.9
Percent change 1946-66					+20.8
population incl. environs				22,757	26,295
intercensal percent change					+15.5
Total employed	5,374	7,057	8,569	n.a.	9,689
Percent in each sector:					
Agriculture and mining	8.2	5.2	6.0		4.5
Manufacturing (incl. misc.)	17.3	16.3	14.4		16.7*
Building and construction	5.8	9.3	5.2		7.5
Services (incl. public utilities)	68.7	69.2	74.4		71.3
Structure of manufacturing sector					
Food: Number of firms	3	4	3	4	6
Number of export firms	0	0	0	0	0
Employment	135	146	104	n.a.	208
Drink: Number of firms	2	2	1	2	2
Number of export firms	0	0	0	0	0
Employment	51	47	5	n.a.	85
Textiles: Number of firms	2	3	3	3	2
Number of export firms	0	0	0	1	2
Employment	173	87	132	n.a.	190
Clothing and footwear: Number of firms	1	1	2	1	1
Number of export firms	0	0	0	0	1
Employment	128	220	343	n.a.	247
Leather: Number of firms	1	1	2	2	1
Number of export firms	0	0	0	0	0
Employment	11	12	9	n.a.	6
Wood and furniture: Number of firms	2	7	12	14	7
Number of export firms	0	0	0	0	0
Employment	132	186	240	n.a.	225
Paper and Printing: Number of firms	1	3	4	5	3
Number of export firms	0	0	0	0	0
Employment	56	73	75	n.a.	150
Chemicals: Number of firms	2	2	1	3	2
Number of export firms	0	0	0	0	1
Employment	76	72	5	n.a.	136
Clay Products: Number of firms	1	4	4	5	2
Number of export firms	0	0	0	1	2
Employment	5	51	n.a.	n.a.	93
Engineering: Number of firms	4	6	5	5	4
Number of export firms	0	0	0	0	3
Employment	147	237	294	n.a.	234
Summary: Total firms	19	33	37	44	30
Total export firms	0	0	0	2	9
Total employment (excl. misc.)	914	1,131	1,207	n.a.	1,577

*See Footnote 19, Chapter 5.

Source: Data derived from author's research.

181

TABLE 47

Wexford

	1926	1936	1946	1956	1966
Population	11,879	12,247	12,308	11,853	11,542
intercensal percent change		+2.9	+0.5	-3.7	-2.6
Percent change 1946-66					-6.2
population incl. environs				12,765	12,744
intercensal percent change					-0.2
Total employed	3,972	4,152	4,713	4,640	4,461
Percent in each sector:					
Agriculture and mining	2.2	2.3	2.1		2.0
Manufacturing (incl. misc.)	27.8	27.1	23.8		29.3*
Building and construction	4.4	7.5	6.8		7.4
Services (incl. public utilities)	65.6	63.1	67.3		61.3
Structure of manufacturing sector					
Food: Number of firms	2	2	2	3	5
Number of export firms	1	1	0	1	0
Employment	172	179	126	n.a.	285
Drink: Number of firms	1	1	1	3	2
Number of export firms	0	0	0	0	0
Employment	60	50	24	n.a.	75
Textiles: Number of firms	2	3	3	3	2
Number of export firms	0	0	0	1	2
Employment	35	4	5	n.a.	257
Clothing and footwear: Number of firms	1	1	1	1	1
Number of export firms	0	0	0	0	0
Employment	189	137	95	n.a.	44
Leather: Number of firms	1	1	1	0	0
Number of export firms	0	0	0	0	0
Employment	12	10	9	0	0
Wood and furniture: Number of firms	3	3	7	6	3
Number of export firms	0	0	0	0	1
Employment	58	64	154	n.a.	73
Paper and Printing: Number of firms	1	2	4	3	1
Number of export firms	0	0	0	0	1
Employment	125	132	80	n.a.	131
Chemicals: Number of firms	0	2	0	1	1
Number of export firms	0	0	0	0	0
Employment	0	6	0	n.a.	7
Clay Products: Number of firms	0	0	1	1	1
Number of export firms	0	0	0	0	0
Employment	0	0	n.a.	n.a.	13
Engineering: Number of firms	3	4	5	5	3
Number of export firms	3	3	2	3	2
Employment	450	535	612	n.a.	409
Summary: Total firms	14	19	25	26	19
Total export firms	4	4	2	5	6
Total employment (excl. misc.)	1,101	1,117	1,105	n.a.	1,294

*See Footnote 19, Chapter 5.

Source: Data derived from author's research.

TABLE 48

Belfast

	1926	1937	1951	1961	1966
Population	415,151	438,086	502,686	529,537	549,939
intercensal percent change		+5.5	+14.7	+5.3	+3.9
Percent change 1951-66					+9.4
Structure of manufacturing sector	(1926)	(1936)	(1946)	(1956)	(1966)
Food: Number of firms	28	34	72	85	62
Number of export firms	6	8	9	5	19
Drink and tobacco: Number of firms	24	22	35	33	21
Number of export firms	11	6	5	5	4
Textiles: Number of firms	109	110	192	250	152
Number of export firms	98	102	99	122	113
Clothing and footwear: Number of firms	56	59	96	143	95
Number of export firms	7	21	19	22	24
Leather: Number of firms	9	7	17	19	14
Number of export firms	1	2	3	3	3
Wood and furniture: Number of firms	32	31	73	96	91
Number of export firms	0	0	3	2	7
Paper and printing: Number of firms	43	42	102	132	140
Number of export firms	3	2	3	6	15
Chemicals: Number of firms	16	17	26	44	43
Number of export firms	2	2	2	2	4
Clay products: Number of firms	17	19	33	40	34
Number of export firms	0	0	6	6	7
Engineering: Number of firms	44	39	45	69	109
Number of export firms	5	10	10	19	43
Summary: Total firms	386	386	704	929	760
Total export firms	133	153	159	192	240

Source: Data derived from author's research.

TABLE 49

Londonderry

	1926	1937	1951	1961	1966
Population	45,159	47,813	50,092	53,762	55,681
intercensal percent change		+5.9	+4.8	+7.3	+3.6
Percent change 1951-66					+11.2
Structure of manufacturing sector	(1926)	(1936)	(1946)	(1956)	(1966)
Food: Number of firms	10	10	14	14	16
Number of export firms	3	3	4	1	3
Drink: Number of firms	0	1	0	2	2
Number of export firms	0	0	0	0	0
Textiles: Number of firms	4	5	7	4	7
Number of export firms	3	3	3	3	2
Clothing and footwear: Number of firms	26	27	33	41	28
Number of export firms	4	14	12	9	10
Leather: Number of firms	2	1	3	3	1
Number of export firms	0	0	0	1	1
Wood and furniture: Number of firms	2	3	5	5	4
Number of export firms	0	0	0	0	0
Paper and printing: Number of firms	5	16	16	12	9
Number of export firms	0	0	0	0	2
Chemicals: Number of firms	2	2	2	3	7
Number of export firms	0	0	0	0	2
Clay Products: Number of firms	0	0	0	4	7
Number of export firms	0	0	0	0	0
Engineering: Number of firms	4	4	4	5	5
Number of export firms	0	0	0	1	2
Summary: Total firms	56	69	84	94	86
Total export firms	10	20	19	15	22

Source: Data derived from author's research.

TABLE 50

Portadown

	1926	1937	1951	1961	1966
Population	13,207	14,803	17,202	18,609	20,710
intercensal percent change		+12.1	+16.2	+8.2	+11.3
Percent change 1951–66					+20.4
Structure of manufacturing sector	(1926)	(1936)	(1946)	(1956)	(1966)
Food: Number of firms	1	2	3	13	11
Number of export firms	0	1	2	4	3
Drink: Number of firms	2	2	1	2	1
Number of export firms	0	0	0	0	0
Textiles: Number of firms	6	7	8	8	11
Number of export firms	1	0	1	1	4
Clothing and footwear: Number of firms	0	1	1	3	5
Number of export firms	0	1	1	1	1
Wood and furniture: Number of firms	0	0	1	3	4
Number of export firms	0	0	0	0	1
Paper and printing: Number of firms	0	1	1	3	4
Number of export firms	0	0	0	0	1
Chemicals: Number of firms	0	0	0	0	2
Number of export firms	0	0	0	0	0
Clay Products: Number of firms	0	0	1	1	7
Number of export firms	0	0	0	0	0
Engineering: Number of firms	0	0	2	5	10
Number of export firms	0	0	1	1	8
Summary: Total firms	9	13	18	38	55
Total export firms	1	2	5	7	18

Source: Data derived from author's research.

185

TABLE 51

Lurgan

	1926	1937	1951	1961	1966
Population	12,975	14,464	16,370	17,872	20,677
intercensal percent change		+11.5	+12.6	+9.2	+15.7
Percent change 1951-66					+26.3
Structure of manufacturing sector	(1926)	(1936)	(1946)	(1956)	(1966)
Food: Number of firms	0	0	0	4	2
Number of export firms	0	0	0	0	1
Drink: Number of firms	0	0	0	2	0
Number of export firms	0	0	0	0	0
Textiles: Number of firms	14	14	9	35	28
Number of export firms	3	8	7	11	10
Clothing and footwear: Number of firms	1	1	1	5	8
Number of export firms	0	0	0	1	2
Leather: Number of firms	0	0	1	0	0
Number of export firms	0	0	0	0	0
Wood and furniture: Number of firms	0	0	0	4	7
Number of export firms	0	0	0	0	3
Paper and printing: Number of firms	0	3	5	9	6
Number of export firms	0	0	0	0	1
Chemicals: Number of firms	0	0	0	0	1
Number of export firms	0	0	0	0	0
Engineering: Number of firms	0	0	1	1	3
Number of export firms	0	0	0	0	3
Summary: Total firms	15	18	17	60	55
Total export firms	3	8	7	12	20

Source: Data derived from author's research.

186

TABLE 52

Newry

	1926	1937	1951	1961	1966
Population	12,226	12,746	13,261	12,429	12,214
intercensal percent change		+4.3	+4.0	-6.3	-1.7
Percent change 1951-66					-7.9
Structure of manufacturing sector	(1926)	(1936)	(1946)	(1956)	(1966)
Food: Number of firms	5	6	7	6	7
Number of export firms	0	2	0	0	2
Drink and tobacco: Number of firms	0	0	0	4	4
Number of export firms	0	0	0	0	0
Textiles: Number of firms	5	5	2	4	7
Number of export firms	0	0	0	0	4
Clothing and footwear: Number of firms	0	0	0	3	4
Number of export firms	0	0	0	0	1
Wood and furniture: Number of firms	1	1	1	1	2
Number of export firms	0	0	1	1	2
Paper and printing: Number of firms	0	7	6	4	6
Number of export firms	0	0	0	0	1
Chemicals: Number of firms	3	4	3	1	1
Number of export firms	0	0	0	0	0
Clay Products: Number of firms	0	0	0	0	4
Number of export firms	0	0	0	0	2
Engineering: Number of firms	1	1	1	1	7
Number of export firms	0	0	0	0	2
Summary: Total firms	15	24	20	24	42
Total export firms	0	2	1	1	14

Source: Data derived from author's research.

BIBLIOGRAPHY

BOOKS AND PERIODICALS

Abrams, C. "Regional Planning Legislation in Underdeveloped Areas,"
Land Economics, XXXV (May, 1954), 85-103.

_____. "Regional Problems in an Urbanizing World," Ekistics,
XVIII, 243-48.

Agarwala, A. N., and Singh, S. P., eds. The Economics of Underdevelopment. New York: Oxford University Press, 1963.

Aigner, D. J., and Heins, A. J. "On the Determinants of Income
Equality," American Economic Review, LVII (March, 1967),
175-81.

Alexander, John W. "The Basic-Nonbasic Concept of Urban Economic
Functions," Economic Geography, XXX, (July, 1954), 246-61, Re-
printed in Mayer and Kohn. Readings in Urban Geography.
Chicago: University of Chicago Press, 1959.

Alexandersson, Gunnar. "City-forming and City-serving Production."
The Industrial Structure of American Cities. Lincoln: University
of Nebraska Press, 1956, 14-20. Reprinted in Mayer and Kohn,
Readings in Urban Geography. Chicago: University of Chicago
Press, 1959.

_____. The Industrial Structure of American Cities. Stockholm:
Almqvist and Wiksell, 1956.

Allison, D. "The University and Regional Prosperity," Ekistics,
XX (September, 1965), 118, 140-43.

Al-Samarrie, Ahmad, and Miller, H. P. "State Differentials in Income
Concentration," American Economic Review, LVII (March, 1967),
59-65.

Amiran, D. H. K., and Shahar, A. "Towns of Israel: The Principles
of Their Urban Geography," Ekistics, XIII (February, 1962),
98-102.

Andrews, Richard B. "Mechanics of the Urban Economic Base,"
Land Economics, XXIX (May, 1953), 161-67.

Andriello, D. "The Physical Planning of Tourism," Ekistics, XIX
(June, 1965), 348-51.

Ash, M. "Physical Planning and the Social Sciences." Report of the Town and Country Planning Summer School, 1966. London: Town Planning Institute, 1967, 90-101.

Attwood, E. A., and Geary, R. C. Irish County Incomes in 1960. Paper No. 16. Dublin: Economic Research Institute, September, 1963.

Aurousseau, M. "The Distribution of Population: A Constructive Problem," Geographical Review, XI (1921).

Bachmura, F. T., and Glasgow, R. B. "Rural Area Development in a Growing Economy," Journal of Farm Economics, XLIII (1963-64), 268-85.

Baker, T. J. Regional Employment Patterns in the Republic of Ireland, Paper No. 32. Dublin: Economic Research Institute, August, 1966.

Balassa, Bela. The Theory of Economic Integration. Homewood, Illinois: Richard D. Irwin, Inc., 1961.

Barzanti, J. Underdeveloped Regions Within the Common Market. Princeton, New Jersey: Princeton University Press, 1965.

Bauchet, Pierre. La Planification Francaise. Paris: Editions du Seuil, 1962.

Beckerman, Wilfred. International Comparisons of Real Income. Paris: Organization for Economic Cooperation and Development, 1966.

Beckman, M. J. "The Economics of Location," Kyklos, VIII (1955), 416-21.

_____. "Some Reflections of Losch's Theory of Location," Papers and Proceedings of the Regional Science Association, I (1955), N1-N9.

Beckman, M. J. and Marschak, T. "An Activity Analysis Approach to Location Theory," Kyklos, VIII (1955), 125-29.

Bell, Gwen. "Change in City Size Distribution in Israel," Ekistics, XIII (February, 1962), 103.

Berry, B. J. L. "City Size Distributions and Economic Development," Ekistics, XIII (February, 1962), 90-97.

_____. "A Method for Deriving Multi-factor Uniform Regions,"
Przeglad Geograficzny, XXXIII, 2 (1961), 263-82.

_____. "An Inductive Approach to the Regionalization of Economic
Development," Research Paper No. 62. Chicago: University of
Chicago, Department of Geography, 1960, 78-107.

Berry, B. J. L., and Garrison, W. L. "A Note on Central Place Theory
and the Range of a Good," Economic Geography, XXXV (1958-A),
304-11.

Berry, B. J. L., and Pred, A. "Central Place Studies: A Bibliography
of Theory and Applications." "Bibliographic Series," No. 1.
Philadelphia: Regional Science Research Institute, 1961.

Bhattacharjee, J. P. "Interaction of Urbanization and Rural Development in India," Ekistics, XVII (1954), 29-32.

Blanco White, M. J. "A Note on Anticipating the Effects of a Regional
Policy," Ekistics, XX (October, 1965), 232-33.

Blouet, B. W. "Town Planning in Malta," Town Planning Review,
XXXV (1964), 183-94.

Bolan, Richard S. 'Emerging Views of Planning," Journal of the
American Institute of Planners, XXXIII, 4 (July, 1967).

Booth, E. J. R. "Inter-regional Income Differences," Southern Economic Journal, XXXI (July, 1964), 144-51.

Borts, G. H. "The Equalization of Returns and Regional Economic
Growth," American Economic Review, L (June, 1960), 319-47.

Borts, G. H., and Stein, J. C. "Investment Return: as a Measure of
Comparative Regional Advantage." Baltimore Committee for
Regional Accounts. Design of Regional Accounts. 1962.

Bos, H. C. Spatial Dispersion of Economic Activity. Rotterdam:
Rotterdam University Press, 1965.

Boudeville, J. R. "A Survey of Recent Techniques for Regional Economic Analysis." Regional Economic Planning: Techniques
of Analysis. Edited by W. Isard and J. H. Cumberland. Paris:
O.E.E.C. 1961, 377-98.

_____. "Frontiers and Interrelations of Regional Planning."
Paper given at the International Congress of Economic Development in Vienna, August-September, 1962.

Boudeville, J. R. Problems of Regional Economic Planning. Edinburgh: Edinburgh University Press, 1966.

Boventer, E. von. "Spatial Organization Theory as a Basis for Regional Planning," Ekistics, XVIII (1964), 130-33.

_____. "Towards a Unified Theory of Spatial Economic Structure," Regional Science Association Papers and Proceedings, X (1963), 163-91.

Brewis, T. N., and Paquet, G. "Regional Development and Planning in Canada: An Exploratory Essay." Paper delivered to the Canadian Political Science Association, Ottawa, June 9, 1967.

Bristow, J. A., and Tait, A. A., eds. Economic Policy in Ireland. Dublin: Institute of Public Administration, 1968.

Broady, M. "Social Change and Town Development," Town Planning Review, XXXVI, 4 (January, 1966), 269-78.

Burns, Leland S. "Cost Benefit Analysis of a Social Overhead Project for Regional Development," Papers and Proceedings of the Regional Science Association, XVI (1966), 155-61.

Bye, Maurice. Industries Anciennes et Regression Regionale. Colloque de Liege, May 22-23, 1964. Librairie Medicis, 1965.

Chapin, F. S. "Selected Theories of Urban Growth and Structure," Journal of the American Institute of Planners, XXX (February, 1964), 51-58.

_____. Urban Land Use Planning. Urbana: University of Illinois Press, 1963.

Chenery, H. P. "The Application of Investment Criteria," Quarterly Journal of Economics, LXVII, 1 (February, 1953), 76-96.

_____. "Patterns of Industrial Growth," American Economic Review, L (September, 1960), 624-54.

_____. "Development Policies for Southern Italy," Quarterly Journal of Economics, LXXVI, (November, 1962), 515-47.

Chernick, S. E. Inter-regional Disparities in Income. Staff Study No. 14, Economic Council of Canada. Ottawa: Queen's Printer, 1966.

Chessa, F. "Depressed Zones and Economic Progress," Kyklos, III (1953), 193-210.

Chib, S. N. "Searching for a Philosophy of Tourism," Ekistics, XIX (June, 1965), 344-45.

Chinitz, B., and Verwon, R. "Changing Forces in Industrial Location," Harvard Business Review, XXXVIII, 1 (January-February, 1960), 126-36.

Chisholm, M. "Tendencies in Agricultural Specialization and Regional Concentration of Industry," Regional Science Association Papers and Proceedings, XX, 10 (1963), 157-62.

_____. "Location of Industry," Ekistics, XV (May, 1963), 286-92.

Christaller, Walter. "The Advantages of a Space-economical Theory for the Practice of Regional Planning," Ekistics, XX (October, 1965), 223-27.

Christaller, W., et al. "Regional Location of Settlements," Ekistics, XX (1965), 223-33.

Chubb, B., and Lynch, P., eds. Economic Development and Planning, Dublin: Institute of Public Administration, 1969.

Clark, C. "The Location of Industries and Population," Ekistics, XIX (1965), 53-62.

Coras Trachtala. Irish Directory of Exporters, Dublin: Coras Trachtala, 1966.

Cullingworth, J. Town and Country Planning in England and Wales: An Introduction, Toronto: University of Toronto Press, 1964.

Davidoff, P., and Reiner, T. A. "A Choice Theory of Planning," Journal of The American Institute of Planners, XXVIII (May, 1962), 103-15.

Davis, Kingsley. "The Urbanization of the Human Population," Scientific American, CXIII, 3 (September, 1965), 42-48.

Davis, K., and Golden, H. H. "Urbanization and the Development of Preindustrial Areas," Economic Development and Cultural Change, III, 1 (October, 1954), 6-26.

Demas, William G. The Economics of Development in Small Countries - with Special reference to the Caribbean. "McGill Center for Developing Area Studies, Keith Callard Lectures, Series 1." Montreal: McGill University Press, 1965.

Denton, Frank T. An Analysis of Interregional Differences in Manpower Utilization and Earnings, Staff Study No. 15. Economic Council of Canada, Ottawa: Queen's Printer, 1966.

Dickenson, R. E. City, Region, and Regionalism: A Geographical Contribution to Human Ecology. London: Kegan Paul, Trench, Trubner & Co., 1947.

✓ Dobrowolska, M. "Functions of Industries in Shaping Socioeconomic Regional Structure," Przeglad Geografienzny (1960), 133-38.

Donaldson, Lorraine. Development Planning In Ireland. New York: Praeger, 1967.

Doxiadis Associates, "Planning for Amenity and Tourism: A Model Study for County Donegal, Ireland," Ekistics, XXIV (April, 1967), 238-45.

Due, J. F. "Studies of State-local Tax Influences on Location of Industry," National Tax Journal, XIV (June, 1961), 163-73.

Duncan, O. D., and Cuzzort, R. P. "Regional Differentiation and Socioeconomic Change," Proceedings of the Regional Science Association, LV (1958), 163-77.

✓ Dunn, E. S. "A Statistical and Analytical Study for Regional Analysis," Papers and Proceedings of the Regional Science Association, XVI (1960), 97-112.

Dyckman, J. W. "The Technological Obsolescence of Planning Practice," Journal of the American Institute of Planners, XXVII (1961), 242-45.

Dyckman, J. W. "Planning and Decision Theory," Journal of the American Institute of Planners, XXVII (November, 1961), 335-45.

England, H.M. Stationery Office. Committee on Compensation and Betterment, England: H. M. Stationery Office, 1949.

Escritt, L. B. Regional Planning, London: Allen and Unwin, 1943.

Eversley, D. E. C. "The Strategy of Industrial Movement," Town and Country Planning (1964), 130-35.

Fisher, J. L., and Revelle, R. "Natural Resources Policies and Planning for Developing Countries," Ekistics, XVI (1963), 324-27.

Fitzgerald, G. Planning in Ireland, Dublin: Institute of Public Administration, 1968.

Florence, P. Sargant. Investment, Location, and Size of Plant, Cambridge: Cambridge University Press, 1948.

_____. "What is Regional Planning for ?" Ekistics, XVIII (1964), 167-69.

Foras Forbartha (National Institute of Physical Planning and Constructional Research). Regional Planning: Proceedings of a National Conference, Dublin: Foras Forbartha, 1965.

_____. Regional Studies in Ireland. By Colin Buchanan and Partners, in association with Economic Consultants Ltd. Dublin: Foras Forbartha, 1968. (The Buchanan Report).

Fouraker, L. "A Note on Regional Multipliers," Papers and Proceedings of the Regional Science Association, I (1955).

Fourastie, Jean,: La Planification Economique en France, Paris: PUF, 1963.

Fox, K. A. "Food and Agricultural Sectors in Advanced Economies," Structural Interdependence, Edited by T. Barna. New York: The Macmillan Co., 1963.

_____. "The Study of Interactions Between Agriculture and the Nonfarm Economy: Local, Regional, National," Journal of Farm Economics, XLIV (February, 1962), 1-34.

France. Preparation du V Plan, Report sur les principales options, Paris: Imprimerie des Journaux Officiels, 1964.

Fredzell, Bo, "Physical Factors of Metropolitan Planning," Ekistics, XIII (April, 1962), 229-31.

Freeman, T. W. Ireland: A General and Regional Geography. 3rd ed.; London: Methuan and Co., 1965.

Friedmann, John. Regional Development Planning, Cambridge:(MIT Press), 1967.

_____. "Regional Planning: A Problem of Spatial Integration," Papers and Proceedings of the Regional Science Association, V (1959), 167-79.

_____. "Regional Policies for Developing Areas," The Regional Science Association Papers, XI (1963), 41-61.

_____. "Planning as Innovation: The Chilean Case," Journal of the American Institute of Planners, XXXII, 4 (1966).

_____. "Economy and Space," Economic Development and Cultural Change, VI (1957-58), 249-55.

_____. "The Concept of a Planning Region," Land Economics, XXXII, (February, 1956), 1-13.

_____. "An Index to Resource Development With Special Reference to Brazil," Land Economics, XXXIV (1958), 298-309.

_____. "Locational Aspects of Economic Development," Land Economics, XXXII (1956), 213-27.

_____. "Economic Growth and Urban Structure in Venezuela," Ekistics, XVII (1964), 316-24.

_____. "Poor Regions and Poor Nations: Perspectives on the Problem of Appalachia," Southern Economic Journal, XXXII (April, 1966), 465-73.

_____. "Regional Development in Post-industrial Society," Journal of the American Institute of Planners, XXX (May, 1964).

Friedmann, J., and Alonso, W. Regional Development and Planning: A Reader. Cambridge: MIT Press, 1964.

Fuchs, V. R. "Changes in the Location of U.S. Manufacturing Since 1929," Journal of Regional Science, I (Spring, 1959), 1-7.

_____. "Statistical Explanations of the Relative Shift of Manufacturing Among Regions of the U.S." Papers and Proceedings of the Regional Science Association, VIII (1962), 104-26

Furtado, Celso. Development and Underdevelopment, Berkeley and Los Angeles: University of California Press, 1964.

BIBLIOGRAPHY

Gallaway, L. E. "Some Aspects of the Economic Structure of Depressed Industrial Areas," Land Economics, XXXV (1959), 337-46.

Gerschenkron, Alexander. Economic Backwardness in Historical Perspective, New York: Praeger, 1965.

Giersch, Herbert. "The Economics of Regional Policy," German Economic Review, III, 1 (November, 1965).

Gittus, E. "The Structure of Urban Areas: A New Approach," Town Planning Review, XXXV (1964), 5-20, 13-24.

Givens, M. B. "Systems of Economic Accounts and Analysis for Urban Regions: Discussion," American Economic Review, LII (May, 1962), 381-83.

Green, F. H. W. "Community of Interest Areas: Notes on the Hierarchy of Central Places and Their Hinterlands," Economic Geography, XXXIV, 3 (1958), 210-26.

Grotewold, A. "Von Thunen in Retrospect," Economic Geography, XXXV (October, 1959), 346-55.

Haar, C., Higgins, B., and Rodwin, L. "Economic and Physical Planning: Co-ordination in Developing Areas," Journal of the American Institute of Planners, XXIV, 3 (1958), 167-73.

Hagen, E. E., and White, S. F. T. Great Britain: Quiet Revolution in Planning. Syracuse: Syracuse University Press, 1966.

Haggett, Peter. Locational Analysis in Human Geography, London: Edward Arnold Ltd., 1965.

Hagood, M. J. "Statistical Methods for Delineation of Regions Applied to Data on Agriculture and Population," Social Forces, XXI (March, 1943), 287-97.

Hagood, M. J., Danilevsky, N., and Beum, C. O. "An Examination of the Use of Factor Analysis in the Problem of Subregional Delineation," Rural Sociology, VI (September, 1941), 216-33.

Hamdan, G. "Capitals of New Africa," Ekistics, XVIII (1964), 426-30.

Hansen, N. French Regional Planning, Edinburgh: Edinburgh University Press, 1968.

Harris, Chauncy D. "Methods of Research in Economic Regionalization," Geographica Polonica, 4 (1964), 59-86.

Harris, Seymour. International and Inter-regional Economics, New York: McGraw-Hill, 1967.

Henderson, J. M. "The Utilization of Agricultural Land: A Regional Approach," Papers and Proceedings of the Regional Science Association, III (1957), 99-114.

Herman, T. "Cottage and Small-scale Industries in Asian Economic Development," Economic Development and Cultural Change, IV (1966), 356-70.

Higgins, B. Economic Development, London: Constable, 1959.

_____. "The Concept of Regional Planning," Canadian Public Administration (June, 1966), 164-76.

Hill, F. G. "Regional Aspects of Economic Development," Land Economics (May, 1962), 85-98.

Hill, T. P. "Growth and Investment According to International Comparisons," Economic Journal, LXXIV (June, 1964) 287-304.

Hirsch, W. Z. "Design and Use of Regional Accounts," American Economic Review, LII (May, 1962), 365-73.

_____. "Regional Fiscal Impact of Local Industrial Development," Papers and Proceedings of the Regional Science Association, VII (1961), 119-30.

Hirschman, A. O. The Strategy of Economic Development, New Haven: Yale University Press, 1959.

Hoover, E. M. The Location of Economic Activity, New York: McGraw-Hill, 1948.

_____. Industrial Loacation and National Resources, Washington, D.C.: Government Printing Office, 1943.

Hoselitz, Bert, ed. Theories of Economic Growth, New York: Free Press, 1960.

Hoselitz, Bert. "The City, The Factory, and Economic Growth," American Economic Review, XLV, 2 (1954), 166-84.

_____. "The Role of Cities in the Economic Growth of Underdeveloped Countries," Journal of Political Economy, LXI (1953), 195-208.

_____. "Urbanization and Economic Growth in Asia," Economic Development and Cultural Change, VI, 1 (October, 1957), 42-54.

Hughes, R. G. "Interregional Income Differences: Self-perpetuation," Southern Economic Journal, XXVIII (July, 1961), 41-45.

Hurter, A. P., and Moses, L. N. "Transportation Investment and Regional Development," Journal of the American Institute of Planners, XXX (1964), 132-39.

Isard, W. Regional Programming, Paris: OEEC, 1960.

_____. Location and Space-economy, New York: John Wiley, 1956.

_____. "Distance Inputs and the Space Economy," Quarterly Journal of Economics, LXV (May, 1951), 188-98.

_____. "General Interregional Equilibrium," Regional Science Association Papers and Proceedings, III (1957), 35-60.

_____. Methods of Regional Analysis, New York: John Wiley, 1960.

_____. "Interregional and Regional Input-output Analysis: A Model of a Space Economy," Review of Economics and Statistics, XXXIII (November, 1951), 318-28.

_____. "Regional Commodity Balances and Interregional Commodity Flows," American Economic Review, XLIII (May, 1953), 167-80.

_____. "The Value of the Regional Approach in Economic Analysis," Regional Income: Studies in Income and Wealth, XXI; Princeton, New Jersey: National Bureau of Economic Research, Princeton University Press, 1957.

_____. "The Scope and Nature of Regional Science," Papers and Proceedings of the Regional Science Association, VI (1960), 9-34.

_____. "Regional Science: The Concept of Region and Regional Structure," Papers and Proceedings of the Regional Science Association, II (1956), 13-26.

_____. "The General Theory of Location and Space Economy," Quarterly Journal of Economics, LXII (November, 1949), 476-506.

_____. "Location Theory and Trade Theory: Short-run Analysis," Quarterly Journal of Economics, LXVIII (May, 1954), 305-20.

Isard, W., and Cumberland, J. H., eds. Regional Economic Planning: Techniques of Analysis for Less-developed Areas, Paris: Organization for Economic Cooperation and Development, 1961.

Isard, W., and Fruetel, G. "Regional and National Production and Their Interrelation," Long-range Economic Projection: Studies in Income and Wealth, XVI; Princeton, New Jersey: National Bureau of Economic Research, Princeton University Press, 1954, 427-71.

Isard, W., and Peck, M. J. "Location Theory and International and Interregional Trade Theory," Quarterly Journal of Economics, LXVIII (February, 1954), 97-114.

Isard, W., and Reiner, T. A. "Regional Science and Planning," Papers and Proceedings of the Regional Science Association, VIII (1962), 1-35.

Israel, Ministry of Labor and Housing Administration, and Doudai, A. "Regional Development and Housing in Israel," Ekistics, XIII, 80 (June, 1962) 384-94.

Jacobs, Jane. The Economy of Cities, London: Jonathan Cape, 1970.

Johnson, H. B. "A Note on Thunen's Circles," Ekistics, XIV (1962), 269-73.

Jones, E. "Aspects of Urbanization in Venezuela," Ekistics, XVIII (1964), 420-24.

Keeble, Lewis. Principles and Practice of Town and Country Planning, 2nd ed.; London: Estates Gazette, 1969.

Kelly and Co. Kelly's Directory of Manufacturers and Merchants, Birmingham: Kelly and Co., 1926, 1936, 1946, 1956, and 1966.

Kindleberger, C. P. The Terms of Trade: A European Case Study, London: Chapman and Hall, 1956.

_____. Foreign Trade and the National Economy, New Haven: Irwin and Co., 1962.

Koldomasou, Y. "The Influence of Transportation on the Geographic Distribution of Industry," Problems in Economics (July, 1958).

Koopmans, T., and Beckmann, M. "Assignment Problems and the Location of Economic Activities," Econometrica, XXV (January, 1957), 53-57.

Kotter, H. "Economic and Social Implications of Rural Industriali-
    zation," Ekistics, XV (January, 1963), 47-50.

Kreditor, A. "The Provisional Plan," In Industrial Development and
    the Development Plan, Dublin: Foras Forbartha, Chapter 8 (1965).

Krueger, Ralph, ed. Regional and Resource Planning in Canada,
    Toronto: Holt, Rinehart, and Winston, 1963.

Krutilla, J. F. "Criteria for Evaluating Regional Development Pro-
    grams," Papers and Proceedings of the American Economic
    Association, XLV, 2 (May, 1955), 120-32.

Kuklinski, A. R. Trends in Research on Comprehensive Regional
    Development, Geneva, October, 1967.

Kurakin, A. F. "Economic Administrative Regions, Their Specializa-
    tion and Their Integrated Development," Soviet Geography
    (November, 1962), 29-38.

Kuznets, Simon. "Quantitative Aspects of the Economic Growth of
    Nations, VIII; Distribution of Income by Size," Economic Develop-
    ment and Cultural Change, XI (January, 1963), 36-45.

_____. "Economic Growth and Income Inequality," American
    Economic Review, XLV (March, 1955), 1-28.

_____. "Quantitative Aspects of the Growth of National Income
    Levels and Variability of Rates of Growth," Economic Develop-
    ment and Cultural Change (October, 1956).

Lampard, E. E. "The History of Cities in the Economically Advanced
    Areas," Economic Development and Cultural Change, III
    (January, 1955); comment, 137-46.

Lean, W. Economic Studies and Assesment of Town Development,"
    Journal of the Town Planning Institute, LIII (1967), 148-52.

_____. Economics of Land Use Planning: Urban and Regional,
    London: Estates Gazette, 1969.

Lefeber, L. "General Equilibrium Analysis of Production, Transpor-
    tation and the Choice of Industrial Location," Papers and Proceed-
    ings of the Regional Science Association, IV (1958), 77-89.

Leontief, W. W., and Strout, A. "Multiregional Input-output Tech-
    niques," Paper presented at the International Conference on
    Input-Output Techniques, Geneva, September, 1961.

_____. "Multi-regional Input Output Analysis," Structural Inter-dependence and Economic Development, Edited by T. Barna, New York: The McMillan Co., 1963.

Leven, C. L. "Establishing Goals for Regional Economic Develop-ment," Journal of the American Institute of Planners, XXX (1964), 100-09.

Levin, Melvin R. "Planners and Metropolitan Planning," Journal of the American Institute of Planners, XXXIII, 2 (March, 1967), 78-90.

Lewis, W. A. Development Planning, London: Allen and Unwin, 1966.

Lichfield, N. "Cost-benefit Analysis in Plan Evaluation," Town Planning Review, XXXV (1964), 159-69.

_____. The Limerick Region, Dublin: Foras Forbartha, 1965.

_____. "Economics in Town Planning," Town Planning Review, XXXIX, 1 (April, 1968), 5-20.

Lisle, E. A. "Regional Planning and Urban Development," Paper given at the International Congress on Economic Development, Vienna, August-September, 1962.

Lopreato, J. "Economic Development and Cultural Change: The Role of Emigration," Ekistics, XV (1963), 51-52.

Losch, August. "The Nature of Economic Regions," Southern Eco-nomic Journal, V (July, 1938), 71-78.

_____. The Economics of Location, New Haven: Yale University Press, 1954.

Lounsbury, F. E. Secondary Manufacturing in the Atlantic Provinces, Fredericton, New Brunswick: Atlantic Provinces Economic Council, 1961.

Luttrell, W. S. "Industrial Complexes and Regional Economic Devel-opment," Paper presented at the Regional Planning Conference Ireland 69, Belfast, March 1969.

Lowry, I. S. Design for an Intra-regional Locational Model, Pittsburgh Regional Planning Association Economic Study of the Pittsburgh Region, Working Paper No. 6, September, 1960.

MacKaye, Benton. New Exploration: A Philosophy of Regional Planning, New York: Harcourt, Brace and Co., 1928.

Madden, Carl H. "Some Spatial Aspects of Economic Growth in the United States," Economic Development and Cultural Change, IV (1956), 371-87.

Mann, L., and Pillorge, G. L. "French Regional Planning (review article)," Journal of the American Institute of Planners, XXX (1964), 155-60.

Mansfield, E. "Size of the Firm, Market Structures and Innovation," Journal of Political Economy, LXXI (1963), 566-76.

Marczewsky, J. Le Take-off vers un Croissance Soutenue, in the Round Table I.A.E.S., Constance, 1960.

Mason, Edward S. "The Financing of Regional Development Programs," Ekistics, XX, 119 (October, 1965), 234-38.

Mason, E., et al. "Administrative Aspects of Regional Development," Ekistics, XX (1965), 234-46.

Massee, P. "L'amenagement du territoire projection geographique de la société de l'avenir," Revue d'Economie Politique, LXXIV, 1 (1964), 3-29.

Mayer, H. and Kohn, C., eds. Readings in Urban Geography, Chicago: University of Chicago Press, 1959.

McDonic G. F. "Growth Points in Scotland," Town and Country Planning (1964), 159-60.

McGovern, P. D. "Planning and Promotion at Shannon," Ekistics, XIII (May, 1962), 361-62.

Meade, James E. The Theory of International Economic Policy, XI: Trade and Welfare, London: Oxford University Press, 1955.

_____. "External Economies and Diseconomies in a Competitive Situation," The Economic Journal, LXII (March, 1952), 54-57.

Meenan, J. F. "Eire," Economics of International Migration, Edited by B. Thomas, London: Macmillan, 1958, Chapter 5.

_____. The Irish Economy Since 1922, Liverpool: Liverpool University Press, 1970.

Meier, R. L. "Measuring Social and Cultural Change in Urban Regions," Journal of the American Institute of Planners, XXV (November, 1959), 180-90.

Meyer, J. "Regional Economics: A Survey," American Economic Review, LIII (1965), 19-54.

Miernyk, W. "Problems and Remedies for Depressed Area Unemployment," Industrial Relations Research Association Proceedings, XIV (December, 1961), 28-36.

Minay, C. L. W. "Town Planning and Regional Development in Scotland," Ekistics, XIX (1965), 296-99.

Mishan, E. J. The Cost of Economic Growth, New York: Praeger, 1967.

Molinari, A. "Some Controversial Questions Concerning Industrial Estates," Ekistics, XIII (May, 1962), 363-69.

Moses, L. N. "A General Equilibrium Model of Production, Interregional Trade and Location of Industry," Review of Economics and Statistics, XLII (November, 1960), 373-97.

_____. "Interregional Analysis," Harvard Economic Research Project, Report on Research for 1954, Cambridge, Mass: Harvard University, 1955.

Mueller, E., and Morgan, J. N. "Location Decisions of Manufacturers," American Economic Review, LII (May, 1962), 204-17.

Mumford, Lewis. "A New Regional Plan to Arrest Megalopolis," Ekistics, XX (September, 1965), 117-20.

Munro, John M. "The Measurement of Interregional Income Disparity in Canada," Paper presented to the Annual Meeting of the Canadian Political Science Association, Ottawa, Ontario, June 8, 1967.

Myrdal, Gunnar. Economic Theory and Underdeveloped Regions, London: Duckworth, 1957.

Needleman, L. Regional Analysis, London: Penguin Books, 1968.

Neff, P. "Interregional Cyclical Differentials: Causes, Measurement and Significance," American Economic Review, XXXIX (1949), 105-19.

Nevin, Edward. "The Case for Regional Policy," Three Banks Review, LXXII (December, 1966), 30-46.

_____. The Ownership of Personal Property in Ireland, Paper No. 1. Dublin: Economic Research Institute (1961).

_____. The Irish Tariff and the E.E.C.: A Factual Survey, Paper No. 3 (1962). Dublin: Economic Research Institute.

_____. The Irish Price Level: Comparative Study, Paper No. 9 (1962). Dublin: Economic Research Institute.

_____. Public Debt and Economic Development, Paper No. 11 (1962). Dublin: Economic Research Institute.

_____. Wages in Ireland, 1946-62, Paper No. 12 (1963). Dublin: Economic Research Institute.

Newcombe, V. Z. "Town and Country Planning in Jordan," Town Planning Review, XXXV (1964), 238-52.

Newman, J. New Dimensions in Regional Planning, Dublin: Foras Forbartha, 1967.

Nez, G. "Methodology for Integration of Economic and Physical Planning," Ekistics, XVII (May, 1964), 297-314.

Nicholls, W. H. "A Research Problem on Southern Economic Development, With Particular Reference to Agriculture," Economic Development and Cultural Change, XI (1952), 190-95.

_____. "Industrialization, Factor Markets, and Agricultural Development," Journal of Political Economy, LXIX (August, 1961), 319-40.

_____. "Some Foundations of Economic Development in the Upper East Tennessee Valley, 1850-1900," Journal of Political Economy, LXIV (1956), 277-302 and 400-15.

_____. "The Effects of Industrial Development on Tennessee Valley Agriculture, 1900-50," Journal of Farm Economics, XXXVIII (1956), 1,636-49.

Nirth, L. "The Limitations of Regionalism," Regionalism in America, Edited by M. Fenson, Wisconsin, 1951.

North, D. C. "Location Theory and Regional Economic Growth," Journal of Political Economy, LXIII (1955), 243-58.

Organization for Economic Cooperation and Development. Development Plans and the Programs, Paris: OECD, I (1964).

_____. Conference on Regional Economic Development, Paris: OEEC, 1960.

Ohlin, Bertil. Interregional and International Trade, Cambridge, Mass.: Harvard University Press, 1935.

Okun, Bernard, and Richardson, R. W. "Regional Income Inequality and Internal Population Migration," Regional Development and Planning: A Reader. Edited by J. Friedmann and W. Alonso. Cambridge, Mass.: MIT Press, 1964, 303-18.

Orr, E. W. "A Synthesis of Theories of Location, of Transportation Rates, and of Spatial Price Equilibrium," Papers and Proceedings of the Regional Science Association, III (1957), 61-73.

Political and Economic Planning, Regional Development in the EEC, London: PEP, 1966.

Perloff, H. S. "New Directions in Social Planning," Journal of the American Institute of Planners, XXXI, 4 (November, 1965).

_____. How a Region Grows, New York; Committee for Economic Development, 1963.

_____. "Problems of Assessing Regional Economic Progress," Regional Income: Studies in Income and Wealth, XXI; Princeton, New Jersey: National Bureau of Economic Research, Princeton University Press, 1957, 35-62.

_____. "Key Features of Regional Planning," Journal of the American Institute of Planners, XXXIV, 3 (May, 1968), 153-59.

Perloff, H. S., and Pazos, F. "Economic Policy Problems in Subnational and Multinational Regions," Ekistics, XXIII (June, 1967), 360-63.

Perloff, H. S., et al. Region Resources and Economic Growth, Baltimore: Johns Hopkins Press, 1960.

Perroux, Francois. L'Economie du XXe Siecle, Paris: PUF, 1961.

Perroux, F., "Note sur La Notion de Poles de Croissance," Economie Appliquée, VII (1955), 307-20.

Peters, G. H. "Industrial Development in Country Towns," Town And Country Planning (1962), 386-89 and 433-35.

Peters, W. S. "A Problem of Locational-demographic Interaction,"
    Papers and Proceedings of the Regional Science Association,
    VI (1960), 139-46.

Pfouts, R., ed. Techniques of Urban Economic Analysis, West
    Trenton, New Jersey: Chandler-Davis, 1960.

Philbrick, A. K. "A real Functional Organization in Regional Human
    Geography," Economic Geography, XXXIII, 4 (October, 1957),
    299-336.

Piperoglou, John. "Comments on the Comparative Usefulness of the
    Economic Base Versus Input-output Analysis," Ekistics, XIII
    (February, 1962), 125-26.

Pitts, F. R. "Urban Systems and Economic Development," Papers and
    Proceedings of the Conference on Urban Systems Research in
    Underdeveloped and Advanced Economies, Eugene, Oregon:
    Business School, University of Oregon, 1962.

Prebisch, R. The Economic Development of Latin America and Its
    Principal Problems. New York: Economic Commission for
    Latin America, 1950.

Pred, A. "Industrialization, Initial Advantage and American Metro-
    politan Growth," Ekistics, XX (September, 1965), 125-31.

Rahman, M. A. "A Linear Programming Model for Investment Allo-
    cation Between Regions or Sectors," Pakistan Economic
    Journal, XII (December, 1962), 14-21.

_____. "Regional Allocation of Investment," Ekistics, XVII
    (1964), 187-89.

_____. "Regional Allocation of Investment: An Aggregate Study
    in the Theory of Development Programming," Quarterly
    Journal of Economics, LXX (February, 1963), 26-39.

Reilly, W. J. "Methods for the Study of Retail Relationships,"
    University of Texas Bulletin No. 2944.

Reiner, T. A. "Sub-national and National Planning: Decision
    Criteria," Papers and Proceedings of the Regional Science
    Association, XIV (1965), 107-36.

Reissman, Leonard. The Urban Process, New York: Free Press,
    1964.

Reynolds, D. J. Road Transport: The Problems and Prospects in
    Ireland, Paper No. 13. Dublin: Economic Research Institute.

_____. Inland Transport in Ireland: A Factual Survey, Paper
No. 10. Dublin: Economic Research Institute.

Reynolds, David R. Rapid Development in Small Economies, New
York: Praeger, 1967.

Rivkin, M. D. "Creation of Growth Regions: Some Experience From
Turkey," Ekistics, XVIII (1964), 146-51.

Robertson, D. J. "Economists and Town Planning," Town Planning
Review, XXXIII (1962), 32-39.

Robertson, R. H. S. "Scotland's Unexploited Resources," Town and
Country Planning (1965), 219-22.

Robinson, E. A. G., ed. The Economic Consequences of the Size of
Nations: Proceedings of a Conference Held by the International
Economics Association, London: Macmillan, 1960.

_____. Backward Areas in Advanced Countries: Proceedings of
a Conference Held by the International Economics Association
at Varenna. London: Macmillan, 1969.

Robinson, K. W. "Processes and Patterns of Urbanization in
Australia and New Zealand," Ekistics, XV (January, 1963).

Rodwin, Lloyd. British New Towns Policy, Cambridge: Cambridge
University Press, 1956.

_____. "National Urban Planning and Regional Capital Budgets
for Developing Areas," Papers and Proceedings of the Regional
Science Association, III (1957), 223-32. Discussion by Bert
Hoselitz (233-39), Stefan Robock (240-42), and Robert Allen
(243-45).

_____. Nations and Cities, Boston: Houghton Mifflin, 1970.

Rodwin, L. "Planned Decentralization and Regional Development
With Special Reference to the British New Towns," Papers and
Proceedings of the Regional Science Association, I (1954), A1-A8.

Rossi, Doria M. "Analysis of Agricultural Structure for Regional
Planning," Regional Economic Planning: Techniques of Analysis
for Less-developed Areas. Edited by W. Isard and J. H.
Cumberland. Paris: Organizatlon for Economic Cooperation
and Development (1960), 239-54.

Rostow, W. W. The Process of Economic Growth, New York:
      Norton and Co., Inc., 1952.

_____. The Stages of Economic Growth, London: Cambridge
      University Press, 1965.

Roterus, Victor. "Centralization or Decentralization of the Economic
      Growth," Ekistics, XX (September, 1965), 121-23.

Roterus, Victor, and Calef, Wesley. "Notes on the Basic-nonbasic
      Employment Ratio," Economic Geography, XXXI (January, 1955),
      17-20. Reprinted in Mayer and Kohn, Readings in Urban
      Geography, Chicago: University of Chicago Press, 1959.

Row, A. "The Physical Development Plan," Journal of the American
      Institute of Planners (August, 1960), 177-85.

Ruttan, V., and Tompkins, L. "The Effectiveness of Location Incen-
      tives on Local Economic Development," Journal of Farm Eco-
      nomics, XLIV (November, 1967), 968-78.

Sah, J. P. and Dutta, S. S. "Economic Development and Spatial
      Planning in India," Ekistics, XXIII (June, 1967).

Schnore, L. F. "Urbanization and Economic Development: The
      Demographic Contribution," Ekistics, XIII (June, 1962), 419-24.

Schultz, Theodore W. The Economic Organization of Agriculture,
      New York: McGraw-Hill, 1953.

Scitovsky, T. "Two Concepts of External Economies," Journal of
      Political Economy, LXII (April, 1954), 143-52.

Seers, Dudley. "The Mechanism of an Open, Petroleum Economy,"
      Social and Economic Studies, XIII, 2 (June, 1964), 233-42.

_____. "A Theory of Inflation and Growth in Under-developed
      Countries Based on the Experience of Latin America," Oxford
      Economic Papers, XIV (June, 1962), 173-95.

_____. "The Stages of Economic Development of a Primary-
      producer in the Twentieth Century," The Economic Bulletin of
      Ghana, VII, 4 (1963), 57-69.

_____. "Economic Programming in a Country Newly Independent,"
      Social and Economic Studies, XI, 1 (March, 1962), 34-41.

Singer, Hans W. International Development: Growth and Change,
New York: McGraw-Hill, 1964.

_____. "The Distribution of Gains Between Investing and
Borrowing Countries, " American Economic Review Proceedings,
II, 2 (1950), 474-79.

Sjoberg, Gideon. "The Origin and Evolution of Cities," Scientific
American, CCXIII, 3 (September, 1965), 54-63.

Social Studies Institute, Papers of the Proceedings of the Workshop
on Regional Development Planning, The Hague: Social Studies
Institute, 1967.

Sonenblum, S., and Stern, L. H. "The Use of Economic Projections
in Planning," Journal of the American Institute of Planners,
XXX (1964), 110-22.

Stefanovic, Dusan. "Metropolitan Planning in Yugoslavia," Ekistics,
XIII (April, 1962), 249-50.

Stevens, B. H. "An Application of Game Theory to a Problem in
Location," Papers and Proceedings of the Regional Science
Association, VII (1961), 143-57.

Stohr, W. "The Definition of Regions in Relation to National and
Regional Development in Latin America," Papers presented to
the first inter-American seminar on the definition of regions
for development planning, Regional Geography Committee of
the Pan-American Institute of Geography and History in Canada,
September 4-11, 1967.

_____. "Planning for Depressed Areas: A Methodological
Approach," Journal of the American Institute of Planners, XXX
(1964), 123-31.

Stopler, W. "Spatial Order and the Economic Growth of Cities,"
Economic Development and Cultural Change, III (1954-55),
137-46.

Stone, P. A. "Decision Techniques for Town Development," Operational Research Quarterly, XV (1964).

Stone, Richard. "A Comparison of the Economic Structure of Regions
Based on the Concept of Distance," Journal of Regional Science,
II, 2 (1960), 1-20.

_____. "Social Accounts at the Regional Level: A Survey,"
Regional Economic Planning. Edited by W. Isard and J. H.
Cumberland, Paris: Organization for Economic Cooperation
and Development 2, (1961), 263-93.

Sufrin, S., et al. The Economic Status of Upstate New York at Mid-
century: With Special Reference to Distressed Communities and
Their Adjustments. Syracuse: Syracuse University Business
Research Center, College of Business Administration, August,
1960.

Symons, Leslie, ed. The General Report of the Land Utilization
Survey of Northern Ireland, London: University of London Press,
1963.

Taylor, G. B. "Services and the City Region," Town and Country
Planning (1964), 215-21.

Teitz, M. B. "Regional Theory and Regional Models," Papers and
Proceedings of the Regional Science Association, IX (1962),
35-50.

Thijsse, J. P. "A Rural Pattern for the Future," Ekistics, XIII
(1962), 104-06.

Thom and Co. Thom's Directory of Manufacturers, Dublin, 1926,
1936, 1946, 1956, and 1966.

Thomas, Brinley. "Labour Mobility, Migration Policy and the
Standard of Living," The Three Banks Review, V (March, 1950),
3-20.

_____. Economics of International Migration, London: Macmillan,
1958.

Thomas, C. Y. "The Balance of Payments and Money Supplies in a
Colonial Economy," Social and Economic Studies, XII, (March,
1963), 27-36.

Thomas, M. D. "Regional Economic Growth and Industrial Development," Papers and Proceedings of the Regional Science Association, X (1963), 61-75.

_____. "The Export Base and Development Stages Theories of
Regional Economic Growth: An Appraisal," Land Economics,
XL (1964), 421-32.

_____. "Economic Activity in Small Areas," Land Economics, XXXVI (1960), 164-71.

_____. "The Economic Base and a Region's Economy," Journal of the American Institute of Planners, XXIII, 2 (1957).

Thompson, Wilbert. A Preface to Urban Economics, London: Oxford University Press, 1966.

Tiebout, C. M. "Exports and Regional Economic Growth," Journal of Political Economy, LXIV (April, 1956), 160-65.

_____. "A Method of Determining Incomes and Their Variation in Small Regions," Papers and Proceedings of the Regional Science Association, I (1955), F1-F12.

_____. "Regional and Interregional Input-output Models: An Appraisal," The Southern Economic Journal, XXIV, 2 (October, 1957), 140-47.

_____. "The Urban Economic Base Reconsidered," Land Economics, XXXII (February, 1956), 95-99. Reprinted in Mayer and Kohn, Readings in Urban Geography, Chicago: University of Chicago Press, 1959.

Tinbergen, J. "Sur un modèle de la dispersion geographique de l'activité économique," Revue d'Economie Politique, Numéro special (janvier-février, 1964), 30-44.

_____. "The Spatial Dispersion of Production: A Hypothesis," Schweizerische Zeitschrift fur Volkswirtschaft und Statistik, XCVII, 4 (1961), 412-19.

_____. "Regional Planning: Some Principles," Revista del Banco Central de Venezuela, 176-178 (octubre-diciembre, 1959).

_____. Shaping the World Economy, New York: Twentieth Century Fund, 1962.

_____. Centralization and Decentralization in Economic Policy, Amsterdam: North Holland Publishing Co., 1954.

_____. "A Method of Regional Planning," Institute of Social Studies. Papers of the Proceedings of the Workshop on Regional Development Programming, The Hague: Institute of Social Studies, 1967.

Ullman, Edward L. "Amenities as a Factor in Regional Growth,"
    Geographical Review, XLIV (January, 1954).

_____. "Regional Development and the Geography of Concentration,"
    Regional Development and Planning: A Reader, Edited by J.
    Friedmann and W. Alonso, Cambridge, Mass: MIT Press, 1964.

United Nations. "Problems of Regional Development and Industrial
    Location in Europe," U. N. Economic Survey of Europe 1954,
    Paris: United Nations, 1954.

_____. "The Establishment of Industrial Estates in Underdeveloped
    Countries," Ekistics, XIII (1962), 130-33.

_____. "Leopoldville and Lagos: Comparative Study of Urban
    Conditions in Africa," Ekistics, XIII (1962), 313-19.

_____. "The Role of Industrial Complexes in Economic Develop-
    ment," Ekistics, XX (September, 1965), 135-39.

Valavanis, S. "Losch on Location: A Review Article," American
    Economic Review, LXV, 4 (September, 1955), 637-44.

Van Sickle, J. Planning for the South: An Enquiry Into the Economics
    of Regionalism. Nashville, Tenn.: Vanderbilt University Press,
    1943.

Various authors. "Regional Problems of Development Planning,"
    Ekistics, XV (1963), 325-41.

_____. "Regional Development Through Land Reform," Ekistics,
    XIV (1962), 175-86.

_____. "Regional Development Through Industrialization," Ekistics,
    XIV (1962), 167-74.

_____. "Processes and Patterns of Urbanization," Ekistics,
    XV (1963), 3-23.

Vicinelli, Paolo. "Experience and Difficulties of Implementing a
    Development Plan," Institute of Social Studies. Papers of the
    Proceedings of the Workshop on Regional Development Program-
    ming, The Hague: Institute of Social Studies, 1967.

Vietorisz, T. V. "Locational Choices in Planning," National Planning,
    Edited by M. F. Millikan. New York: National Bureau of Economic
    Research (1967), 104-11.

Vining, R. "Regional Variation in Cyclical Fluctuation Viewed as a Frequency Distribution," Econometrica, XIII (July, 1945), 183-213.

_____. "The Region as an Economic Entity and Certain Variations to be Observed in the Study of Systems of Regions," American Economic Review, XXXIX (May, 1949), 89-104.

_____. "The Region as a Concept in Business Cycle Analysis," Econometrica, XIV (July, 1946), 201-18.

_____. "Delimitation of Economic Areas: Statistical Conceptions in the Study of the Spatial Structure of an Economic System," Journal of the American Statistical Association, XLVIII (January, 1953), 44-64.

_____. "A Description of Certain Spatial Aspects of an Economic System," Economic Development and Cultural Change, III (1954-55), 160-65.

_____. "Location of Industry and Regional Patterns of Business Behaviour," Econometrica, XIV (July, 1946), 37-68.

Viot, Pierre. "Regional Aspects of French Planning" in Regional Planning Proceedings of National Conference, Dublin: (Foras Forbartha), 1965.

Voorhes, A. M. "The Nature and Use of Models in City Planning," Journal of the American Institute of Planners, XXV (May, 1959), 57-60.

Walker, David. Local Government Finance in Ireland: A Preliminary Survey, Paper No. 5. Dublin: Economic Research Institute (1962).

_____. The Allocation of Public Funds for Social Development, Paper No. 8. Dublin: Economic Research Institute.

Ward, Barbara. "Political Implications of the Science of Ekistics," Ekistics, XVIII (October, 1964), 198-205.

Warntz, W., and Nept, D. "Contributions to a Statistical Methodology for Areal Distributions," Journal of Regional Science, II, 2 (1960), 47-66.

Waterson, A. Development Planning: Lessons of Experience, Baltimore: Johns Hopkins Press, 1965.

Watts, K. "How to Make an Urban Planning Survey," Ekistics, XIII (1962), 300-12.

_____. "Small Town Development: The Problem and Possibilities in the Context of South and South-east Asia," Ekistics, XVII (1964), 24-25.

_____. "Urbanization and Planning in Nigeria," Town and Country Planning (1963), 474-75.

Webber, M. M. "Comprehensive Planning and Social Responsibility: Towards an AIP Consensus on the Profession's Role and Purpose," Journal of the American Institute of Planners, XXIX (1963), 232-41.

Weber, Alfred. Ueber den Standort der Industrien, Part 1; Reine Theorie des Standorts, Tubingen, 1909. Translated by C, J. Friedrich as Alfred Weber's Theory of the Location of Industries. Chicago: University of Chicago Press, 1928.

Weddle, A. E. "Rural Land Resources," Town Planning Review, XXXV (1965), 267-84.

Weitz, R. Rural Planning in Developing Countries: Report on the Second Rehovoth Conference Israel, 1963, London: Routledge and Kegan Paul, 1966.

_____. "A New Approach in Urban-rural Relationships in Developing Countries," Paper presented to the International Seminar on Social and Cultural Integration in Urban Areas, Haifa, 1964.

_____. "Rural Development Through Regional Planning in Israel," Journal of Farm Economics, XLVI (1965), 634-51.

_____. Regional Development Programming, Washington, D.C.: Organization of American States Studies and Monographs, VII, 1966.

_____. Spatial Organization of Rural Development, Rehovoth: National and University Institute of Agriculture, Settlement Study Center, 1968.

Whalen, H. "Public Policy and Regional Development: The Experience of the Atlantic Provinces," The Prospect of Change, edited by Abraham Rotstein. Toronto: McGraw-Hill, 1965.

Wibberly, G. P. "The Economic and Social Role of the Country Town," Town and Country Planning (January, 1960), 411-14.

Wilhelm, P. A. "Industrial Development Planning," Journal of the American Institute of Planners, XXVI (1960), 216-23.

Williams, A. "Fiscal Policy and Interregional Resource Allocation," Public Finance, XVI, 2 (1961), 133-51.

Williamson, J. "The Equilibrium Size of Marketing Plants in a Spatial Market," Journal of Farm Economics, XLIV (November, 1962), 953-67.

_____. "Regional Inequality and the Process of National Development: A Description of the Patterns," Economic Development Cultural Change, XIII, 4, Part 2 (July, 1965), 1-84.

Wilson, Thomas, ed. Papers on Regional Development, Oxford: Basil Blackwell, 1965.

_____. Policies for Regional Development, "University of Glasgow, Social and Economic Studies" Occasional Paper No. 3, Glasgow: Oliver and Boyd, 1964.

_____. "First Economic Plan for Northern Ireland," Discussion paper presented at the Regional Planning Conference Ireland 69 in Belfast, March, 1969.

Wise, M. J. "Industrial Location: A Geographical Approach," Inaugural Lecture, London, 1960.

_____. "Economic Factors of Metropolitan Planning," Ekistics, XIII (April, 1962), 232-34.

Woodbury, C. "Economic Implications of Urban Growth," Town and Country Planning (January, 1960), 7-17.

Wright, H. H. "National and Regional Planning," Ekistics, XVI (1963), 20-23.

Wright, Myles. The Dublin Region, Dublin: Foras Forbartha, 1967.

_____. "Dublin Regional Advisory Plan," Paper presented at the Regional Planning Conference Ireland 69, Belfast, March, 1969.

Wrobel, A. "Some Observations on the Regional Concept," Geographia
     Polonica, I (1964), 231-39.

GOVERNMENT PUBLICATIONS

Ireland. Agriculture in the Second Programme for Economic Expansion,
     Dublin: Stationery Office, 1964.

_____. Census of Industrial Production, Dublin: Stationery Office,
     1926, 1936, 1946, 1956, and 1966.

_____. Census of Population, Dublin: Stationery Office, 1926,
     1936, 1946, 1956, and 1966.

_____. Commission of Enquiry into Banking, Currency, and Credit,
     Dublin: Stationery Office, 1938.

_____. Commission on Emigration and Other Population Problems,
     1948-54, Dublin: Stationery Office, 1955.

_____. Current Trends and Policies in Housing, Building and
     Planning, Dublin: Department of Local Government, 1969.

_____. Economic Development: First Programme for Economic
     Expansion, Dublin: Stationery Office, 1958.

_____. Free Trade Area Agreement and Related Agreements,
     Exchange of Letters and Understanding, Dublin: Stationery
     Office, 1965.

_____. National Income and Expenditure, Dublin: Stationery Office,
     published annually.

_____. Report on Vital Statistics, Dublin: Stationery Office,
     published annually.

_____. Second Programme for Economic Expansion, Dublin:
     Stationery Office, 1964.

_____. Statistical Abstract of Ireland, Dublin: Stationery Office,
     published annually.

_____. Survey of Grant-aided Industry, Dublin: Stationery Office
     Office, 1967.

_____. The Trend of Employment and Unemployment. Dublin: Stationery Office, published annually.

National Industrial Economic Council, Report on Arrangements for Planning at Industry Level, Dublin: Stationery Office, 1966.

_____. Report on Economic Planning, Dublin: Stationery Office, 1965.

_____. Report on Full Employment, Dublin: Stationery Office, 1967.

_____. Report on Industrial Adaptation and Development, Dublin: Stationery Office, 1968.

_____. Report on Manpower Policy, Dublin: Stationery Office, 1964.

_____. Report on Physical Planning, Dublin: Stationery Office, 1969.

_____. Review of 1968 and Outlook for 1969, Dublin: Stationery Office, 1969.

Committee on Industrial Organization. A Synthesis of Reports by Survey Teams on 22 Industries, Dublin: Stationery Office, 1965.

_____. Third Interim Report, Creation of Adaptation Councils to Promote Measures of Rationalization, Co-operation, etc. in Individual Industries, Dublin: Stationery Office, 1962.

Northern Ireland. Annual Report of the N. I. Tourist Board, Belfast: H. M. Stationery Office.

_____. Annual Report of the Registrar General, Belfast: H. M. Stationery Office.

_____. Belfast Regional Plan 1962, Report by Sir Robert Matthew, 2 vols.: Belfast: H. M. Stationery Office, 1964.

_____. Capital Grants to Industry: Report of the Chief Inspector of Factories, Belfast: H. M. Stationery Office, published annually.

_____. Census of Population, Belfast: H. M. Stationery Office, 1926, 1937, 1951, 1961, and 1966.

_____. Census of Production, Belfast: H. M. Stationery Office, published annually.

_____. Digest of Statistics, Belfast: Stationery Office, published annually.

_____. Economic Development in Northern Ireland, (The Wilson Report.) Belfast: H. M. Stationery Office, 1965.

_____. Northern Ireland Economic Report, Belfast: Stationery Office, published annually.

_____. Report of the Ministry of Development, Belfast, H. M. Stationery Office, published annually.

_____. Report on the Census of Production of Northern Ireland 1966, Belfast, H. M. Stationery Office, 1968.

_____. The Trade of Northern Ireland, Belfast: Ministry of Commerce, published annually.

_____. Ulster Year Book, Belfast: H. M. Stationery Office, published annually.

_____. Who Makes What in Northern Ireland, Belfast: H. M. Stationery Office, 1966.

ABOUT THE AUTHOR

   Helen O'Neill, a native of Ireland, is a lecturer in the Department of Political Economy and in the Department of Town Planning in University College, Dublin.

   Dr. O'Neill is a commerce graduate of University College, Dublin, and received her M.A. and Ph.D in economics from McGill University, Montreal.

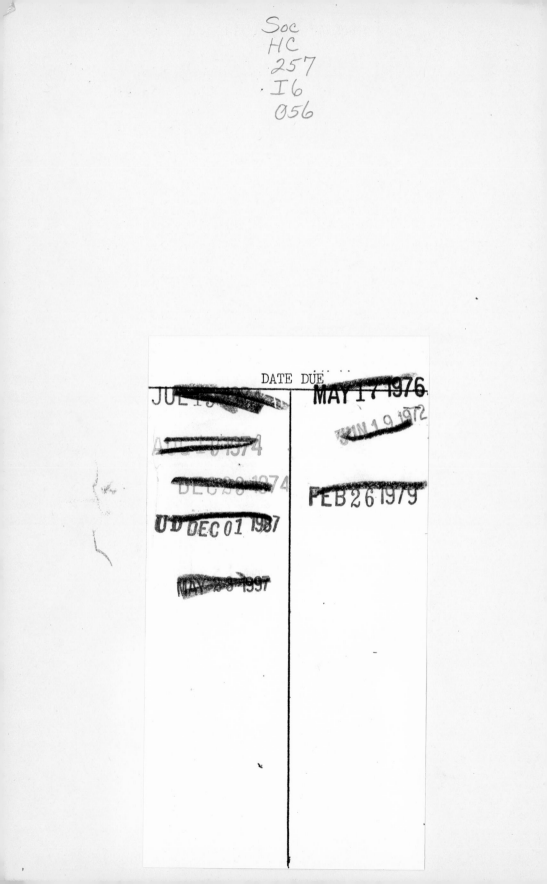